RECEIVING THE GIFTS
OF EVERY MEMBER

KOOS TAMMINGA

Receiving the Gifts of Every Member

A Practical Ecclesiological Case Study on Inclusion and the Church

Summum

This edition was made possible by donations of:
Stichting Greijdanus-Kruithof Fonds, Steunfonds GKv, Sint Jacobs Godshuis, Stichting SPZ.nl.

Sponsored by **STICHTING AFBOUW KAMPEN**

Cover design: Brainstorm

ISBN 9789492701114

Copyright 2020 © Summum Academic Publications, Kampen, The Netherlands.

All rights reserved. No part of this publication may be reproduced, translated, stored in a retrieval system, or transmitted in any form by any means, electronic, mechanical, photocopying, recording or otherwise, without prior written permission from the publisher.

To
Geranne,
for doing the things that I think about in this book
in ways that precede and surpass description and reflection.

Contents

List of Figures & Tables	xiii
A Note on Language	xv
Foreword	xvii

1 Introduction   1
- 1.1 Sharing Life, Not Just a Roof 1
- 1.2 Statement of the Problem 4
  - 1.2.1 Church in Transition 4
  - 1.2.2 Society in Transition 7
  - 1.2.3 Interaction Between Church and Society 10
- 1.3 Research Goal 11
- 1.4 Research Questions 13
- 1.5 Overview of the Project 16
- 1.6 Relevance 17

2 Theoretical Framework: Potential Roles of Churches and Ecclesiology for Disability Inclusion   19
- 2.1 Introduction 19
- 2.2 A Turn to Inclusion 20
  - 2.2.1 Inclusion in Policy 21
  - 2.2.2 Inclusion in Two Webs of Practices: Education and the Job Market 23
  - 2.2.3 Reflection on Inclusive Policy and Practice ... 26
- 2.3 A Third Web of Practices: The Church 27
  - 2.3.1 The Turn to Inclusion in Vathorst 29

		2.3.2	Reflection on Community as Intrinsic to the Life of the Church	29
	2.4	Theology and Inclusion		32
		2.4.1	How-Engagement	33
		2.4.2	Maximal Why-Engagement	34
		2.4.3	Minimal Why-Engagement	36
		2.4.4	Non-correlative Engagement	39
	2.5	Concluding Reflections		41

3 Practical Theological Position & Methodology — 45

- 3.1 Introduction . . . 45
- 3.2 Theological Paradigm . . . 47
  - 3.2.1 Empirical Research and Reformed Theology . . 48
  - 3.2.2 Defining Reformed Theology . . . 50
  - 3.2.3 Points of Contact Between Reformed Theology and Empirical Methodology . . . 53
  - 3.2.4 Summary . . . 55
- 3.3 Basic Understanding of Practical Theology . . . 55
  - 3.3.1 A Typology of Practical Theological Approaches . . . 55
  - 3.3.2 What is Practical Theology? . . . 58
  - 3.3.3 Qualitative Research Methods and Practical Theology . . . 62
  - 3.3.4 Summary . . . 65
- 3.4 Basic Theory of Discipline . . . 66
  - 3.4.1 Practical Theological Ecclesiology . . . 66
  - 3.4.2 Theological Ethnography . . . 69
  - 3.4.3 Summary . . . 70
- 3.5 Practice Theory — Research Methods . . . 71
  - 3.5.1 Research Model . . . 71
  - 3.5.2 Single Case Study Research . . . 72
  - 3.5.3 Participant Observations . . . 74
  - 3.5.4 Interviews . . . 76
  - 3.5.5 Data Analysis . . . 78
  - 3.5.6 Validity and Reliability . . . 79
  - 3.5.7 Limitations . . . 79

4 Four Perspectives on the Ontmoetingskerk — 81

- 4.1 Introduction . . . 81

	4.2	Four Perspectives on Faith Communities	82
	4.3	Context	84
		4.3.1 Micro Context	84
		4.3.2 Meso Context	92
		4.3.3 Macro Context	100
	4.4	Identity & Culture	109
		4.4.1 Hart van Vathorst: Sharing Life	109
		4.4.2 The Ontmoetingskerk: Discovering Christ	113
		4.4.3 Ongoing Reflection: An Emerging Theology of Inclusion	120
		4.4.4 Summary of Identity & Culture	124
	4.5	Structure & Resources	125
		4.5.1 Organization	125
		4.5.2 People	130
		4.5.3 Summary of Structure & Resources	132
	4.6	Leadership	133
		4.6.1 Leadership in HVV	133
		4.6.2 Leadership in the Ontmoetingskerk	134
		4.6.3 Summary of Leadership	137
	4.7	Summary	138

5 Practicing Church in the Ontmoetingskerk — 139

	5.1	Introduction	139
	5.2	Leitourgia	141
		5.2.1 Church Services in the Ontmoetingskerk	141
		5.2.2 Adaptations in Liturgy?	151
		5.2.3 Summary Leitourgia	158
	5.3	Diakonia	159
		5.3.1 Concrete Support and Practical Care	159
		5.3.2 Diakonia and Leitourgia	160
		5.3.3 Diakonia and Koinonia	161
		5.3.4 Summary of Diakonia	162
	5.4	Martyria	163
		5.4.1 Church Services	163
		5.4.2 Teaching Practices	164
		5.4.3 Missional Practices	166
		5.4.4 Summary of Martyria	167
	5.5	Koinonia	168

		5.5.1	Intentional Connections 168
		5.5.2	Encounter Groups 169
		5.5.3	Unity or Subgroups? 174
		5.5.4	Developments in Koinonia 176
		5.5.5	Summary of Koinonia 178
	5.6	Summary 178

6 Putting Inclusion into Practice — 181
    6.1 Introduction 181
    6.2 Interaction 181
        6.2.1 Interaction During Communal Gatherings . . . 182
        6.2.2 Individual Interaction 188
        6.2.3 Experienced Benefits of Interaction 193
        6.2.4 Summary of Interaction 198
    6.3 Commitment 199
        6.3.1 Different Levels of Commitment 199
        6.3.2 Formal Commitment 199
        6.3.3 Informal Commitment 202
        6.3.4 Motivations 204
        6.3.5 Summary of Commitment 208
    6.4 Resistance 209
        6.4.1 Forms of Resistance 209
        6.4.2 Changes and Communication 210
        6.4.3 Practical Concerns 212
        6.4.4 Conceptions of Disability 216
        6.4.5 Summary of Resistance 226
    6.5 Summary 227

7 Conclusions & Discussion — 229
    7.1 Introduction 229
    7.2 Conclusions 229
        7.2.1 Descriptive Subquestions 229
        7.2.2 Interpretative Subquestions 232
        7.2.3 Main Question 234
    7.3 Discussion 236
        7.3.1 Inclusion - What's New? 237
        7.3.2 Organization and Leadership Towards Inclusion 246
        7.3.3 Inclusive Celebration 257

7.3.4		Inclusive Church in the World	265
7.3.5		Theological Reflection	270

Appendix A Code Groups   **277**

Bibliography   **279**

Index   **297**

List of Figures & Tables

1.1	The Four Voices of Theology.	15
2.1	Quality of Life Framework at a Glance	22
2.2	Approaches to the Use of Inclusion Language in Theology	33
3.1	De Ruijter's levels of practical theological reflection.	46
3.2	Research model	73
3.3	Overview of Interviewees	78
4.1	A comparison of the perspectives in three congregational studies approaches.	83
A.1	Distribution of code groups over chapters	277

A Note on Language

If there is anything I have learned in embarking on a journey through disability studies and disability theology, it is that our naming of phenomena is not neutral. When we name something, we take ownership of it in a way. By naming it in a certain way, we predispose ourselves to think about it in specific ways, making it possible if not likely that we will end up overexposing some aspects, while underexposing others or overlooking them altogether. One could therefore argue that the act of naming includes a necessary element of violence. When we name things, that violence is unhelpful, as it prevents us from fully understanding the things we name. When we name people (or groups of people), that violence is not only unhelpful for our understanding, but also painful and potentially dangerous, as the people we name may feel misunderstood and may even be mistreated on the basis of the wrong naming applied to them in their situation. For people with disabilities, these pains and dangers are not just hypothetical in nature. The fact of the matter is that names of disabilities tend be used more often as cuss words than they are to help a person to participate and belong. So too certain understandings of disability, such as that which turns disability into a threat to the strength of a society or race, have led to eugenic programs which put millions of human lives in true danger and continue to do so even today.

Notwithstanding my own awareness of the potentially unhelpful, painful, and dangerous elements in naming, I have had to make choices in the way I name people and things. I have tried to be as open as possible to correction from the people involved. I have tried not to impose names that the people themselves did not recognize. As a rule of thumb, I opted to use *person-first language* (e.g. 'a person with a disability', rather than 'the disabled'). I made this choice to ensure that in our speaking of different 'groups' of people, I as a writer and you as a reader first explicitly note our common humanity, instead of starting with those things that make us different. Some would even argue that we should get rid of the denominator 'disabled' altogether for its inadequacy. However, the social issues (such as exclusion and injustice) frequently faced by people with disabilities are in my opinion too serious not to name them. When I use the term 'disabilities', I therefore refer primarily to the ways in which human differences can become negativized due to particular social, political, or theological discourses and interpretations that underly said harmful social issues.

A second issue concerning language is related to the international and ecumenical character of the present study's academic audience. In my Dutch context, the use of male language for God is very common, in line with what we find in much of Scripture. However, other contexts remind me that this has the potential of projecting human constructs of masculinity on God and perpetuating these sometimes illegitimate human constructs by our legitimation of them in the image we have of God. In places where I interact with authors or respondents, I have chosen to follow the language they themselves use (e.g. sometimes 'God reveals himself'). In places where I make my own theological argument, I have chosen to use a more neutral language (e.g. 'God reveals God-self').

I hope that my readers will be sympathetic to these and other linguistic choices I have had to make. I remain open to correction, and am hopeful that linguistic errors on my part will not prevent anyone from interacting with this work.

Foreword

Completing this book and the years of study that preceded it, marks a moment of heartfelt gratitude. The past years have brought so many good things to be thankful for. I have been able to discover new things, to grow in academic skills, but also as a disciple of Jesus Christ. I received so many surprising gifts of grace. Therefore, first of all, I want to thank God for all God's goodness shown to me.

I thank God for the gift of a supportive circle of family and friends around me. First and foremost, I must mention my wife Geranne, to whom this book is dedicated. I am not going to say that she has had to suffer much while I was doing the work of this research. Mostly, I have experienced doing this work as a joy, and I have refused to take my worries over the project home with me too much. Nonetheless, as I wrote in the dedication, besides being a stable factor at home, Geranne was also an example of many of the values and practices that I describe in this book. She is a star at making contact with others, and always willing to go the extra mile with them. While I was working on this project, Geranne and I received two sons, Toon and Wiebe. They made coming home after work every day extra joyful. Toon and Wiebe, I hope you grow up in a community in which your God-given gifts are discovered, valued, and cherished. I also want to mention my parents and parents-in-law for their continued support. I am thankful for friends like Chris van Zwol, Matthijs van der Welle, Tom Waalewijn, and Yoo Eun Seong, who have all become ministers while I was doing my research, for their friendship and for the opportunity to keep a close connection to the messiness of everyday church life, hopefully preventing me from chasing abstract idealisms. I am thankful for all those other friends and family members, who have helped me remember that life is so much more than study, even if the study is concerned with a subject as awesome as theology.

I thank God for the gift of critical and constructive academic friends, colleagues, and supervisors. My primary supervisor Hans Schaeffer has been very diligent in turning me into a structured practical theologian. His efforts in doing so and his patience are remarkable. Any conceptual coherency in this book is undoubtedly the result of his critical remarks. Most of these remarks were placed in the context of our research meetings together with colleagues Jasper Bosman and Attila Csongor Kelemen. I have fond memories of the many hours we spent on scrutinizing each other's texts. It was truly a joy to know that the difficulties I faced in my research were not unfamiliar to both of you. I have been able to use a lot of your hard work for my own benefit. I hope that pleasure was mutual. My secondary supervisor John Swinton has done much to encourage me and to prevent me from falling into the many pitfalls I did not immediately see as a rookie in disability theology. I am very honored he wanted to be a part of my project. I am thankful for the critical readers who have served on the assessment board. I am thankful for the Theological University in Kampen, where I have studied and worked for ten years and was given tremendous opportunities to learn and grow. The university is filled with wonderful and inspiring people, not in the least place those that inhabit our 'Ph.D. Attic' like my roommate Jung-Hun Seo. I am thankful for the critical feedback and stimulating conversations within the university's research group Reformed Traditions in Secular Europe (RTSE), and the Center for Church and Mission in the West (CCMW). My participation within The Netherlands School for Advanced Studies in Theology and Religion (NOSTER) has proven to be very fruitful. I wish to thank especially Marcel Barnard and Carl Sterkens who have both led Noster's seminar on the empirical study of religion, where I learned much. A final academic community I want to mention here is the Institue on Theology and Disability. This group has not only been a tremendous academic inspiration to me, but also a place of friendship and endless surprises. I have to mention the name of Bill Gaventa here, who has worked very hard over the years to build this community. Also, I must mention the Institute's Ph.D. seminar, in which I was able to participate four times. Hans Reinders, a Dutchman whom I met primarily in the United States, showed me how academic rigor and a commitment to disability are in no way mutually exclusive.

Foreword

I thank God for the gift of generous sponsors, both individuals, and foundations. Not only have they made it possible for me to devote my attention to the project that resulted in this book - by supporting this project, they underscored that is was important, not only to me but to a wider audience. I am thankful for the work of Tjerk Bos who prepared the way for me to do this research in terms of fundraising. I am also thankful for those who have helped me along the way with preparing this book, like my neighbor and friend Wolter Rose, Kampen's one and only LaTeX-pert. I also thank Albert Gootjes for correcting the English of my manuscript. He hasn't seen this foreword, so rest assured: things will be better from here on. Of course, all remaining mistakes are my own.

Last but certainly not least, I thank God for the surprising gifts I received through meeting so many people. It was a joy to discover that reflection on faith and disability is a field to which many people have already devoted themselves wholeheartedly. I have met many of them, and they have greatly inspired me. The many encounters I had in Hart van Vathorst, about which you are to read a bit more in the following pages, have been life-changing. I thank all my interviewees for their openness, and their willingness to talk to me, even if I asked difficult or impertinent questions. I am especially thankful for Tjerk Busstra and Joost Smit, two people who have trusted me enough to let me see how things were really going in Vathorst. I hope and pray that Hart van Vathorst will continue to be a place of surprising encounters, and that its story inspires others. Hopefully, my telling of this story in this book will make you, as a reader, curious for more.

Let the name of the LORD be praised, both now and forevermore.

Koos Tamminga
Kampen, Summer 2020

Chapter 1

Introduction

1.1 Sharing Life, Not Just a Roof

In August 1986, the celebrated Dutch catholic theologian and priest Henri Nouwen had an encounter that would forever change his life. The encounter is described in Nouwen's famous book *Adam: God's Beloved*. Adam Arnett was a young man with profound intellectual and physical disabilities, who could not speak or move without assistance. Henri met Adam at the Daybreak community in Ontario, Canada, where he had moved after his career as a professor of theology. While Henri had been asked to care for Adam, soon, in his own words, "the tables were turning, Adam was becoming *my* teacher, taking *me* by the hand, walking with me in my confusion through the wilderness of *my* life."[1]

This story of a theology professor who becomes the student of a man with severe intellectual disabilities is remarkable in many ways. It runs counter to many prevalent ideas of what it means to learn. One's IQ, or even the ability to speak, is apparently not decisive for what one human being can teach another. In fact, what Henri Nouwen learned most from Adam Arnett was the relative value of words: "My many words, spoken or written, always tempted me to go up into lofty ideas and perspectives without keeping me in touch with the dailyness and beauty of ordinary life. Adam didn't allow this. It was as if he said to me, 'Not only do you *have* a body like I do, Henri, but you *are* your

---

[1] Nouwen, *Adam*, p. 36.

body. Don't let your words become separated from your flesh. Your words must become and remain flesh.'"[2]

An important lesson from Nouwen's encounter is thus the possibility of deep reciprocity between people who are very different. (Dis)ability does not have to lead to unequal relationships in which the roles of giver and receiver are predetermined. This notion goes well with current-day developments in reflection on disability and its social context, as the word 'integration' has come to be replaced by 'inclusion'. Briefly stated, whereas integration is a term that highlights the outsider's responsibility to become an insider, inclusion demands much more attention for reciprocity. In relation to people with disabilities, inclusion demands not only that they be present in society, but also that there be room for their contributions.

Still, Nouwen's description of his encounter with Adam goes one step further than this broadly applicable emphasis on reciprocity. Nouwen writes that the impact of his encounter with Adam can only be properly understood in its full value in relation to the life of Jesus. Nouwen does not claim that Adam is a second Jesus, but he does observe a remarkable similarity in their life stories. Adam's life, so he writes, is an *embodiment* of the story of Jesus.[3] Through this hermeneutic lens of the story of Jesus, Henri Nouwen begins to understand *why* this encounter had so much impact on him. In Adam, Henri encountered something of Jesus. This faith perspective therefore provides a powerful narrative for what one could call an 'inclusive community'.

The encounter between Henri and Adam is not an isolated phenomenon. It took place in Daybreak, which is part of a network of communities called L'Arche. L'Arche's goal is to *share life* communaly, with people 'with' and 'without' disabilities.[4] Although Nouwen's book is unique because of its eloquence and inspiring character, the kind of encounter that lies behind it is not. L'Arche and communities like it are a rich source of encounters that are similar in structure and impact. These communities are therefore remarkable; imagine what

---

[2] Nouwen, *Adam*, pp. 36–37.

[3] Ibid., pp. 112–113.

[4] Reinders, "Being with the Disabled" gives an account of L'Arche founder Jean Vanier's mission of sharing life and its theological implications. See also Wall, *Welcome as a Way of Life*.

1.1. Sharing Life, Not Just a Roof

the encounter meant to Adam, what it meant to Henri, what it still means for so many others who read Nouwen's book. Not only did Adam and Henri find a sense of fulfilment and wholeness in their relationship, which enriched *both* of their lives in fascinating ways – but through their encounter, something of Jesus also came to revelation.

Regardless of the specific theology adhered to by a given church or denomination, it would seem like those two things ought to be part of its vision: meaningful communion between its members, and a process of deeper discovery of who Jesus is as a result. Although L'Arche is not a church, it seems clear that churches that seek to reflect on how to live faithfully in this world have much to learn from its experiences and those of similar communities. In fact, the American ethicist Stanley Hauerwas and L'Arche's founder Jean Vanier co-authored a book on what L'Arche could mean for churches in their ecclesiological reflection.[5]

> In February 2020, as the research described in this thesis was already finished, the terrible news about Jean Vanier's sexual abuse of at least six women without disabilities came out. The news left many devastated, as the legacy of Vanier, especially visible in the L'Arche communities he helped to found, was an inspiration to them all. Vanier's actions must be strongly condemned, all the more because they contradict his ideal of non-violent and safe communities. Although Vanier himself betrayed the trust of the women involved, and therefore also that of those who looked up to him as a spiritual example, the life of the L'Arche communities and his reflections on this life do not lose their value. Therefore, this thesis will still refer to his work. Notwithstanding, new questions will need to be asked as to the roots of Vanier's actions and to which degree these are connected to the core and fabric of L'Arche.

One might ask, however, whether experiences like Nouwen's are not a 'step too far' for the average congregation. Would this not work only

---

[5]Hauerwas and Vanier, *Living Gently in a Violent World*.

in high-commitment settings, where people have a specific predisposition for such community life? This is the question that the research project seeks to put to the test. We will trace the developments in Hart van Vathorst, a project in which a local church - a very 'average congregation' - teamed up with a number of disability service providers. In their reflection on what this would mean for their community life, they read Vanier and Hauerwas's book and participated in the production of a Dutch translation. After much deliberation, they decided that they would not only share the roof of their new building, but also strive to share their lives. By tracing how this dream became reality, I hope to contribute to reflection on the way transformatory encounters like that of Adam and Henri can help shape the church's life.

1.2 Statement of the Problem

In this section, I will introduce the problem addressed by the present study as an *ecclesiological* problem. There are two reasons that make it ecclesiological in nature. First of all, the twenty-first century church in the Netherlands finds itself in transition, and ecclesiological reflection seems to be needed to wrestle through this transition in a responsible way. Secondly, like many societies in the West, Dutch society is itself also in transition, and this transition is intertwined with the situation of the churches in many ways. In the following, I will describe the changes in church and society in broad lines, showing that they are intertwined and call for ecclesiological reflection on the level of *community*.

1.2.1 Church in Transition

In this twenty-first century, the churches in the Netherlands are experiencing a decline in their numbers.[6] At the same time, for many who are still in the church, larger ecclesial structures like denominations have become meaningless.[7] This is not just a national trend. Traditional mainline Protestantism in the West appears to be declining on the level of church membership and congregational vitality, as

---

[6] Bernts and Berghuijs, *God in Nederland*.
[7] Geertsema, *Jaarplan 2016*.

1.2. Statement of the Problem

well as the level of the church's influence on society, culture, and politics.[8] However, in the European context, the Swedish sociologist of religion Per Pettersson has observed that it is not in all respects that the church's presence is declining:

> Our data tells us that there is both an increasing and a decreasing role for the majority churches in contemporary Europe. On the one hand, churches have a steady, and possibly increasing role to play both in social cohesion and as welfare agents. At the same time however, their membership is diminishing. But even with their reduced capacity (financial as well as human), they are expected to handle increasing social needs.[9]

Given the changed social circumstances that we will sketch in the next subsection, the Dutch situation appears to resonate with this larger European and Western perspective. There are increasing expectations, but decreasing membership and capacities. In a 2004 study from the Dutch sociologist of religion Ton Bernts and others, expert interviewees identified the same problem: churches are increasingly expected to deliver professional support for the communities around them, while human and financial resources are scarce.[10] The picture of the state of the Church in the West is thus not an unequivocal one. The church does not appear to be on a straight path to total evanescence; as Pettersson argues, there are indeed important roles for the church to play. Yet it seems clear that there are also many challenges. Pettersson and Bernts identified these challenges in terms of numbers, both financial and human. The core of the challenges, however, seems to lie even deeper. Pettersson may have made no recommendation on the roles the churches *should* or *should not* play, or where they should invest their reduced capacity. Such a statement was, however, made by the Dutch politician Wim Deetman, one of the people Bernts interviewed for study: "the churches' primary task is to preach the Word of God. Do not walk away from that task."[11] If the church is really to be

---

[8]Cahalan, "Three Approaches"; Pew Research Center, *America's Changing Religious Landscape*.
[9]Pettersson, "Church as Welfare Agent", p. 15.
[10]Bernts, *Boodschap aan de kerken?*, pp. 185–186.
[11]Ibid., p. 45.

served in its life as a church, the question of priorities is an important one to consider. After all, the church has historically not presented itself as just another 'welfare agent', but as a community with a specific identity or calling. And to ask and answer questions about the church's identity and calling is to practice ecclesiology.

The American theologian Bryan Stone defines ecclesiology as follows:

> Ecclesiology is a discipline that undertakes critical and constructive reflection on the Christian community as a distinct social body in the world and as a particular people in history. This community understands itself to be the 'body of Christ', the 'temple of God', and a living 'sacrament' that, because of its union with Christ, reveals to the world something of God's very nature and purpose. At the same time, the church is also and always an imperfect, social and historical institution: constantly subject to change; reflective of the cultures in which it is to be found; and created, organized, and maintained by particular human beings in specific times and places.[12]

The first thing Stone's definition shows is that ecclesiology is both critical and constructive. It can be *critical* in its description and analyses of the church as it is, and *constructive* in pointing out ways forward. The critical task of ecclesiology could be considered a descriptive and analytical task. The constructive task of ecclesiology can also be a *strategic* or *normative* task. Secondly, the definition points out an important theme in ecclesiology, namely the relationship between theological statements about the church and its actual reality.

Ecclesiology can be practiced by focusing on one of the aspects of its task as described by Stone. There are ecclesiological approaches that limit themselves to sociological description, others that invest in theological – often systematic theological - analysis, and yet others that concern themselves primarily with the strategic or normative aspects of ecclesiology.[13]

The challenges that today's church faces, as presented above, fall

---

[12] Stone, *Ecclesiology*, p. 1.

[13] Examples of sociological descriptions are: Bainbridge, *The Sociology of Religious*

1.2. Statement of the Problem

under the strategic aspect of ecclesiological inquiry; to use Pettersson's terminology, the question is how the church ought to invest its reduced capacity. This is a question of strategy, calling for normative ecclesiology. However, it is clear that in order to deal with the challenges on a normative level, we must first adopt a vision for the church's identity. What *is* the church - what is it in real life, and what *should* it actually be?

Since these questions are intrinsically related, the problem cannot be easily solved by focusing on only a single aspect of ecclesiology. The current state of the church demands fundamental reflection with the actual churches in view, because they are the communities actually facing the challenges. However, a theological level of inquiry is needed as well, since discernment on the investment of the church's reduced capacities is motivated in terms of how the community understands itself to be a *church* rather than just another welfare organization.

The first half of the problem can thus be summarized as follows: The twenty-first century church in the Netherlands is in transition and fundamental ecclesiological reflection is needed. The nature of this reflection should not be one-sided (favoring either the church's concrete sociological or its abstract theological identity), but rather comprehensive in its approach so as to be able to truly serve the church as a community discerning where it might best invest its reduced capacity.

1.2.2 Society in Transition

A lot is happening in Dutch civil society.[14] In broad lines, we can observe a decentralization of social policy. Beginning in 2015, parliament accepted a number of bills relating to health care, youth care, accessible employment, and education. These bills show a common trend in terms of their program of decentralizing responsibilities from the national government to local, municipal governments, and down

---

Movements, Pickel and Müller, *Church and Religion in Contemporary Europe*. A very influential and oft-quoted example of ecclesiological analytical reflection based on theological models is: Dulles, *Models of the Church*. We find the more normative and strategic level in missional ecclesiologies like: Keller, *Center Church*, Piper, *Let the Nations Be Glad!*

[14]The term 'civil society' can be interpreted in various ways. Following Martin van der Meulen, I use the following definition: "In a minimal sense, civil society is

to the informal communities around the people in need of care or assistance.[15] There are multiple reasons for this policy, including financial ones. Yet a strong ideological argument is also being made, using the terminology of participation and inclusion. In his 2013 national address, King Willem Alexander of the Netherlands coined the term 'participation society' as a description of the new and ideal society.[16] This term is understood as a 'dot on the horizon', an ideological dream for society. While the above bills are not to be mistaken for this society, they are indeed meant to support a deeper cultural and societal change. Participation society was described as "a society in which citizens together shape 'good lives', and in which professionals may offer support wherever the citizens' abilities require such support."[17]

It is thus clear that a lot of emphasis is being placed on the power of citizens and local communities to live 'good lives' together, over against a larger role for the government in social policies. The participation society is a turn away from government dependency to a more self-sufficient and accessible form of social community. This fits within broader, international contexts in which the terms participation and inclusion are being used as well. The 2006 UN Treaty on the protection and promotion of the rights and dignity of persons with disabilities is an important example of this. The main goal of this treaty, its 'dot on the horizon', seems to be for people with disabilities to live "independently and [to be] included in the community."[18] In 2016, the treaty was ratified by Dutch parliament, as part of the larger push toward a more participatory and inclusive society.[19] The debates on this matter have not been settled yet, as will emerge from the discussion in chapter 2. Important questions are still being raised as to the expected

---

a network of associations of citizens that try to achieve common goals set by themselves. This network can be distinguished, but not separated from the domains of state, market and the private sphere. In a stronger sense, civil society promotes the 'civility' of society by strengthening communicative action, solidarity and the diffusion of power." See Van der Meulen, *Vroom in de Vinex*, p. 174. I use the term in its 'minimal sense'.

[15]Kooiman et al., *Leren transformeren*, p. 3.

[16]"Troonrede 2013". Online sources are cited by title only. The full URL can be found in the Online References section of the bibliography at the end of this volume.

[17]Kooiman et al., *Leren transformeren*, p. 8, translation KST.

[18]United Nations, *Rights and Dignity of Persons with Disabilities*, p. 19.

[19]*Dutch senate ratifies UN treaty*.

1.2. Statement of the Problem

power of citizens and the strength of communities in Dutch civil society: Are they really ready to take over a significant amount of work from the professionals who have been doing it up till now? Can these communities become inclusive, and what does that actually mean?

Questions about the nature of Dutch civil society have sparked some interest in the position that churches are to assume within this field of social communities. When existing social structures are dismantled, the church may prove to be of service to local governments in need of partners in civil society. Research shows that some local governments have quite easily and naturally partnered up with churches, while others have found it less self-evident to partner up with religious organizations like churches.[20] The churches themselves have sometimes recognized the challenges and opportunities that these transitions in society present. In an open letter published in 2016, René de Reuver, a leading figure of the mainline Protestant church in the Netherlands (PKN), and Gerard de Korte, one of the leading bishops of the Roman Catholic church in the Netherlands, identified a twofold role for the church. On the one hand, the church is the government's ally in offering support to those in need. On the other hand, the church has a critical voice, calling upon the government to prevent society from heading towards a big divide between "those who participate and those who are left on the side."[21] The letter was written in reaction to research showing a significant increase in the social support offered by churches due to the rise in Dutch poverty rates.[22]

Dutch Christian thinkers have devoted extensive study to the societal developments and linked them primarily to the church's practices in terms of diaconate.[23] Another potential theological discipline for studying these developments is that of missiology. The societal changes may, after all, present new possibilities and challenges for

---

[20]Noordegraaf, *Kerk en Wmo*, pp. 109–115.

[21]De Korte and De Reuver, "Kerk als bondgenoot en luis in de pels".

[22]Crutzen and Van der Linden, *Armoede in Nederland 2016*. When this research was repeated in 2019, it showed that poverty rates were still on the rise; see Bolwijn, *Armoede in Nederland 2019*. The 2019 report sparked similar responses from De Korte and De Reuver in which they criticized the way in which the ideal of autonomous citizenship has become a leading ideal in governmental policymaking; see De Korte, "Armoedebestrijding" and De Reuver and De Korte, "Zelfredzaamheid".

[23]Crijns, *Diaconie*; Noordegraaf, *Kerk en Wmo*; Noordegraaf, *Betrek kerken bij Wmo*; Jager-Vreugdenhil, "Zo hoort het".

sharing the gospel with people in our communities. The two theological disciplines of diaconiology and missiology share at least two common tendencies: they focus on what we *do* as a church, and they can therefore become disconnected from the church as a whole. Noordegraaf, a Dutch specialist in diaconate studies, describes his field as "a department of the church", one of the churchly activities.[24] And Dutch missiologist Stefan Paas calls his work "the Research & Development department of the church."[25] Missiology and diaconiology are by trade outward-looking disciplines.

Even though local governments may have specific requests for churches that can be met with diaconal projects and possibly answered also with missiological concerns in mind, society's actual challenges still seem to lie elsewhere. As shown by the current debates introduced above, which we will investigate in much greater detail in chapter 2, there is uncertainty regarding the strength of communities within civil society. Will they really hold when the pressure rises? Will civil society prove to be strong enough? What do communities need to become inclusive? To respond to these challenges, churches must reflect not just on what they can do, or on which 'department' should be the one to act. Rather, the focus must be on the kind of community the church *is*. Can the church be a community that is sufficiently reliable for a 'participation society'? Does it have resources to live out a communal life that is rightfully 'inclusive'? To answer such questions, ecclesiological reflection is needed: fundamental, comprehensive, and theological.

1.2.3 Interaction Between Church and Society

As noted above, it is not just society as an outward phenomenon that gives reason to study ecclesiology. Such reflection is not only needed to communicate with those 'outside', but also called for by the church's own inner life. The transitions in church and society are not happening independently of one another. As an ironic example, it has been argued that in the Netherlands roughly up until the Second World War, before the implementation of the so-called welfare state, churches had clearly defined roles in society. When the government took over social

---

[24]Noordegraaf, *Kerk en Wmo*, p. 11.
[25]Paas, "Ecclesiology in Context", p. 147.

legislation and the church's care was no longer needed, the church's self-evident position changed. This development, so it has been argued, led to a less prominent place for the church within Dutch society and may even have played a role in the internal struggles which churches consequently experienced in terms of their numbers and influence.[26] There is no doubt that factors of context (on the micro, meso, and macro levels) play an important role in church life.[27] Now that the welfare state seems to be coming to its end, the same questions are being asked again: What kind of a community is the church? What role and capacity does it have in society?

In short, there are two reasons for ecclesiological reflection on the way the church can be a reliable and inclusive community in its particular context: the church's own situation, and the appeal which society has made on the church. These two reasons are interrelated in various ways, and they seem to point towards a common, deeper problem relating to the nature and capacity of the communities we live in.

1.3 Research Goal

As indicated above, the problem we have identified is not easily solved. Thinking through various theories of community might provide us with some useful insights, but that exercise could easily remain disconnected from reality and be arbitrary in its selection of theories. Furthermore, there are many existing theories on churches and inclusion that have arisen from contexts other than the Dutch. These contexts often shine through in theories in ways that are potentially unhelpful for their application in other contexts. For the present project we therefore strive to engage the problem of community in a different way, namely by focusing on the practices of a single, concrete community as it strives to become a more inclusive community in its own context. As noted in section 1.1, the case study revolves around a congregation in the Vathorst neighborhood in the Dutch town of

---

[26]Kennedy, *Stad op een berg*, p. 18; Sol, "De geschiedenis van de gereformeerde diakonie, 1945-1964"

[27]27 It is not surprising, then, that many recent approaches in the field of congregational studies include context as one of the key factors for reflection; cf. Ammerman et al., *Studying Congregations*; Cameron, *Studying Local Churches*; Brouwer et al., *Levend lichaam*. Cf. ch. 4.

Amersfoort called the Ontmoetingskerk, which translates into English as 'Encounter Church'. The Ontmoetingskerk has become involved in 'Hart van Vathorst' (lit. 'Heart of Vathorst'; henceforth: HVV), and is a cooperative project of the Ontmoetingskerk, an 'inclusive daycare center' for children, and two disability service providers. About 100 people with various disabilities, ranging from Down syndrome to traumatic brain injury and dementia, live in HVV. Together, the Ontmoetingskerk and disability service provides have built a new, shared building, committing themselves to sharing not only a roof, but also their lives.[28]

This investigation departs from the expectation that this case study will be particularly useful for dealing with the present problem, given that Hart van Vathorst is intrinsically connected with the two sides of the problem as identified in section 1.2: as health care agencies, they are part of the broader societal shifts; and, as a church, they face the same challenges that other contemporary churches in the Netherlands face. The path that Hart van Vathorst and the Ontmoetingskerk have chosen to respond to the challenges appears to be that of community: In a society in which words like inclusion and participation are frequently used but questions still remain as to their actual practical value, this community has set out to live together with a group of people who would normally live quite separate lives. What does the successful young urban professional have to do with the middle-aged man who has suffered brain damage and is unable to work a paid job? Will the Ontmoetingskerk prove to be a different, more inclusive kind of community that could answer the needs of people both within and outside the church? Will it be a community in which all members have a proper place (inclusion) and can actively contribute to it (participation)? If it becomes such a community, will it then extend its welcome to the surrounding society? Will it function as an inspiring example? The nature of this study made it impossible to offer an answer to any one of these questions at the outset. Yet the path that the Ontmoetingskerk has chosen seemed worthy of further study even before any outcomes became visible. Questions and struggles regarding the inclusive sharing of life can surface anywhere in society, but since a large number of people in HVV faced this new way

---

[28] *HVV's website.*

of living together without much preparation or prior motivation, the expectation was that these questions would surface in great numbers and with much urgency.

The goal of this study is to track the path of this community with special attention to the theology at work in it. The Ontmoetingskerk is not just a social partner, it is a church. This is why we will attempt to unearth what this means in practice and how it engages the society around it. In other words, we are looking for a kind of contextualized ecclesiology. Will a concept like inclusion be part of such an ecclesiology? If so, what will it look like when embodied in specifically Christian practices? By identifying this implicit and operant ecclesiology and its outworking, the church and its surrounding society can learn valuable lessons. This one case study is thus meant as an exploration of existing theory. Rather than looking for some blueprint that might show all churches and communities exactly what to do, this case will allow us to identify strengths and weaknesses in both theory and practice that can function as learning points for other communities facing similar questions and challenges.

1.4 Research Questions

The central question for this study will be:

What contribution does the example of Hart van Vathorst make to theological reflection on the inclusion of people with disabilities in the church?

Some of the terms in this main question require further explanation. As argued above (see 1.2), this study concerns itself with *ecclesiology*. This means we are not just looking for what people say about the church (descriptive), but strive to find truly theological, normative results. Nicholas Healy and others have convincingly argued that the study of the church's concrete praxis should be part of ecclesiological reflection.[29] This is why the Ontmoetingskerk represents an *example* worthy of further study. It is not the only possible example, but for reasons mentioned above (1.3), it does seem to be a fitting one. Using

---

[29] Healy, *Church, World, and the Christian Life*; P. Ward, *Perspectives* This point will be further elaborated in chapter 3

the term example does not mean that it stands beyond reproach. This study does not mean to erect a monument for the Ontmoetingskerk or to tell a story of success; this would be totally contrary to the way Healy speaks about practical ecclesiological reflection. Rather, an example (or 'case', in methodological terms) can be used to generate the kind of knowledge that abstract theory cannot provide. Research has shown that the type of knowledge from which people learn is very often concrete and practical in nature, rather than purely abstract and theoretical.[30] Hence, the kind of *contribution* that the present study wants to make is on the level of the church's concrete praxis. This means that the results cannot be easily generalized in a classical sense or summarized, but, as we will argue in more detail in chapter 3, it *does* make a contribution by challenging and sometimes falsifying existing theories and paradigms, and inspiring new approaches and experiments.[31]

Part of the answer to the main research question will be descriptive in nature, leading to the following subquestions:

1. What does the praxis of the Ontmoetingskerk in the Hart van Vathorst context look like?

2. What operant ecclesiological voices relating to inclusion can be heard?

3. What espoused ecclesiological voices relating to inclusion can be heard?

4. What formal ecclesiological voices relating to inclusion can be heard?

5. What normative ecclesiological voices relating to inclusion can be heard?

These questions are meant to structure the description of the Ontmoetingskerk and its practices. Subquestion 1 is general, a simple and short question with a very long and complex answer. Even though a

---

[30]Flyvbjerg, "Five Misunderstandings About Case-Study Research".

[31]Flyvbjerg, "Five Misunderstandings About Case-Study Research"; Campbell-Reed, "The Power and Danger of a Single Case Study in Practical Theological Research".

1.4. Research Questions

full answer may elude us, this question is an important one to ask because a general feel for the story of the Ontmoetingskerk is essential to understanding more specific descriptions of certain parts of its life. Subquestions 2-5 are more clearly defined. They build upon the Theology in Four Voices model introduced by Helen Cameron and others.[32] Their model is helpful in understanding how theology and practice relate. As summarized in figure 1.1, the authors state that theology comes in four voices: normative, espoused, formal, and operant.

Normative Theology Scriptures The creeds Official church teaching Liturgies	**Formal Theology** The theology of the theologians Dialogue with other disciplines
Espoused Theology The theology embedded within *a group's articulation of its beliefs*	**Operant Theology** The theology embedded within *the actual practices of a group*

Figure 1.1: The Four Voices of Theology.

These four voices are always interrelated. However, it is worth distinguishing between them and discovering where they differ from and challenge each other. Listening carefully for each distinct voice makes it possible to engage the voices in a meaningful conversation at a later stage. We will discuss this model of theology in four voices in greater detail in section 3.3.2.

Apart from a descriptive part, this study also requires a thick anal-

---

[32] Cameron, Bhatti, and Duce, *Talking About God*, p. 54. This model will be further introduced and discussed in section 3.3.2.

ysis of the case and more 'normative' or 'strategic' conclusions in order to reach its goal. This makes a second set of subquestions necessary:

6. How can the Ontmoetingskerk's approach for applying inclusion to church life in the Hart van Vathorst context best be understood in relation to existing theory?

7. How can the Ontmoetingskerk's praxis in the Hart van Vathorst context be understood in relation to this approach?

8. What lessons can be learned from the Ontmoetingkserk in the Hart van Vathorst context?

Subquestion 6 is a question of analysis. To describe this case and learn from it in a meaningful way, it is necessary to connect it to existing theory. Due to the inductive nature of this research, it is important for the theories and concepts applied not to be used as preconceived matrices. Subquestion 7 seeks to reflect critically on the practices of the Ontmoetingskerk: how do vision and practice relate? The final question (8) is a question about strategy. What lessons can be learned and implemented following thorough analysis and reflection?

1.5 Overview of the Project

While an in-depth methodological account will be given in chapter 3, the current section is intended to offer a general outline of the project and to describe the structure of this dissertation. There is a difference between the research project as process and this dissertation as product. The research as a whole was structured much like the subquestions above indicate. A large part of the research time was invested in watching, listening, and observing (subquestion 1). This data collection phase started at the very outset of the project, even before a detailed research proposal had been drawn up. Given the inductive nature of this research, the intention was to have the analysis and evaluation of the material (the second set of subquestions) be guided naturally by the data collected. This took the shape of an iterative process, from data to interpretation and back to data again. Subquestions 2-5 were meant as a way to organize the data. The research project's main lens is ecclesiology, hence its central position in the main question. The respective theological voices in subquestions 2-5 serve to distinguish between the different types of data acquired. Due to the iterative nature of this study, the approach was theological from the very beginning, notwithstanding the use of methods from the social sciences. These issues will discussed at greater length in chapter 3.

Whereas the process itself was a mix of interpreting and collecting data, in the actual dissertation a greater distinction will be maintained between the two. After this introductory chapter (ch. 1), a second chapter will discuss the main theoretical surroundings of this research (ch. 2). A third chapter will present the practical theological embedding of this research and the methodology employed in the empirical parts of this study (ch. 3), followed by three chapters of a descriptive nature (chs. 4, 5, and 6). These descriptive chapters will treat subquestions 1-5, along with subquestion 6. Together, these chapters present the results of data collection over a period of two-and-a-half years of field work. The final chapter (ch. 7) provides a conclusion and discussion in which also subquestions 7 and 8 are addressed.

1.6 Relevance

As a dissertation project, this study has *academic* relevance in the way it introduces two fields of reflection to each other that in the past have rarely been combined, namely practical theological ecclesiology and disability theology.[33] Furthermore, within the Dutch theological context there has been little academic theological reflection on the inclusion of people with disabilities.[34] With its focus on practices, the present project introduces existing theories from other contexts to the Dutch context, with an awareness of their contextual nature. One therefore becomes aware in practice how the Dutch socio-political context is very different from the American context, for example, from which much reflection on the matter stems.

Besides its academic relevance, this research project also has a

---

[33] In chapter 2 we will explore the little that has been done on the intersection of these two fields.

[34] Besides some more popular resources which will be reviewed in chapter 2, the main contribution comes in the form of the following collection of essays: Meininger, *Van en voor allen*.

wider relevance. This applies first of all on the *ecclesial* level. Churches in the West find themselves in a situation of transition and need to reflect on their life in new and creative ways to rediscover their identities and to find faithful ways of being church in their rapidly changing contexts. This research project may serve as one example of the way churches can look in perhaps unexpected directions for finding new and faithful ways of being church.

Lastly, there is a broader *societal* dimension to this project's relevance. As we have already noted in section 1.2 (see also ch. 2), society at large also finds itself in transition. It wants to become somehow 'inclusive', but often does not know what this entails. A critical theological perspective may aid society at large in gaining clarity on this matter. Additionally, many governments (on both local and supra-local levels) are looking to churches to partner with them in neighborhood social work. The present study may thus help them to understand more about the church's unique nature, opening the way to more fruitful cooperation.

Chapter 2

Theoretical Framework: Potential Roles of Churches and Ecclesiology for Disability Inclusion

2.1 Introduction

This chapter[1] provides an overview of the theoretical background to the case study presented in this dissertation. Such a theoretical background or framework is necessary to gain a better understanding of the case and to learn from its study.

People with disabilities have often been marginalized and discriminated. This is true in society at large, but also in the church. The place of people with disabilities in communities is not self-evident. Much of the conversation surrounding the concept of disability and the place of people with disabilities in society today is framed in terms of inclusion. In the following section (2.2), we will examine how this concept of inclusion is being used and reflected upon. We will illustrate this in two webs of practices: education, and the job market.[2] The sub-

---

[1] This chapter is a revised and updated edition of: Tamminga, Schaeffer, and Swinton, "Potential Roles of Churches and Ecclesiology for Disability Inclusion". It is used here with permission from the publisher, De Gruyter.

[2] We borrow the term 'web of practices' from Reinhard Hütter, who speaks about

sequent section (2.3) will sketch out how inclusion functions in yet another web of practices: the church. We will show what theological (or practical theological) reflection on the church's practices may bring to the table. Section 2.4 will then explore the intersection of reflections on inclusion and ecclesiology. The final section (2.5) provides some concluding thoughts.

The research presented in this dissertation was carried out from a Dutch perspective. Even though conceptual discussions are connected to broader international debates, it is impossible to write about a concept like inclusion disconnected from a specific context. This explains the presence of some examples from the Dutch context as well as the selection of a number of Dutch authors who have reflected on the notion of inclusion. But every reader is invited to read her own examples and context into the text.

2.2 A Turn to Inclusion

The inclusive turn taken by society has already been noted above. This turn applies not only to reflection on the place that people with disabilities take in society, but also for the position assumed by other minorities. Inclusion seems thus to have become a magical word of sorts, representing a dream of the ideal society in which everybody belongs and participates equally. In this section, we will explore the way the concept of inclusion functions in policymaking, looking at how it plays out in two fields of practice (i.e. the job market, and education), and describe a number of persistent questions that remain when it comes to the implementation of a more inclusive society. Our focus will be on the inclusion of people with disabilities.

---

the church as "a web of core practices" in Hütter, "The Church", p. 35. In section 3.3.2, we will offer a deeper exploration of what we mean by 'practices'. For now, it is important to note that we understand practices as complex social activity, which is both informed by convictions and constitutive of those convictions. Hence, the study of practices reveals more than just the observable behavior; it points at underlying values and convictions. By referring to education, the job market, and the church as 'webs of practices', we seek attention for the complex nature of these fields and underline why their study yields important results for understanding what is believed and practiced in them with regard to inclusion.

2.2. A Turn to Inclusion

2.2.1 Inclusion in Policy

One of the most influential contexts in which inclusion is conceptualized in its current use is the quality of life framework (QOL), summarized in figure 2.1 on page 22. This framework, developed by Robert Schalock and others, consists of three *factors: independence, social participation, and wellbeing*. These factors can be broken down into a number of *domains* that can be distinguished based on *exemplary indicators*. Social inclusion is perceived as a domain within the factor of social participation. Exemplary indicators include involvement and roles in communities.[3] QOL has become very influential in disability policy and in the broader field of health care, a circumstance which appears to constitute one reason for the prominent place the concept of inclusion currently has in reflection on the place of people with disabilities in society.

Another important driving force behind inclusive policy making with respect to people with disabilities is the *UN Convention on the Protection and Promotion of the Rights and Dignity of Persons with Disabilities*.[4] This convention is a legal text without explicit underlying values. However, what stands out when the domains of Schalock's model are compared with the UN treaty is that the domains of rights and social inclusion both appear in seven of the treaty's articles, while other domains surface far less frequently (with a maximum of three).[5] The convention can therefore be seen as a strong force driving more inclusive practices in society. In the convention, inclusion seems to be primarily a matter of involving people with disabilities in all aspects of life. This makes the term inclusion almost synonymous with *accessibility*. As such, inclusion becomes a term defined by its antonym; society is inclusive as long as it does not *exclude* people, whether physically or otherwise.

QOL and the UN treaty seem thus to represents the two major conceptual backgrounds that policymakers and activists refer to when they argue for more inclusive practice. However, within public debates, inclusion seems to encompass much more than just accessibility (UN). It has greater significance than simply being the *domain* of

---

[3] Schalock et al., "Cross-Cultural Study of Quality of Life Indicators".
[4] United Nations, *Rights and Dignity of Persons with Disabilities*.
[5] As demonstrated by Van Loon and Steglich-Lentz, *Geloven in inclusie*, p. 38.

Factor	Domain	Examplary Indicators
Independence	Personal Development	Personal skills, adaptive behavior.
	Self-determination	Choices, decisions, autonomy, control.
Social Participation	Interpersonal Relationships	Social networks, friendships, social activities.
	Social Inclusion	Involvement in community, community roles.
	Rights	Equal opportunities, respectful treatment, legal access, and due process.
Well-being	Emotional Well-being	Safety and security.
		Positive experiences, success.
	Physical Well-being	Health and nutritional status.
		Recreation, physical exertion.
	Material Well-being	Income, possessions.

Figure 2.1: Quality of Life Framework at a Glance

2.2. A Turn to Inclusion

one of the three *factors* of QOL. Rather, inclusion is often the only factor mentioned, without much in the way of explanation of its meaning. Many policymakers and activists strive for an inclusive society and inclusive cities.[6] According to the psychologists Lynn Martin and Virginie Cobigo, inclusion is a concept that has to do with "complex interactions between personal and environmental factors, including social and cultural factors."[7] Martin and Cobigo argue for the necessity of a developed definition of the term 'inclusion', given that the term is explained in many different ways. Educationalist Sarah Hall conducted qualitative research in order to identify the elements that are important in the social inclusion of people with disabilities. She found the following six elements: being accepted, having meaningful relationships, being involved in activities, having fitting living accommodations, having employment, and having support systems.[8] Hall's research shows that inclusion is indeed a complex concept, with implications on all levels of individual and communal life.

2.2.2 Inclusion in Two Webs of Practices: Education and the Job Market

But what does inclusion really look like in real life? Over the course of roughly two years, we tracked a number of Dutch newspapers with specific attention for the theme of disability.[9] The word 'inclusion' showed up numerous times in many different contexts. In what follows, the two contexts of education and the job market will be discussed briefly as examples.

There were many newspaper articles that addressed the implementation of more inclusive education in the Netherlands. Oftentimes a tension was identified between an inclusive ideal that everyone (or almost everyone) shared, and practical considerations that got in the way of this ideal. An example of this tension can be seen in the case involving Kubo, a young boy with Down syndrome.[10] Kubo at first at-

---

[6] Schippers and Van Heumen, "Inclusive City".
[7] Martin and Cobigo, "Definitions Matter in Understanding Social Inclusion".
[8] Hall, "The Social Inclusion of People with Disabilities".
[9] Three newspapers were studied in detail: the *Nederlands Dagblad*, *Trouw*, and the *Reformatorisch Dagblad*. All three have a specific interest in religion and the church in the Netherlands.
[10] See for example Bezemer, "Steunt mensenrechtencollege schoolkeus?"; Bezemer,

tended a regular elementary school, but one day this school concluded that it was no longer able to provide the extra support Kubo needed to attend classes. The Netherlands has a system of special schools for children with developmental disabilities, to which Kubo was then referred. Kubo's parents, however, thought their son would benefit more from education in a regular school context, and so they contested the school's decision, making reference to the UN treaty in the process. Kubo's father said, "People are different, that should be normal. How do you want to create a participation society if you begin by segregating children?" And, "We cannot imagine there to be no regular school where Kubo fits in. Definitely not in a city that calls itself inclusive."[11] After a judge ruled in the school's favor, Kubo's parents appealed their case before the Netherlands Institute for Human Rights. It ruled that, even though it favored more inclusive education and considered that the UN treaty demanded developments accordingly, the school could not be blamed for the decision it had made since the national government had not yet translated the inclusive principles of the un treaty into concrete policy and practice, making it impossible for the school to offer sufficient support.[12] There are also other cases similar to that of Kubo, and all witness the same tension: nobody opposes inclusion, but teachers complain that they just cannot offer the necessary support in classrooms which are already filled beyond capacity. According to the government agency for education (DUO), this produces negative effects for children who need extra support (because they do not get it) as well as for the other children in the classroom (because their teacher is busy trying to provide extra support).[13] Reflecting on this, one teacher said, "The government has beautiful ideas, but it's strange if you don't provide the means necessary for these ideas."[14]

Our search unearthed many other newspaper articles on the creation of accessible jobs in the pursuit of a more inclusive job market. The Dutch government has pledged to work towards an inclusive job market aimed at enabling as many people as possible to par-

---

"'Kubo leert het meest op een gewone school'"; Trouw, "Terecht verwezen"; ANP, "Welk Recht Heeft Kind Met Down?"

[11]Bezemer, "'Kubo leert het meest op een gewone school'".
[12]Trouw, "Terecht verwezen".
[13]Van der Woud, Van Bokhoven, and Van Grinsven, *Monitor*.
[14]Dujardin, "Leraren zuchten".

2.2. A Turn to Inclusion

ticipate in 'normal jobs'. To this end, the government implemented the *Participatiewet* (Participation Bill) in 2015. Three years later, the Netherlands Institute for Social Research (SCP) calculated that unemployment amongst people with disabilities had risen 40% since the implementation of this new legislation.[15] Together with employers, the government has since pledged to create 125.000 jobs for people with disabilities by the end of 2025. These jobs were to be divided between the two parties: private employers were to create 100.000 jobs, the government 25.000. By 2019, private employers had created 40.000 of those jobs, while the government was falling far behind. Depending on the method of calculation, some reports suggested the government had created about 8000 jobs,[16] while others reported numbers as low as 600 (!).[17] Since then, the government has decided to abandon the distinction between jobs created by the government and jobs created by private employers. However, it still insists it wants to keep its promise of creating 125.000 accessible jobs by 2025.[18] The developments in this quest for a more inclusive job market are accompanied by heated debates on the method of calculation: Which jobs count for which sector? And what kinds of jobs are to be counted?[19] Recent research shows that many so-called accessible jobs turn out not to be so accessible after all. Many employees with disabilities only managed to hold their job for a short time, or else they worked for low salaries and limited social benefits.[20] A 2019 final evaluation of the Participation Bill by the Netherlands Institute for Social Research concluded that the legislation's aims have not been reached: while the chances of employment increased slightly for young people with disabilities, their income and job security actually declined. For others, there was no increase in employment opportunities at all.[21]

---

[15] Sadiraj, Hoff, and Versantvoort, *Participatiewet*.
[16] Waterval, "Wat bedrijven kunnen".
[17] Weel, "Creatieve constructies overheid"; Julen, "Arbeidsbeperkte pion".
[18] ANP, "Overheid zoekt banen".
[19] Debated issues include, for example, who exactly is considered to 'have a disability'. Sometimes, the definition is altered so as to either include or exclude more people; cf. Weel, "Blinde en dove mensen".
[20] Weel, "Werk zonder rechten"; Weel, "Arbeidsbeperkten even werk".
[21] Van Echtelt et al., *Eindevaluatie*.

2.2.3 Reflection on Inclusive Policy and Practice

Our explorations of inclusive policy and practice show that inclusion has clearly become a buzzword. Nobody seems to have anything against inclusion as an ideal. Yet when this ideal is translated into practice, problems do arise. As a recent study carried out by an alliance of disability advocacy agencies concludes, despite the ratification of the UN treaty and a push for more inclusive policy, unemployment amongst people with disabilities has gone up since ratification, as has the number of children excluded from the regular school system.[22] We thus observe a tension between lofty ideals and lacking means necessary for the implementation of these ideals. We also saw that it is often unclear what exactly the term 'inclusion' means. Sometimes it is understood in a 'shallow' or technical way, but it also can include much more profound elements (Hall). Some scholars have observed that the implementation of inclusive legislation in the Netherlands runs the risk of interpreting social participation mainly in terms of rights, while overlooking the social elements that are a necessary part of it. They therefore stress the importance of "genuine community inclusion"[23] or state that "true social inclusion requires connection to others."[24]

The question that needs to be asked is what such statements mean for an 'inclusive society'. Inclusion is often reflected upon within a given discipline (e.g. inclusive education), but there is no such thing as 'inclusion studies' in which the concept itself is studied and subjected to critique. The Australian ethicist and disability scholar Jayne Clapton recognizes that such fundamental theoretical reflection on the practice of inclusion is nonetheless important, writing that "'inclusion' is not only a dualistic term in a dichotomous relationship with 'exclusion', but also [...] a multifaceted, complex concept which commands a socio-ethical critique."[25] In her work, Clapton shows that we need to distinguish between four different levels in our reflection on inclusive practice:

---

[22]Visser, "Positie verslechterd"; Visser, "Toegang".
[23]Parmenter, "Inclusion and Quality of Life".
[24]Schippers and Van Heumen, "Inclusive City".
[25]Clapton, *Transformatory Ethic of Inclusion*, p. 2. Cf. the way in which the UN

1. Profound exclusion

2. Technical inclusion

3. Legislative inclusion

4. Ethical inclusion

Profound exclusion refers to a state of segregation and inequality. Technical inclusion can be explained as practical adjustments to promote accessibility. One can think here, for example, of the above pursuit for a more inclusive job market. The legislative level refers to the grounding of these inclusive practices in legal documents and conventions on rights. These three levels are quite easily recognizable in public discourse on disability inclusion. Reflection on the final level of ethical inclusion, however, is harder to find. This is the level of motivation and attitudes.

We can therefore conclude that inclusion is a buzzword in society. While there may be some reflection on this term, this reflection remains scattered across many different academic disciplines. Yet as Clapton argued, the concept itself is also deserving of critique and has many layers. In particular, the fourth level of inclusion (i.e. the ethical level) and its impact on social practice need to be explored and discussed. The examples of education and employment we noted above reveal that the use of inclusive language itself is not enough to ensure true inclusion. Even the creation of inclusive policy (technical level) and inclusive bills of law (legislative level) do not ensure such true inclusion. What is necessary is a fundamental debate on how inclusive values fit in with other values driving political decision-making (ethical level).

2.3 A Third Web of Practices: The Church

We have looked at the origin and definition of the term 'inclusion' as it functions in society and looked at two webs of practices to see how this concept functions in real life. In this section, we turn to the church as yet another web of practices. The church has often followed

---

treaty uses the word inclusion.

societal terminology and approaches to people with disabilities. Disability was long perceived as a medical issue, to be treated in hospitals, segregated from public and church life. Later on, the terminology of 'integration' became influential in both society and church; people with disabilities were expected to benefit from more interaction with others without disabilities. This interaction was often perceived as working in one direction, as people with disabilities could learn to adapt their behavior so as to become part of the 'normal' world. As soon as inclusion became an important concept in social policies, also the church started working with this term. The pursuit for inclusion in churches has historically undergone significant influence from greater societal dynamics, specifically the human rights movements in the 1960s and subsequent reforms in education and other spheres of society.[26] Although certainly not all congregations have made the turn to inclusion, as some remain focused on an 'integration-perspective' or might even best be described as 'exclusive', on the whole a shift towards inclusion can be observed. The existence of a growing body of literature assisting faith communities in their pursuit of more inclusive practice testifies to this shift. In the Netherlands, for example, a number of academic and non-academic books have been published over the last decades, specifically aimed at helping churches become more inclusive.[27] Outside the Netherlands, a vast amount of such literature is available.[28] In these sources, inclusion is seen as the next step forward from an 'integration-perspective'. All kinds of strategies and tips are presented to surpass the level of simply making churches accessible, and to pursue a new level of actually becoming a single community and of reciprocal learning. Much of this literature operates on Clapton's technical level, but there is also some attention for the ethical level.[29] Apart from the available literature, there are also

---

[26]R. Kunz and Liedke, *Handbuch Inklusion in der Kirchengemeinde*, pp. 11–18; Brock, "Theologizing Inclusion", p. 151.

[27]Smit, *Sociale integratie in de geloofsgemeenschap*; Smit, *Zo gewoon mogelijk*; Smit, *Vademecum voor een inclusieve kerk*; Meininger, *Van en voor allen*.

[28]To name just a few: Carter, *Including People with Disabilities* in the United States, Bach, *Ohne die Schwächsten ist die Kirche nicht ganz* and R. Kunz and Liedke, *Handbuch Inklusion in der Kirchengemeinde* in Germany and Hull, *Disability* in the UK.

[29]Erik Carter, for example, states that one of the requirements for becoming a "welcoming congregation" is a change in that community's *motivations*; see Carter, *Including People with Disabilities*, pp. 30–31.

disability advocacy groups in churches suggestive of more inclusive practices. So although the term 'inclusion' does not necessarily find its origin within the church, it is still frequently used in its life and self-reflection.

2.3.1 The Turn to Inclusion in Vathorst

When the Ontmoetingskerk became involved in Hart van Vathorst, a committee was formed to reflect on the project's vision. Even though the vision statement drawn up by this committee is very concise, inclusive values can still be clearly recognized in it. From the interviews I conducted with members of the congregation it also became clear that many of them were using the terminology of inclusion, even when I as interviewer had deliberately refrained from doing so. People in leading positions in the church as well as the other participating partners all explicitly mentioned the concept of inclusion when asked to reflect on how people with and without disabilities should relate to one another. In the denominational annual review for 2018, the Ontmoetingskerk was similarly described as an *inclusive congregation*.[30]

What remains to be seen, of course, is how this concept of inclusion was understood by the members of the congregation, by those in leading positions, and by others. Even more important is the question of how the concept has been *embodied* in the practices of Hart van Vathorst. These questions form the subject of our investigations in the following chapters, where I will describe, analyze, and discuss the results of the empirical research. For now, it is important to note that the concept of inclusion was indeed used by the project respondents to describe Hart van Vathorst and the Ontmoetingskerk, making it an important part of the theoretical background to this case study.

2.3.2 Reflection on Community as Intrinsic to the Life of the Church

One of the things that make this third web of inclusive practices different from the two above is that the church, in contrast with society, intrinsically reflects on Clapton's fourth level (i.e. ethical inclusion). It is virtually impossible to find a commonly accepted, comprehen-

---

[30] J. Kuiper, *Handboek 2018*, p. 482.

sive normative vision on how society as a whole should be structured, and on the values and motivations that should guide this process. The church could be seen as a society within society, albeit a society with a specific nature; it is in some way structured by the question of who Jesus Christ is and what His person and work mean for the life of the church and the world. This means that, whereas society as a whole might not invest very heavily on the 'ethical level' due to the wide variety of convictions and values present in public discourse, the church does by its very nature invest heavily in these questions. These questions are at the root of its existence.

Fundamental reflection on the communal life of the church takes place in the discipline of ecclesiology. Such reflection is called for in relation to inclusion for three reasons. First, as we observed, Clapton's fourth level of ethical inclusion requires a fundamental reflection on motivations and values. If we only aim at the first three levels identified by Clapton, ecclesiological reflection might seem superfluous. However, if we include the fourth level, fundamental theoretical reflection is indeed demanded. Secondly, since it takes the specific nature of the church into account, ecclesiological reflection makes it possible to draw the contours of a truly theological account of inclusion that would better fit the practices of the church than the 'importing' of a standard or common sense account of inclusion would. A third, related reason is formed by the many conflicts of interest that come up in practice. For example, some churches have specific cognitive requirements for full membership and participation in the Eucharist. These requirements may acquire an almost sacred status within a community, making it very difficult for that community to become more welcoming to people with cognitive impairments. Ecclesiology can thus help us to explore and negotiate these conflicting interests.

Ecclesiological reflection exists in many forms. Some approaches depart from a normative framework, derived from the Bible or the tradition. Others are more involved in the church's lived reality. Catholic theologian Nicholas Healy wrote an extensive critique of what he calls 'blueprint ecclesiologies'. According to Healy, such ecclesiologies create "twofold construals" in which the true identity of the church is detached from the reality of its life in this world. Describing how such construals work, Healy writes:

2.3. A Third Web of Practices: The Church

> In spite of appearances to the contrary, the concrete church is a realization of something hidden within it that is more basic and perfect, something constituted by God's gracious and saving presence. Thus, we might claim that the church is, in spite of its evident sinfulness, *really* unlike other institutions, since they do not have this reality at their core. The church is then both unique and superior, for it is the only religious body that cannot be adequately described in purely sociological terms. Only a theological perspective can access its primary reality.[31]

Healy argues that such an understanding of the church does not actually help the church to live out its calling in this world because the lived reality in a sense becomes totally irrelevant. For this reason, he suggests a theodramatic approach to ecclesiology that

> is not governed by the blueprint criteria of completeness, normativity, universal application and systematic coherence. Rather, it is judged by how well it promotes the church's practical coherence with the principle laid down by Paul, that the church boast in the Cross of Jesus Christ, and only in the Cross of Jesus Christ. Its assessment is therefore in terms of how well it fosters the church's truthful witness and its members' discipleship within this particular context, as well as its practical-prophetic force and application within a particular scene of the theodrama.[32]

In Healy's approach, ecclesiological reflection is not expected to yield a blueprint for some kind of perfect, inclusive church. Such a church does not exist. Rather, when we apply Healy's approach to our interest in inclusion, ecclesiology comes to be seen as reflection on the church's concrete practices and on concrete practices of inclusion in a critical conversation. This means that ecclesiology is not just the terrain of systematic theology, but that the practices of the church and reflection on these practices (practical theology) have important con-

---

[31] Healy, *Church, World, and the Christian Life*, p. 30.
[32] Ibid., p. 76.

tributions to make to ecclesiological reflection. We will return to this point in section 3.4.1.

2.4 A Map of Theological Positions Pertaining to Inclusion

In the previous sections, we have explored the way in which the concept of inclusion (for people with disabilities) is used in society and the church. We have also discussed the possible contribution that ecclesiology can make. In this section, it is time to map out what has already been done on the intersection of ecclesiology and inclusion. The use of the word inclusion in theology has not passed uncontested. Some people are immediately triggered to think of 'theological inclusivism', the belief that "all that has been touched by the truth and goodness of Christ is in some way embraced within the church's reality."[33] Others have questioned the theological significance of the concept of inclusion. John Swinton, for example, argues that inclusion is primarily a political term and is not concerned with the *reasons for* the inclusion of people with disabilities. He makes a distinction between love and inclusion, writing: "It is the ability to love, not the ability to include or tolerate, that is a primary mark of discipleship."[34] Evidently, theological discourse witnesses a variety of responses to the terminology of inclusion. We have arranged these responses into three main streams as shown in the figure below. It depicts whether and how theologians engage with the terminology of inclusion in their scholarly work. In the following subsections, we will discuss the main streams I have outlined and offer a few of examples.[35]

---

[33] Healy, *Church, World, and the Christian Life*, p. 130.
[34] Swinton, *Friends of Time*, p. 93.
[35] It must be noted here that we can only give very short accounts of the theological responses that follow, meaning we cannot do full justice to the thorough work that lies behind many of them. Organizing positions in flowcharts leaves out the temporal aspect; some of the approaches labeled 'how-engagement' might build further on the work of others that could be labeled 'why-engagement'. Nonetheless, our conviction is that a model like this helps one to gain a grasp on the field before getting to know all its complexities.

2.4. Theology and Inclusion

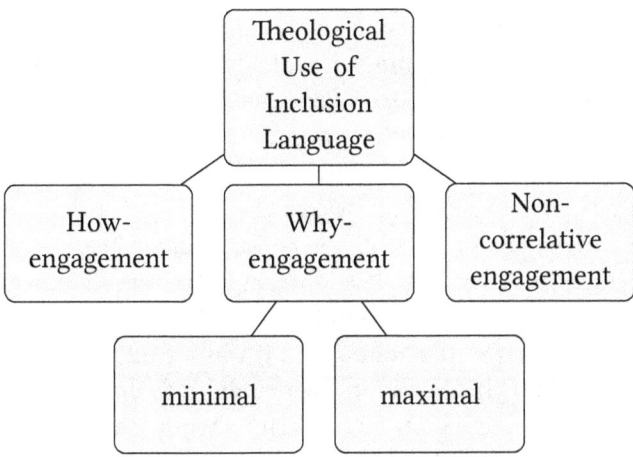

Figure 2.2: Approaches to the Use of Inclusion Language in Theology

2.4.1 How-Engagement

Some theologians use the discourse of inclusion to undergird existing practices within the church, such as diaconal efforts or community building, and provide a theoretical framework for these practices without theological language, striving for creative collaboration between Christian faith communities and non-Christian partners in civil society or government partners. In the Dutch context, for example, Herman Noordegraaf has connected diaconal work with the discourses of inclusion and participation in society, looking for fruitful collaboration.[36] Johan Smit specifically connects the inclusion of people with disabilities in society with what churches can contribute to this inclusion and how churches themselves can become more inclusive. Most of his work lacks a specifically Christian theological rationale for inclusion, and rather presupposes that inclusion is a goal to pursue.[37] Internationally, there are more examples of resources,

---

[36]Noordegraaf, *Betrek kerken bij Wmo*; Noordegraaf, *Kerk en Wmo*.

[37]Smit, *Zo gewoon mogelijk*; Smit, *Vademecum voor een inclusieve kerk*; Smit, *Sociale integratie in de geloofsgemeenschap*. In his Ph.D. dissertation, Smit focusses on pastoral competencies for communicating with people with intellectual disabilities as a key for more inclusion in faith communities; see Smit, "Competenties voor de pastorale communicatie met mensen met een verstandelijke beperking".

which mainly connect inclusion and theology on the level of practice, such as the previously mentioned work of Eric Carter in the USA and the *Handbuch Inklusion in der Kirchengemeinde* in Germany.[38] These 'how-to-books' often do not mention the theological complexities of inclusion, mainly because that lies beyond their confines as practical companions. In some cases, however, the theology is right there below the surface. In the first chapter of the *Handbuch*, for example, we read about the historical development of the term 'inclusion'. The author argues that it is connected to the civil rights movement of the 1960s in the United States, adding that it was meant to implement the values of the French revolution for people with disabilities as well. Another example can be found in Carter's work. In *Including People with Disabilities in Faith Communities*, he recognizes the importance of an explicit and specific religious motivation for inclusive practice, although he himself only describes it in general terms.[39] These examples show how, even though inclusion may initially seem to be a theologically neutral term, there still are theological choices that need to be made: the historical context sketched by the *Handbuch* demands theological reflection and evaluation, as does the religious motivation of faith communities noted by Carter. This theological dimension is not reflected upon in the 'how-stream' of theological engagement with inclusion.

2.4.2 Maximal Why-Engagement

In the center of the model are theological approaches that provide a specifically Christian rationale for inclusion, responding to the question why Christians should be promoting inclusive practice. We have divided these approaches into maximal and minimal approaches. Maximal approaches make inclusion a major theme of ecclesiology, or even something like a single guiding principle. Here we can think of theological inclusivism, but also of approaches in which the Gospel is equated with the liberation or full inclusion of marginalized groups, such as people with disabilities. Examples of such theology can be found in the work of Steven Shakespeare and Hugh Rayment-Pickard.

---

[38] Carter, *Including People with Disabilities*; R. Kunz and Liedke, *Handbuch Inklusion in der Kirchengemeinde*.

[39] Carter, *Including People with Disabilities*, pp. 30–31.

2.4. Theology and Inclusion

In their *The Inclusive God*, inclusion becomes Christianity's central motif. Main themes like creation, revelation, and Christology are then retold from an inclusive perspective.[40] Similarly, Brett Webb-Mitchell describes the Church as a fundamentally inclusive community. When he paints the biblical theological picture of inclusion, he does so under the heading "Scriptural Resources for Inclusiveness".[41] Such a heading suggests that the primary reason for incorporating a certain biblical text or motif as *resource* depends on its promotion of inclusive practice. As a result, there is little attention for more complex themes and texts in the Bible where disability is spoken of in arguably problematic ways or where the boundaries of the people of God are seemingly exclusionary.

Theology in which inclusion becomes a central motif can also be found within the field of disability theology. Some strands of disability theology, like disability studies, perceive disability mainly as a social construct.[42] It argues that much of the suffering resulting from disabilities is not caused by the impairment itself, but by the accompanying social stigmatization and marginalization. Hence, disability theologians strive for liberation much like other proponents of liberation theology do.[43] The best-known example of such disability theology can be found in the work of Nancy Eiesland. Her theology looks at the Christian tradition, including Scripture, from a disabled perspective, identifying and resisting discriminating elements in it. In doing so, she seeks to promote a more just society. Eiesland's conviction is that the church should be a model of justice, leading the way for such a society: "access for people with disabilities [...][is] a prerequisite for equality and the foundation on which the church as model of justice must rest."[44] Much like Eiesland, John M. Hull argues that disability adds an important perspective to theology. If the voices of people with disabilities are not heard, theology as a whole and the

---

[40] Shakespeare and Rayment-Pickard, *The Inclusive God: Reclaiming Theology for an Inclusive Church*.

[41] Webb-Mitchell, *Beyond Accessibility*, pp. 28–33.

[42] For an overview of the field of disability studies, see Watson, Roulstone, and Thomas, *Routledge Handbook of Disability Studies* and especially the introduction to the handbook in Roulstone, Thomas, and Watson, "The Changing Terrain of Disability Studies". For an introduction to the social model of disability, see Barnes, "Understanding the Social Model".

[43] Swinton, "Disability, Ableism, and Disablism".

church as a whole will both become narrow-minded, forgetting that the able-bodied, so-called normal perspective is just one perspective among many.[45]

2.4.3 Minimal Why-Engagement

The minimal approaches do stress the importance of inclusion as a quality of the Christian church, but balance it with other interests. Hence, there is a taxonomy in the application of inclusion that is not present (or less present) in the maximal approaches. Jennie Weiss Block, for example, critiques liberation theologies of disability, herself pursuing what she calls a "theology of access". In her proposal, which clearly seeks to achieve more inclusive faith communities, she also wrestles with problematic biblical passages as well as the less-than-inclusive parts of the Christian tradition, since she wants to remain in dialogue with the whole of this tradition.[46] So too the Dutch ethicist Hans Reinders accepts and uses the terminology of inclusion, while also criticizing the inclusion discourse, specifically for its focus on rights. Reinders comments that

> ...rights claims can only do as much for vulnerable people as can be enforced on others. The recognition of rights includes people in the community of citizenship, but it does not, per se, include them in the community of the good life.[47]

Reinders's words seem to reflect a discontentment with a shallow interpretation of inclusion in terms of rights, resembling Swinton's criticism of inclusion as a predominantly political term, as described above. The point here is that such understandings of inclusion do not go far or deep enough and need to be complemented with theological considerations of a more fundamental nature. The same intention can

---

[44]Eiesland, *The Disabled God*. Cf. Eiesland and Saliers, *Human Disability and the Service of God*. Somewhat in the line of Eiesland's normative description of the church as a "model of justice", Kevin Timpe writes that the church "ought to be a beacon of inclusion"; Timpe, *Disability and Inclusive Communities*, p. 104.

[45]Hull, "Open Letter"; Hull, "Inly Blind?"; Hull, *Disability*; Hull, "Blindness and the Face of God"; Hull, "A Spirituality of Disability".

[46]Weiss Block, *Copious Hosting*.

[47]Reinders, *Receiving the Gift of Friendship*, p. 126.

2.4. Theology and Inclusion

be detected in other theological approaches, as in the work of Thomas E. Reynolds.[48]

Another illuminating example of a minimal why-engagement with inclusion can be found in the work of Leo Koffeman, a Dutch scholar specialized in church polity. He develops four quality markers in order to assess "to what extent the *una sancta* can be expressed and recognized in church life."[49] These quality markers relate to the four attributes of the Church (catholicity, apostolicity, unity, holiness) as they can be found in the Nicene Creed. Koffeman connects the catholicity of the church to the quality marker of inclusivity:

> As a community [the church] is called to, and it longs to embrace all people. If a church tries to live up to its destination, it cannot accept any limitation beforehand. So-called 'self-evident' boundaries, like social, cultural and economic dividing lines cannot be decisive. A church even knows of the relativity of its own historical limitations: it reaches out, beyond borders, and it is missionary and diaconal in nature.[50]

Because inclusivity represents one of four quality markers for Koffeman and is not the single guiding principle, his approach leaves room for tensions arising in practice. For example, the holiness of the church, translated into the quality marker of integrity, implies that "although [...] no limitation can be accepted at the outset, it is [...] true also that not 'everything goes' within the church. The Gospel implies limitations. Sometimes a clear 'no' has to be there, most of all in its internal life."[51] Koffeman does not want to pronounce this 'no' in places where the church has pronounced it at times throughout its history, as in the case of its homosexual members. Rather, for Koffeman, the 'no' has to be spoken to ensure that the church is "utterly reliable", that its "doctrine and life really match", and that ministry is exercised in an "unimpeachable" way.[52]

Theological rationales for inclusion also arise from other theolog-

---

[48]Reynolds, *Vulnerable Communion*.
[49]Koffeman, *In Order to Serve*, p. 132.
[50]Ibid., p. 132.
[51]Ibid., p. 133.
[52]Ibid., p. 215.

ical disciplines. Frank Anthony Spina, for example, uses the themes of insiders and outsiders as a lens for an Old Testament theology of inclusion. After a careful and rigorous reading of a selection of Old Testament stories that seem quite exclusionary by modern standards, Spina concludes that the core of these stories nonetheless calls for a more inclusive way of being God's people. For example, after discussing the story of Naaman and Gehazi (2 Kings 5), Spina concludes:

> Ethnicity, geography, social status, prior religious commitment or understanding, and political standing are not the most decisive factors in being part of Israel. Religious commitment and theological comprehension are the primary factors. That is why an outsider such as Naaman can actually become a part of Israel in the most important way, and, conversely, an insider such as Gehazi can find his access to God cut off even though in other ways he remains part of Israel.[53]

Inclusion thus concerns all sorts of marginalized groups. Spina sums up a few factors that may play a role, among them ethnicity, geography, social status, prior religious commitment or understanding, and political standing. Other scholars, however, have shown that what we now call 'disability' can also be such a factor.[54]

While Spina writes from an Old Testament perspective, close readers of the New Testament have also been making important contributions to the biblical theological reflection on inclusion. A central text in the discussion is chapter 12 of Paul's first letter to the Corinthians, where the apostle discusses the church as the body of Christ. Brian Brock has offered a reading of this chapter with a specific interest in the theme of disability. He argues that the main point of Paul's argument is not that 'all should be accepted', but that God has given each and every member of the church specific charismata. Inclusion is thus not only a sensitivity towards people's needs and wants, but most of all a discerning eye for the gifts of the Spirit. These gifts cannot be equated with natural abilities or disabilities, because they are spiritual gifts. Brock thus warns us to not jump to quick conclusions

---

[53] Spina, *The Faith of the Outsider*, p. 93.
[54] Yong, *The Bible, Disability, and the Church*, Chapter 2.

by identifying people with disabilities as the weaker members of the body, thereby limiting their gifts or charismata to that of being a reminder of our dependence on God and on one other. As is true for every other member of the congregation, the gifts of a person with disabilities are diverse and surprising. The congregation will miss out on these gifts if it fails to recognize them.[55]

2.4.4 Non-correlative Engagement

On the right-hand side of the model, there are those who do not use the word 'inclusion' for fear of being co-opted by a common sense understanding of the term. These theologians clearly share some goals with the inclusion movement, but avoid the terminology of inclusion. One field in which such critical avoidance can be found is that of political theology. Luke Bretherton thus points to the dubious relationship between communitarian thought and neoliberal politics in today's society. He is speaking in the first place about the UK, but the same can be said about the Netherlands and large parts of the Western world. The same people who use the communitarian language of participation, inclusion, and the like are also pursuing a liberal agenda which seeks to highlight and promote the individuality of citizens. For Bretherton and others, church and theology must think twice before using this terminology or cooperating with partners on the basis of such discourse.[56] What do politicians actually mean when they say *inclusion*? Are they thinking of genuine solidarity, or of budget cuts? One of the most concise formulations of such concerns can be found in Shakespeare and Rayment-Pickard's The Inclusive God, a work we introduced above as an example of maximal why-engagement:

> Can those of us who make the case for a church we call 'inclusive' really come to the table with an ecclesiology worthy of the name? Or are we simply the pale reflections of the liberal settlement, mimicking the world's love of tolerance, individual freedom and rights?[57]

---

[55]Brock, "Theologizing Inclusion".
[56]Bretherton, *Christianity and Contemporary Politics*, pp. 32–37.
[57]Shakespeare and Rayment-Pickard, *The Inclusive God: Reclaiming Theology for an Inclusive Church*, p. 156.

Shakespeare and Rayment-Pickard answer the first question with a resounding 'yes' when they place their concern for an inclusive church within a wholly inclusive theology. The title of their book draws a connection between the nature of God himself (*theology proper*) as inclusive and the consequences of this inclusivity for the communal life of the church. Miroslav Volf, however, offers a different answer to the question of inclusion. He deliberately avoids the term in the title of his *Exclusion & Embrace*, arguing that the widespread use of inclusion language in today's society makes it look as if exclusion is something barbaric, from a faraway past. As such, our eyes are closed to our own exclusionary practices and to the way they are deeply nestled within our social and individual identities. Volf writes:

> exclusion [...] is not about barbarity 'then' as opposed to civilization 'now', not about evil 'out there' as opposed to goodness 'here'. Exclusion is barbarity within civilization, evil among the good, crime against the other right within the walls of the self.[58]

Volf goes on to pinpoint some of the philosophical backgrounds to what he calls the 'dubious triumph of inclusion' in today's postmodern Western society, identifying Foucault as a major impetus. Foucault had asserted that modern selves are constituted by the exclusion of the other and consequently proposed to eliminate these excluding boundaries. Volf reflects on the impossibility of life without some kind of boundaries and concludes: "A consistent pursuit of inclusion places one before the impossible choice between a chaos without boundaries and oppression with them."[59]

Thus, while Volf promotes a social order and a vision of the Christian message that might rightfully be labelled inclusive by others, depending on their conception of inclusion, he himself does not attach that term to it in order to avoid being pulled into either one of the camps in the heated debates surrounding this terminology.

---

[58]Volf, *Exclusion & Embrace*, p. 60.
[59]Ibid., 63f.

2.5 Concluding Reflections

In this chapter, we drew a map of potential theological engagements with the terminology of inclusion and their ecclesiological consequences. Looking at this map, a number of characteristics stand out. We have seen that inclusion has become a buzzword in society and in the church. It has an almost magical ring to it, making it all but impossible to express disagreement with an inclusive vision for society. However, additional theoretical reflection on inclusive practices did prove to be necessary. The use of inclusive language alone is no guarantee for meaningful change, as illustrated in the examples of education and the job market. Jayne Clapton's four levels tell us that practical adjustments do not suffice to achieve true inclusion; neither does legislation. What is needed is reflection on what Clapton calls 'ethical inclusion'. Such reflection was indeed encountered in some areas, although it remained scattered across many different disciplines and could therefore be considered an emerging field. In this respect, the church differs from society at large, since it is implicitly involved with questions on Clapton's fourth level. Asking questions of the fourth level is part of the church's specific nature. Furthermore, there is a commonly accepted source to turn to in search of answers to these questions – namely, Scripture and the theological tradition resulting from reflection on Scripture. This gives the church a unique advantage over a society that does not have such a shared source. Yet the reality of church life testifies how difficult it is to come to agreements even with this advantage, as Scripture is read in a variety of ways and theological traditions differ. It is the task of ecclesiology to help churches to be faithful to their specific nature and calling. Ecclesiology can do this best when it combines theological considerations with attention for the lived reality of the church in this world.

As we have seen, such ecclesiological reflection can yield objections against the use of the terminology of inclusion for the practices of the church. These objections show us that Christianity has its own story regarding diversity and community, whether that story be told on the basis of the Cross on which enemies (the ultimate others) are once again taken up in communion with God, or traced back to the very nature of God as the Trinity in which the boundaries between self and other are fluid due to perfect, mutual self-giving love, or told from yet another perspective. There is truth in Swinton's claim that 'love' is a better description of faithful discipleship than 'inclusion' (p. 32). Using the term *inclusion* in theology runs the risk of unintentional association with an anthropology that is more neo-liberal than Christian and with a problematic view of boundaries that leads to chaos instead of freedom. Co-operation with governments on the basis of this discourse might jeopardize the church's prophetic role in exposing where inclusion-talk is nothing more than a clever pitch for budget cuts. Furthermore, if inclusion is understood from a perspective of equality and civil rights, the question remains whether it leaves room for true otherness and actual diversity. It is thus clear that the use of the concept of inclusion in theological discourse is not neutral or without risk.

These considerations lend themselves to an ecclesiology that could be described as *countercultural*. With respect to inclusion, such an approach implies that true inclusion is not possible in a world governed by neo-liberal values. In this line of thought, the church would be the place where genuine inclusion becomes possible, because in the church it is other values that lead the way. However, an ecclesiology that is only countercultural might overlook how the church is always comprised of people who are (at least partly) shaped by the values of the world they inhabit. In other words, the church is not a safe haven, untouched by its surrounding context. The church relates to the culture around it in at least four ways. First, the church is transcultural: the Gospel transcends cultural boundaries. Secondly, the church is contextual: it is always marked by its specific location in place and time. Thirdly, the church is cross-cultural: it provides a space where elements from every culture can be brought in and valued as meaningful contributions that serve to glorify God. Fourthly, the church is countercultural: it critiques elements of every culture that are counter to the Gospel.[60] These four perspectives remind us that the lines between the church and the surrounding culture (i.e. the world) are fluid. Certainly, the church should speak with a prophetic voice against the exclusionary practices of a society that claims to be inclusive, but at

---

[60] This terminology had been taken from the Nairobi Statement, which addresses specifically the practice of worship; here we have applied the terminology to the life of the church in general. See Lutheran World Federation, "Nairobi Statement on Worship and Culture".

2.5. Concluding Reflections

the same time it should be aware that it is in itself in many ways not so very different from the world.

When the fluidity of the borders between church and world is taken into account, together with the fact that the terminology of inclusion *is* used in church practice (see 2.3), it seems that theologians ought to engage with the terminology of inclusion in at least some way, even if theological questions remain. Theology, as a second-order activity, reflects critically on first-order beliefs and practices. This reflection may take the shape of a conversation in which theologians have the opportunity to show and explain how an embodied Christian version of inclusion might differ from a secular version. Such a conversation seems relevant to help both society and the church in their further reflection on the meaning of inclusive practices for communities.

This research project sets up such a conversation on inclusion and the life of the church, while remaining close to the church's lived reality. In section 2.3.2, we argued for such practical ecclesiological reflection. In the following chapter (3), we will further develop the concept of practical theological ecclesiology and describe the methodology behind the present case study in greater depth. In chapters 4, 5, and 6, we will present the material for the conversation: the results from our case study on the way inclusion is understood and realized in Hart van Vathorst and the Ontmoetingskerk, based on the data gathered. In the final chapter (7), we will return to the theory presented in this current chapter and the next, and bring it into conversation with the case study. In doing so, we are setting up the kind of practical ecclesiological conversation we believe is needed for a better and deeply theological understanding of inclusion as well as a more faithful practice.

Chapter 3

Practical Theological Position & Methodology

3.1 Introduction

This third chapter will lay out the methodology of this study. Its goal is twofold:

1. to situate the chosen approach within the wider theological (or practical theological) landscape.
2. to describe the methodological tools I used for observing and interpreting the object of this study (i.e. the Ontmoetingskerk), and how I used this knowledge to formulate constructive theological proposals.

In order to reach these goals, I have structured this chapter in four sections, corresponding to the four levels of reflection at work in practical theological research as established by the practical theologian Kees de Ruijter. The complexity of this research lies in its exploratory nature, which makes it necessary to adopt a broad methodology that is open to the complexities of everyday church life in Vathorst. De Ruijter's model helps in formulating and structuring the methodological questions that must be addressed when we interact with the complex reality of church life as practical theologians.

The 0-level is the level of prereflexive activity. Although this is in many ways the most meaningful level (because this is 'where it hap-

4. Theological paradigm
3. Basic understanding of practical theology
2. Basic theory of discipline
1. Practice theory
0. Actual practice

Figure 3.1: De Ruijter's levels of practical theological reflection.

pens') as well as an important source for practical theological reflection, the activity on this level is itself not yet understood as theology. Rather, it becomes theology when it is reflected upon, regardless of *who* is doing this reflection. Theology is not restricted to academia alone, and yet I do understand it as a form of reflection, or a 'second order activity'.[1] From this 0-level on up, there are four levels of abstraction that De Ruijter identifies as (1) practice theory, (2) the basic theory of the discipline in question (e.g. pastoral studies, homiletics, diaconiology, etc.), (3) the basic understanding of practical theology, and (4) the theological paradigm. Each level is informed by the other levels.[2] The use of this model could make it seem like the theological paradigm is the 'highest' level that controls the others, leaving us with a normative-deductive kind of practical theology. That, however, is not how this model is being used. Rather, it is used as a structure to guide the reflexivity of the researcher. Theological considerations play a part in methodology, and De Ruijter's model presents a paradigm showing that the various levels of reflective abstraction in practical theology are always interrelated.

In the following, I will first describe the theological paradigm in which this study situates itself. Since this project is theological in nature, it raises the important question of what we mean by theology. That is the question which will be addressed in section 3.2. I do realize that a universal definition of theology is difficult to formulate.

---

[1] In section 3.3.2, I briefly discuss the view that practice itself can be understood as theology.

[2] See De Ruijter, *Meewerken met God*, pp. 85–88. Next to the theological paradigm, De Ruijter also includes the 'interdisciplinary paradigm' in his fourth level. I have chosen not to include it as a separate section because the fourth level is to me about the basic presuppositions guiding the research, which, for a theologian, are always theological in nature.

Instead of trying to formulate such a definition, I will describe one specific branch of theology as the theological paradigm operant in this research. Consequently, I will position this study as a form of practical theology, discuss a number of issues that are raised on the third level of reflection, and then reflect on my own position within that field (3.3). I will then further specify my basic disciplinary theory as practical theological ecclesiology, which I understand to be a sub-discipline of practical theology (3.4). In the final section, I will address a number of issues related to the practicalities of this research project, which is the first level in De Ruijter's model. It is important for these things to be well-documented from the perspective of the researcher's ethics; if what I have done and the rules according to which I have played are clearly defined, my findings can be properly understood and evaluated (3.5). Hence, more than just a statement of research method, this chapter can be seen as an extension of the theoretical framework constructed in the previous chapter.

3.2 Theological Paradigm

The academic landscape of theology is vast and diverse, and the meaning of the term 'theology' differs accordingly, especially when it comes to the difficult question of the mutual relationship between theology and empirical research. Within the context of this methodological chapter, it is neither possible nor necessary to give a full overview of the theological landscape.[3] Nevertheless, we will still have to reflect on what we expect theology to be doing and how it relates to empirical research.

In this section, I will reflect on my own position within the field of theology as grounded (both theologically and biographically) in the Reformed tradition. First, I will zoom in on a potential problem that this tradition presents in relation to the present research project, namely its ambiguous relationship with empirical research (3.2.1). I will then identify certain aspects of Reformed theology that nonetheless seem fruitful for this research project (3.2.2). In that light, I will turn and revisit the question of Reformed theology and empirical re-

---

[3]For a concise overview of this landscape, see De Roest, *Collaborative Practical Theology*, pp. 116–128.

search (3.2.3). This section will conclude with a short summary (3.2.4).

3.2.1 Empirical Research and Reformed Theology

I was born, raised, and educated in Reformed circles. The Ontmoetingskerk is a Reformed congregation. I wrote this dissertation at a Reformed theological university, notwithstanding its intention to serve a broader academic audience. Hence, it is hardly surprising that my underlying theological paradigm is also Reformed in nature.

Unsurprising as the choice for this paradigm may seem, I did not find it altogether unproblematic. Reformed theology has been quite shy about the application of empirical methods in theology, making it difficult to connect the paradigm of this study to its methodology. Reflecting on what constitutes Reformed theology (cf. 3.2.2), there seem to be at least three reasons for its reservations:

1. The notion of the *sufficiency of scripture*: According to this idea, what we need to know about God can be found in scripture.[4] Hence, even if it were possible to see God's work in human history, it would teach us nothing new, since the knowledge of God and his work we might gain from it could also be found in Scripture.

   We note, however, this idea of the sufficiency of Scripture must be understood against the backdrop of the Reformation and as a response to a Roman Catholic understanding in which, according to the Reformers, the tradition became a separate source of knowledge of God apart from Scripture.[5] It was never meant to downplay the importance of God's activity in history.

2. The perceived *effects of sin* on the human capacity for knowledge of God: This Reformed position holds that, even though God (or aspects of God) can be known through his work in creation, human wickedness and limitations prevent us from com-

---

[4]The notion of the sufficiency of Scripture is related albeit not synonymous with inerrancy. In the theological world, there are heated debates on how this inerrancy is to be precisely understood, but sufficiency is not so much about whether the Bible can be wrong but whether it tells us everything we need to know.

[5]For the sufficiency of Scripture, see Bavinck, *Gereformeerde dogmatiek*, Part 1, Chapter 2, Section 14 E and Calvin, *Institutes*, Book 4, Chapter VIII.

3.2. Theological Paradigm

ing to full knowledge of Him in this way. Hence, it is necessary for God to reveal himself in Scripture and to illuminate believers with His Holy Spirit so that they might receive true knowledge of him.[6]

However, it seems theologically arbitrary to reckon with the effects of sin when it comes to the empirical study of reality, but to downplay this factor when it comes to the interpretation of the Bible. Recent developments in Reformed biblical hermeneutics have also called for attention to this inconsistency, so that it is now argued that our understanding of the Bible must be drawn into the realm of soteriology: understanding the Word of God is always a gift of grace.[7] The same can be said about the study of created reality and the church *in its relation to the Triune God*. As Reinhard Hütter writes:

> Our knowledge of God is subject to the same eschatological condition to which our whole being is subject. We find ourselves engaged by and in the Spirit's beginning and increasing work (opus inchoatum) of sanctification. The knowledge of God we are thereby drawn into is saving, yet not total; concrete, yet not complete; distinct, yet not comprehensive; "clothed" by embodied practices and normative doctrine, thus perceived "like in a mirror dimly", yet still not "face to face".[8]

3. The *debates around theological epistemology and method* have sometimes been polarized, leading to caricatures of strictly theological approaches (like radical orthodoxy) or strictly empirical approaches (like the study of material religion). It is as if there are two rocks in the empirical theological landscape, a Scylla and Charybdis. On one side there is the rock of a methodologically rigorous empirical approach that excludes the presence and activity of God from study on the grounds that it cannot be

---

[6] E.g. ibid., Book 1, Chapters IV and V.
[7] Burger, "Theologische Hermeneutiek in Soteriologisch Perspectief".
[8] Hütter, "The Church", p. 46.

objectively established.⁹ On the other side, there is the rock of orthodox theology in which empirical research is met with suspicion.¹⁰ If the choice is between holding on to Scripture and doctrinal theology or giving up on them so as to explore reality empirically, the Reformed theologian does not seem to have much of a choice.

These reasons illustrate the difficulties involved in designing an empirical research project with a Reformed theological paradigm. In the next subsection, I will outline why I have nevertheless decided to make this connection.

3.2.2 Defining Reformed Theology

As indicated in the previous subsection, notwithstanding its somewhat troublesome relationship with empirical research, Reformed theology does represent a logical place for this research project to start; it is both part of my own theological formation as a researcher, and the theological tradition of the people I have studied.¹¹ The articulation of a theological framework is relevant to this study because I do not merely want to describe and interpret, but also to contribute to enhanced practice.¹² In Richard Osmer's terms, I aim to attend to the descriptive, interpretative, normative, and strategic tasks of practical theology.¹³ The final two listed tasks cannot be accomplished without the articulation of some kind of theological framework.¹⁴

---

⁹In a helpful article, Rein Brouwer described the work of the Dutch practical theologian Hans van der Ven as an example of such an approach. Van der Ven raises the theological notion of God's transcendence as an argument for excluding God's presence and performance from empirical research: God can never be measured by human concepts, research models, etc. (Brouwer, "Detecting God in Practices"). For a wider description of the empirical turn in practical theology, see De Roest, *Collaborative Practical Theology*, pp. 100–106.

¹⁰De Ruijter, professor emeritus of practical theology at the Theological University Kampen, has written a chapter on the theological backgrounds to this suspicion in De Ruijter, *Meewerken met God*, pp. 96–115.

¹¹This ecclesial background will be introduced in somewhat greater detail in section 4.3.2. The name of the denomination is Gereformeerde Kerken vrijgemaakt (Reformed Churches Liberated, or RCL for short).

¹²Cf. the research question in 1.4.

¹³Osmer, *Practical Theology*.

¹⁴The same is arguably true for the first two tasks, but that is not a matter we need

3.2. Theological Paradigm

Within the denomination associated with both the researcher and the participants, a widely accepted definition of the task of theology is the following:

> Theology concerns itself with
>
> 1. God in the reality of His revelation,
> 2. The life of the Christian church in the world,
> 3. And Creation
>
> In their mutual relations.[15]

This is the definition used as an introduction to theology at the institution where the denomination's pastors are trained. Another widely accepted introduction to theology follows along similar lines, describing theology as "respectfully and decently reflecting on God, man and the world."[16] In contemplating these two broad definitions, there are two things that stand out: In the first place, in both cases the object of theology clearly includes God-self. The object of theology in this tradition thus cannot just be the church as a sociological group or human religious experience as a psychological phenomenon. Secondly, this focus on God-self as the object of theology clearly does not entail a neglect of human experience or the life of this world. Both definitions demanded attention for these matters as objects of theology as well. In the first definition, the question of human experience is divided into two categories: church and creation. In the second definition, the church does not appear as a separate category. According to these two definitions, then, theology is about finding proper language describing the connection that God has established between creation and God-self. Even though theology seems in these definitions to be primarily a human effort, the definitions rest on the belief that God reveals God-self through the Scriptures and the Holy Spirit. In this conception, theology is relevant because the study of the connection

---

to address here.

[15]De Bruijne, *Gereformeerde Theologie Vandaag*, p. 17, translation KST.

[16]Van den Brink and Van der Kooi, *Christelijke dogmatiek*, Chapter 1. In the English translation of this work, the Dutch word 'fatsoenlijk', which I have translated as 'decently', is translated as 'disciplined'. Cf. Van den Brink and Van der Kooi, *Christian Dogmatics*, Chapter 1.

that God has established, God's revelation, will lead to deeper insight into who God is, who we are, and what we are to make of the lives we have been given to live in this world. This idea of theology's task may well be contestable, but it is widely found throughout the Christian tradition, from Thomas Aquinas to John Calvin and contemporary voices.

Understood this way, theology is clearly distinct from religious studies. This distinction is one that surpasses the methodological distinction between *etic* and *emic* perspectives.[17] A religious studies approach might very well be emic in nature. Yet it would most likely not work from the basic presupposition that research leads to deeper insight into who God is and who we are. The religious studies scholar studies religions. The (Reformed) theologian studies God and the world in their mutual relationship.

To be able to say anything meaningful about God (or, as Van den Brink and Van der Kooij put it, to speak *decently* about God), Reformed theology has biblical revelation as its anchor point. It speaks about God "in the reality of His revelation". Here we recognize the *Sola Scriptura* of the Reformation. This does not mean that the Bible is the only source of knowledge with which theologians concern themselves.[18] However, Reformed theology seeks to understand reality by reflecting on it from a biblically informed hermeneutical framework.[19]

---

[17] The distinction between theology and religious studies is sometimes framed this way. Theology's specific 'added value' to empirical studies is then conceived as its inside knowledge of religious terminology, context, and history, making it a fitting discipline for giving rich emic descriptions. But empirical theological studies may very well be both emic and etic; see, for an example, Cartledge, *Testimony in the Spirit*, pp. 19–20.

[18] 18Reformed theology has an open eye for the revelatory work of God in creation, as can be witnessed, for example, in article 2 of the Belgic Confession, one of the three important confessional texts in Reformed churches. Recently, a doctoral dissertation was written, tracking the way in which this article has functioned in Reformed theology; see A. Kunz, "Als een prachtig boek". Additionally, Reformed Theology is attentive to the work of God in human beings and to the distinct role of the Holy Spirit, even if Spirit and Word have always been kept closely together. E.g. Calvin, *Institutes*, Book 1, Chapter IX; Book 2, Chapter IV; Book 3, Chapter I. Reformed Reformed Theology thus has a wider scope than just the Bible text. Indeed, its scope is as wide as creation, to recall the definition of theology given above.

[19] This approach is not confined to Reformed thought alone. Many other theological approaches function along similar lines. I do not mean to exclude them, but chose to be as specific as possible in naming my own theological background.

3.2.3 Points of Contact Between Reformed Theology and Empirical Methodology

The definitions of theology which we discussed above show why this branch of theology seems potentially fruitful for our research project. With this theological paradigm as a framework, I can do justice to the reality of church life in Vathorst as a place where God's work can be encountered, while also making constructive proposals from a shared normative framework.

Section 3.2.1 showed, however, that the relationship between Reformed theology and empirical research is not an unambiguous one. All the same, in recent years a number of practical theologians from various Reformed backgrounds in the Netherlands have tried to formulate proposals that are both truly theological in the sense described above, and also open to empirical methodology as a valuable asset to theology. Kees de Ruijter, for example, has found inspiration in the work of Gerben Heitink and therefore opted for a bipolar model of practical theology as an alternative for what he calls the 'normative-deductive model', in which there is no room for the empirical voice, and for the 'humanities model', in which no real theological voice is heard. Here the two rocks of the theological landscape as I portrayed it above are easily recognized. According to De Ruijter, this bipolar model takes both the empirical and the theological perspective seriously.[20] For him, this double perspective is given with the very nature of God as Trinity: Father, Son, and Spirit are all intimately connected to our world (through creation, incarnation, and inspiration). Yet creation also has its own existence, which can be studied through empirical models. As such, the object may be one and the same (e.g. the practices of the church), but it can still be studied from two separate perspectives.[21]

De Ruijter's successor, Hans Schaeffer, has observed that his predecessor's bipolar model leaves an important question unsolved – namely, which one of the two poles is the most important one? The bipolar model seems to imply a rivalry between the two perspectives, especially if they lead to different interpretations of the same reality, even if that may not be what De Ruijter intended. To escape this

---

[20]De Ruijter, *Meewerken met God*, pp. 58–79.
[21]Ibid., pp. 41–57.

conflict, Schaeffer turned to the theology of creation that has been so influential in the Reformed, neo-Calvinist tradition. Faith in God as Creator, so he argues, has implications for the nature of the connection between theology and the humanities. Six points Schaeffer makes can be paraphrased as follows:[22]

1. Creation is not only a moment in history, God still sustains his creation. He does so in a *mediated* way.

2. This mediation means that human activity and divine activity cannot be neatly separated from and contrasted with each another.

3. The liturgy of the Christian church is, among other means, meant to teach believers to perceive the world around them as creation.

4. This liturgy, consequently, puts an appeal on people's lives to live in accordance with God's creative activity.

5. Because creation is not only a moment in history, but an ongoing activity of God, it can be understood as a historical narrative that is outlined in the Bible, but it also entails our lives in this world.

6. At the heart of this narrative, we find the cross of Jesus Christ, confronting us with the devastating effects of sin. These effects make the discernment of God's mediated speaking in our world an ambiguous task.

For Schaeffer, these points imply that empirical methods have valuable contributions to make to theological reflection. There is no easy way of defining the human and the divine component in the life of the church due to the *mediated* nature of God's activity as well as the effects of sin. However, this does not mean that nothing can be said about God's presence and activity in this world. Rather, the use of empirical methods, involvement with lived reality, will help us to gain deeper, more systematic insights into our world as God's creation.

---

[22] Schaeffer, "Theologie en etnografie".

3.2.4 Summary

My position as researcher in this study is rooted in the Reformed branch of theology. This means that the *theological* nature of this study can be understood as the pursuit of deeper insight into God, the world, and human life in this world through revelation. If the object of this project in some way includes God's presence and activity, then we need to make room for such a form of theology. Otherwise, we end up with only half of the story. Or less. Obviously, this understanding of theology is broader than just strictly 'Reformed'. I have chosen to describe this specific tradition in order to be as concrete as possible. Yet my hope is that theologians from many traditions will be able to identify with this approach. Although I have shown that the Reformed tradition has had its questions regarding the legitimacy of empirical methods in theological projects, I have also shown there to be many points of contact between the two. In this respect, I follow Schaeffer and De Ruijter. Of course, this point of departure makes the research 'biased' in a way, which is why I have given a lot of attention to the researcher's reflexivity and positionality, and opted for a methodology that gives room for positionality (cf. 3.4.2).

3.3 Basic Understanding of Practical Theology

Now that I have explained my theological paradigm, it is important to outline how this study is a practical theological study. First, I will take up my position within the broad field of approaches to practical theology. I will do so by presenting a typology of the field developed by Kathleen Cahalan, and identifying my position in it. Consequently, I will outline my approach in close relation to the approach developed by John Swinton and Harriet Mowat.[23] The approaches chosen here are compatible with the theological paradigm as it was described above.

3.3.1 A Typology of Practical Theological Approaches

In her article *Three Approaches to Practical Theology, Theological Education, and the Church's Ministry*, Kathleen A. Cahalan divided the land-

---

[23] Swinton and Mowat, *Practical Theology and Qualitative Research*.

scape of academic practical theology into three contemporary, 'postmodern' streams which she derived from the theologian Paul Lakeland:[24]

1. **The late modern option** continues the enlightenment quest for universal principles to ground morality and politics, although the idea of an autonomous subjectivity has been replaced by more attention for the situatedness of the subject. According to Lakeland, philosophers like Jürgen Habermas and Charles Taylor fit into this category.

   For practical theology, this means that tradition is subject to criticism in terms of rationality and is not placed on a higher level than secular, contemporary life. Cahalan identifies this approach in Don Browning's revised correlational method, for example.

2. **The countermodern option** is largely associated with the work of Alasdair MacIntyre, and offers a critique of individual autonomy as has it has developed in modernity as the source of many problems in society. It strives to re-discover values forgotten by modernity by focusing on practices and narratives of religious or cultural traditions.

   Cahalan finds a practical theological example of this countermodern option in Craig Dykstra and Dorothy Bass's *Practicing Our Faith*.[25] Whereas the late modern option seeks to align the practices of the church and the secular world, the countermodern option seeks to invest in distinctly Christian practices to serve a Christian identity. Without necessarily becoming fundamentalist, it gives a significant amount of attention to tradition as 'wisdom from the past', thereby distinguishing it from a correlational approach. In another work, co-authored with Miroslav Volf, Bass writes that Christian practices are "things Christian people do together over time to address fundamental human needs in response to and in the light of God's active presence for the life of the world."[26]

---

[24]Cahalan, "Three Approaches"; Lakeland, *Postmodernity*.
[25]Bass and Dykstra, *Practicing Our Faith*.
[26]Volf and Bass, *Practicing Theology*, p. 18.

3.3. Basic Understanding of Practical Theology

3. **The true or radical postmodern option**, lastly, can be found in the work of Foucault, Derrida, Lyotard, and others. Like the countermodern option, it subjects modernity to critique. But instead of looking to pre-enlightenment times and rediscovering traditional narratives there, it aims to deconstruct all meta-narratives. Lakeland admits that there are only a few theologians who work from this radical postmodern option, and finds them predominantly in the corner of liberation theology. Summarizing Lakeland, Cahalan writes that these theologians "are not 'death of God theologians' but they have certainly pronounced the death of the White-male European theologically-constructed God."

When it comes to this approach in practical theology, Cahalan identifies an example in the work of the feminist theologian Rebecca Chopp. Her work uses 'critical theory' as a method to show how contextual and particular theological constructs are, and to 'deconstruct' them in this way. Her constructive proposals stem from women's experiences in theological education and the church. Although Cahalan does not mention this, there are also such approaches to the theme of disability. One can think, for example, of the work of Nancy Eiesland and John Hull. Both of these theologians deconstruct parts of the Christian tradition and try to bring to the fore constructive elements from a 'disability perspective'.[27]

In line with the theological paradigm selected, the approach of the present project can best be understood as *countermodern*. Biblical revelation is understood to strengthen and deepen our understanding of this world. It is the meta-narrative that guides our interpretations. This meta-narrative is open to reinterpretations and rereading, so to speak, but it is not deconstructed, since in our theological paradigm the meta-narrative of revelation is understood to provide deeper insight into reality and is therefore needed. This strikes out the true or radical postmodern option as a viable option for conducting this study. On the other hand, the attention which our theological paradigm gives to particularity and its openness to the work of the Creator Spirit in

---

[27]E.g. Eiesland, *The Disabled God*; Hull, *Disability*.

creation, combined with an awareness of the limitations of the human capacities as a result of sin, disqualifies the late modern approach which pursues universal principles.

3.3.2 What is Practical Theology?

In the preceding section, we opted for what Cahalan calls a countermodern approach to practical theology. This approach is characterized, amongst other things, by a heavy investment in Christian practices. In the current section, I will present the approach of John Swinton and Harriet Mowat as a countermodern way of doing practical theology that is both in line with my theological paradigm and potentially fruitful for this project.

Swinton and Mowat define practical theology as follows:

> Practical theology is critical, theological reflection on the practices of the church as they interact with the practices of the world, with a view to ensuring and enabling faithful participation in God's redemptive practices in, to and for the world.[28]

From this short definition it is clear that even though Swinton and Mowat have an eye open for interaction between the practices of the church and those of the world, their approach is not correlationist in a 'late modern' way. Nor is it deconstructive in a 'radical postmodern' way, though still critical.

Swinton and Mowat adopt Alasdair McIntyre's definition of *practices* as

> any coherent and complex form of socially established cooperative human activity through which goods internal to that form of activity are realised in the course of trying to achieve those standards of excellence which are appropriate to, and partially definitive of, that form of activity, with the result that human powers to achieve excellence, and human conceptions of the ends and goods involved, are systematically extended.[29]

---

[28] Swinton and Mowat, *Practical Theology and Qualitative Research*, p. 7.
[29] MacIntyre, *After Virtue*, p. 187.

3.3. Basic Understanding of Practical Theology

Practice, then, is not merely what people do over against theory, as what people think. Nor is it only 'technical'. Such a limited conception of practice would reduce the task of practical theology to a pure description of what people do, or to the writing of technical instructions for how people should do what they do. For Swinton and Mowat, the primary task of practical theology does not lie in *application*, but, in line with Bass and Dykstra's theological appropriation of McIntyre's definition,[30] in deepening understanding of God and Creation. According to Swinton and Mowat, "The dominant question for practical theology is not 'what difference will this make in the pulpit and pew?' but rather 'who is God and how does one know more fully His truth?'"[31]

Swinton and Mowat thus do not limit the task of practical theology to a description or even an 'enhancement' of practice. They are after truth. Christian truth, in their opinion, is always embodied, or, to use Reinhard Hütter's words as cited above, it is "'clothed' by embodied practices".[32] In this, they follow the American theologian Stanley Hauerwas, who speaks about faith as *performance*, rather than 'a set of ideas'. In dramaturgical terms, one could therefore describe the task of practical theology in terms of revealing and negotiating the tensions between *script* and *performance*. This makes it a critical, albeit also truly theological discipline. Within a critical dialogue that uses tradition and revelation in Jesus Christ as a hermeneutical framework, script and performance are carefully discerned. The objective is to support faithful practice (or performance). But to understand what faithful practice actually *is*, discernment is needed, including knowledge of the script. This is why Swinton and Mowat, while recognizing the reality of sin and its impact on human knowing, still stress the importance for practical theology to find *truth*.[33]

Contrasting terms like *script* and *performance* might make it seem as if there is a clear and simple way of distinguishing the two. The British Catholic theologian Clare Watkins describes this seeming simplicity of distinction as a "temptation of much systematic theology [...] to assume that the places of practice are the loci of the problems

---
[30] Bass and Dykstra, *Practicing Our Faith*.
[31] Swinton and Mowat, *Practical Theology and Qualitative Research*, p. 26.
[32] Hütter, "The Church", p. 46.
[33] Swinton and Mowat, *Practical Theology and Qualitative Research*, pp. 10–11.

and that the theological tradition is a treasure trove of answers".[34] Resisting this temptation, she counters that "practices are bearers of theology",[35] or even that practices *are* to some extent theology, as "the things Christians do together, to express their faith, are examples of 'faith seeking understanding'."[36] However, calling everything theology obscures the conversation; many things Christians do - even when they desire to do them to express their faith - simply do not align in a fruitful way with things other Christians do or believe. If practical theology is interested in finding theological truth, as Swinton and Mowat claim, we need more than just 'describing practices' (even though proper description is indeed an important and time-consuming task). Watkins recognizes this. Like a number of other theologians, she argues that taking serious account of practices as places for discovering truth makes it necessary to adopt approaches like *action research*.[37] However, what she also recognizes is that this action research too needs to be *theological*.[38] Watkins was part of a team of theologians who carried out such theological action research in churches and Christian organizations. To safeguard the theological nature of their work, they designed the model of theology in four voices, which has already been briefly introduced in section 1.4. The distinction between normative, espoused, operant, and formal theological voices makes it very clear that, even though all these voices do bear theology, they are indeed very different from one another.[39] For the present study, we have used this theology in four voices model to structure the research questions. It provides us with a structure to organize the various theological voices we encounter in our research. Despite the difficulties often involved in making clear-cut distinctions between the different voices, together with the possibilities of identifying even more or other voices, this model does do justice at once to the fact that all voices bear theology and to the differences between them. The task of practical theology is to engage the different voices

---

[34] Watkins et al., "Practical Ecclesiology", p. 176.

[35] Ibid., p. 177.

[36] Ibid., p. 170.

[37] Ibid., p. 178. See also Swinton and Mowat, *Practical Theology and Qualitative Research*, pp. 260–266, and P. Ward, *Introducing Practical Theology*, pp. 83–86.

[38] Watkins et al., "Practical Ecclesiology", p. 178.

[39] Cameron, Bhatti, and Duce, *Talking About God*.

3.3. Basic Understanding of Practical Theology

in a meaningful conversation. This conversation, in turn, enables theologians to continue their pursuit of the truth. The present research project is best described in terms of the identification of the different theological voices pertaining to ecclesiology and inclusion in the HVV case study in chapters chapters 4, 5, and 6, followed by the construction of a conversation between them in chapter 7. Although the model was designed in the context of theological action research, it can also be applied in our research even if it is less action-oriented, since the model itself is mostly descriptive.[40]

For Swinton and Mowat, practical theology can be characterized by these six points:[41]

1. It is interested in finding **finding truth** and **supporting faithful practice**. It is never enough simply to gain understanding; the understanding gained should always lead to changed practice. This is why Swinton and Mowat devote the final conclusion of their book to practical theology as action research.[42]

2. It is a **cyclical** discipline, moving from practice to reflection and back, over and over again.

3. It is **attentive to context** because the Christian faith is performed within the history of this world.

4. It is an **interpretative** discipline and is not satisfied with bare description. Rather, it seeks rich description. This means it has an eye for the complexity of reality and tries to find ways to understand this complexity, for example by learning from other theological disciplines. In this way, practical theology complexifies situations and helps people to look behind the veil of normality.[43]

5. Although practical theology does formulate theory, it stays **close to experience** and seeks *phronesis*, a form of practical wisdom, instead of knowledge for its own sake.

---

[40] Cf. Bosman, *Celebrating the Lord's Supper in the Netherlands*, pp. 9–10.

[41] Swinton and Mowat, *Practical Theology and Qualitative Research*, pp. 24–26.

[42] Ibid., pp. 260–266. Cf. De Roest, *Collaborative Practical Theology*, pp. 196–215 for an overview of action research, participatory action research, participatory research, and theological action research in relation to practical theology.

[43] Swinton and Mowat, *Practical Theology and Qualitative Research*, pp. 13–15.

6. It always seeks to be **missional** in the sense that it seeks to connect practice to God's mission or practices of redemption in the world.

For our study, the approach outlined seems to be a fruitful one for doing practical theology. Swinton and Mowat's proposal creates room for a balanced conversation between practice and the theological tradition. We will now look at how practice can be studied concretely according to this approach.

3.3.3 Qualitative Research Methods and Practical Theology

Swinton and Mowat's proposal for doing practical theology thus makes room for the inclusion of contributions from empirical research. In this, they opt specifically for *qualitative* empirical research. Defining qualitative research is not an easy task, but following some of the main figures in the field (e.g. Denzin, Lincoln, Guba), Swinton and Mowat state that two of its important characteristics are 1) an open eye for the complexity of situations; and, relatedly, 2) the aim of *understanding* situations rather than immediately suggesting 'solutions' to problems. This aligns very nicely with their understanding of practical theology's task of complexification.[44]

Qualitative research seeks so-called *ideographic* knowledge, in contrast with the *nomothetic* knowledge many of the sciences are seeking. Nomothetic knowledge needs to pass the tests of falsifiability, replicability, and generalizability, whereas the concept of ideographic truth means that knowledge that really matters and has the power to transform is often unique and non-replicable in nature.[45] Ideographic truth "assumes that it is not possible to step in the same river twice; that the very action of stepping in the river shifts the river bed, displaces the water in ways which mean it will never be the same again."[46] Swinton and Mowat point out that the transformative core truths of Christianity (such as cross and resurrection) are ideographic in nature.

---

[44]Swinton and Mowat, *Practical Theology and Qualitative Research*, pp. 27–67.
[45]The issue of the generalization of this research will be revisited in section 3.5.6.
[46]Swinton and Mowat, *Practical Theology and Qualitative Research*, p. 41.

3.3. Basic Understanding of Practical Theology

Despite all these points of contact between practical theology and qualitative research, Swinton and Mowat also see some areas of tension. These areas center largely around epistemology and the perceived nature of reality. Qualitative research often works from a social constructionist paradigm. In such a paradigm, truth and knowledge are perceived mainly in terms of how they are constructed by individuals and communities. Reality itself is perceived to be (largely or fully) inaccessible, or even irrelevant or as such non-existent. Here a link emerges with Cahalan's third category of true or radical postmodern approaches. This poses important questions, so Swinton and Mowat write, because, "if reality is totally inaccessible, then so is revelation, a suggestion that leads to obvious and complicated theological problems. We would therefore argue that reality is both real and, in principle, accessible."[47] The level of the theological paradigm therefore shows itself to be closely related to our understanding of practical theology. Swinton and Mowat's position amounts to a kind of critical realism in which reality is understood to be real and human constructs help to gain knowledge of this reality. However, the constructs themselves are always provisional and open to change.

Because of these areas of tension, Swinton and Mowat are careful and rigorous in defining the relationship between qualitative research and practical theology. Their approach is not correlationist, as we already saw above. But they do acknowledge that the critical correlational method has strong points in terms of its open eyes for God's work in the world and its prophetic critical qualities. However, their main point of criticism centers on the fundamental asymmetry between theological truth and other forms of truth that Swinton and Mowat assume. They write, "theology does not acquire its ultimate significance from the data of qualitative research. [...] Within the process of practical-theological research, qualitative research data *does* acquire its significance from theology. Theology's significance is therefore logically prior to and independent of qualitative research data."[48]

Therefore, Swinton and Mowat find themselves more on the side of Van Deusen Hunsinger's proposal for a revised model of mutual

---

[47]Ibid., p. 35.
[48]Ibid., p. 83.

critical correlation.⁴⁹ Her model is inspired by Karl Barth's account of the Chalcedonian formulation of the divine and human natures of Christ. An important element in her work is the *logical* priority of theology. This means that theology claims to be of meaning in the realm of qualitative research, but not the other way around. Therefore, theology has *logical* priority - although this does not mean that it is always right or can never be challenged. However, by acknowledging this logical priority, the practical theologian can do justice to the fundamental asymmetry we described above. This point of theology's logical priority corresponds to what I noted about the *Sola Scriptura* and the central place of revelation in section 3.2.2. In this respect, Alister McGrath opts for what he calls a cataphysic approach to theology. To his mind, methodology should always follow ontology; the methodological approach has to match the nature of the reality of the object. Hence, sociological explanations of realities that include metaphysical aspects, for example, can never give a complete account of these realities.⁵⁰

Swinton and Mowat accept Van Deusen Hunsinger's proposal with the one critical remark that theology itself is not available in a 'pure' form. Accordingly, theological truths and convictions cannot be exempt from critical reflection. The existence of many different theological systems worldwide and across denominations testifies to this observation. Therefore, Swinton and Mowat argue for *critical faithfulness* in which the "divine givenness of scripture and the genuine working of the Holy Spirit" is taken seriously, while still maintaining a realistic and critical position towards the "interpretative nature of our grasping after divine revelation and to recognize that truth is, at least to an extent, emergent and dialectic."⁵¹

All of these considerations lead Swinton and Mowat to formulate three rules of thumb for a fruitful use of qualitative research methods in practical theology:⁵²

1. **Hospitality**: The practical theologian should welcome methods from outside his or her own discipline, while being a con-

---

⁴⁹See Van Deusen Hunsinger, *Theology and Pastoral Counseling*
⁵⁰McGrath, *Science of God*; McGrath, *A Scientific Theology: Reality*.
⁵¹Swinton and Mowat, *Practical Theology and Qualitative Research*, p. 89.
⁵²Ibid., pp. 86–88.

3.3. Basic Understanding of Practical Theology

fident host. Giving up one's own values does not make one a good host.

2. **Conversion** is a result of the logical priority of theology, as in Van Deusen Hunsinger's approach. It means, for example, that the epistemic framework cannot be methodologically atheistic or agnostic if the research works from a theistic theological paradigm, because this will exclude parts of the research object.[53]

3. **Critical faithfulness** means that there is room for criticizing the tradition, based on the assumption that such criticism will promote more faithful practice.

These three points show how qualitative empirical research can be a valuable and constructive element of the present practical theological research project. Even if theology is given *logical* priority, there still is room for criticism from practice, respecting the results of empirical research. To use the word of the Dutch practical theologian Henk de Roest: "practical theology needs to steer a middle course to avoid the pitfalls of mystification, idealisation and prescriptive models on the one hand and surrender to social scientific understandings on the other hand."[54]

3.3.4 Summary

In the terms of Cahalan's typology for practical theology, this project can best be understood as countermodern in its approach. Following Swinton and Mowat, I see practical theology as "critical, theological reflection on the practices of the church." In practical theology, the theological has logical priority, but it is also subject to criticism. This is why it is important to use a model like Cameron's Four Voices of Theology model (which this project has adopted) to properly structure and evaluate the various voices that are uncovered in the study of a complex reality. I understand qualitative research to be of aid in the discovery of these voices and the discernment of their meaning.

---

[53]Cf. footnote 50 on page 64.
[54]De Roest, *Collaborative Practical Theology*, p. 129.

3.4 Basic Theory of Discipline

Up to this point, we have considered the theological paradigm of this research project and the conception of practical theology it uses. It is now time to focus on De Ruijter's second level: the basic disciplinary theory. First, I will describe the discipline at hand as *practical theological ecclesiology* (PTE) (3.4.1). Consequently, I will describe *theological ethnography* as a suitable method for conducting PTE (3.4.2).

3.4.1 Practical Theological Ecclesiology

In section 2.3.2 we have already discussed ecclesiology and shown Nicholas Healy's discontent with so-called *blueprint ecclesiologies*.[55] Blueprint ecclesiology does not need practical theology nor qualitative research as it works from a purely systematic or biblical theological understanding. Healy's argument amounts to a call for an ecclesiology that does justice to the *struggles* of the church in the world while also acknowledging the specific identity of the church. Thus, a classic correlationist approach does not suffice for Healy: "The church cannot be correlated with 'the' culture, for neither church nor world can be reduced to clearly defined positions."[56] Healy's work can be seen as an important impetus for developing practical theological reflection on the church (Practical Theological Ecclesiology, in short: PTE). PTE strives to go beyond sociological description of the church. Rather, in line with Swinton and Mowat's conception of practical theology in general, PTE reflects critically and aims to promote more faithful practices. In this sense, PTE can be seen as "chastening of the church's doctrinal self-understanding."[57] This is important because, as we have stated above and as Stanley Hauerwas so powerfully puts it: "Christianity, like peace, is not an idea; rather, it is a bodily faith that must be seen to be believed."[58] Hence, what is at stake in PTE is a *plausible*

---

[55]Healy, *Church, World, and the Christian Life*.

[56]Ibid., p. 175.

[57]Healy, "Ecclesiology, Ethnography, and God", p. 183. Cf. De Roest's warning for "the pitfalls of mystification, idealisation and prescriptive models" (De Roest, *Collaborative Practical Theology*, p. 129).

[58]Quote from a speech by Stanley Hauerwas, published in Hauerwas, "Seeing Peace", p. 113.

3.4. Basic Theory of Discipline

ecclesiology.[59] Reality matters theologically, for if the church is called to witness, what this witness looks like in practice and how truthfully and faithfully this witness is performed are relevant issues.[60]

The Norwegian theologian Harald Hegstad observes a significant rise of interest for such empirical theological reflection on the church, which he calls surprising given the wide theological suspicion against human experience as a source of theological knowledge. Hegstad links this suspicion primarily to Barthian approaches to theology,[61] and it can also be recognized in the Reformed suspicion as described above in section 3.2.1. The theologian John Webster, who was heavily influenced by the work of Barth, offers a strong criticism of approaches like PTE. Based on his fundamental understanding of the church as primarily a work of God, Webster questions whether it really is possible to 'see' the church from an empirical stance. What we see when we look at the church's immanent and temporal life on earth is connected to God's transcendent and eternal work.[62] Human experiences of the church must therefore be relativized: "though they are encountered in particular concretizations of practice in the history of the church, fundamental forms are not wholly identical with those practices. Talk of the church's fundamental forms thus has a critical or relativizing function with respect to the empirical life of the church."[63] This statement contrasts sharply with Healy's definition of PTE as a chastening of the church's doctrinal self-understanding. The underlying question is: what is real? While Healy proposes a 'reality check' to 'test' doctrine, Webster argues that our human immanentized understandings of reality are deserving of such a 'reality check'. Webster recognizes Healy's fear of idealization in speaking about the church, but is hesitant to turn to empirical methods to turn this danger aside. According to Webster, the sociological reality is not the only 'real' in this world; rather, "for Christian dogmatics, God is *ens realissimum*, God's acts are *acta realissima*."[64] Therefore, Webster urges theologians who makes use of empirical research methods like ethnography (see

---

[59] P. Ward, *Perspectives*, pp. 4–5.
[60] Swinton, "Where Is Your Church?", p. 74.
[61] Hegstad, "Ecclesiology and Empirical Research", p. 34.
[62] Webster, "In the Society of God", pp. 214–220.
[63] Ibid., p. 216.
[64] Ibid., p. 203.

3.4.2) to be cautious: "The church is not simply social nature but created and fallen social nature re-created by the saving missions of the Son of God and the Holy Spirit and so reconciled to God and on the way to its perfection. This already means that the ethnography of such a society will be irregular, even aberrant, utterly enigmatic if we restrict the matter of ethnography to purely natural motion."[65] In sum, for Webster empirical research on the church's life has limited value, while bearing massive risks.

To avoid those risks, it is important to be mindful of the theological nature of PTE. Honoring Webster's criticism does not have to result in the triumph of doctrine over practice. As we discussed above (3.3.2), it can be helpful to view theological reflection as a conversation involving different, albeit all fully theological voices. Even if this does complexify the theological conversation, it also moves theology ahead in its quest for 'the truth about church'. As Clare Watkins writes, "practical ecclesiology finds its fullest expression [...] not in a simple, single voice, but in the dynamism of ongoing conversation and multivoiced reflections. It is here that the truth about church will be disclosed."[66] In this conversation, the different voices may criticize and relativize one another. Healians might be afraid that Websterian doctrinal corrections will lead to *twofold construals*, but they can also be *formal* questions inviting fresh *operant* and *espoused* responses. Websterians, in turn, might fear that Healian *chastening of dogma* misjudges the divine essence of the life of the church, but it can also be an *operant*-inspired question demanding new *normative* or *formal* answers. As Harald Hegstad suggests, the formal and normative theological perspectives do not compete with the empirical perspective. Rather, formal or normative theological statements, as well as empirical statements, both address the same human community that is the church. What matters theologically is that this community is "understood in light of its future, as a sign and an anticipation of the fellowship between God and humans that will be brought about by the coming kingdom of God. Statements about the church as one and holy must not be understood as statements about an invisible church behind the visible, but about the church in light of its eschatological destiny."[67]

---

[65]Webster, "In the Society of God", p. 220.

[66]Watkins et al., "Practical Ecclesiology", p. 181.

[67]Hegstad, "Ecclesiology and Empirical Research", p. 40. See also Hegstad, *The Real*

3.4.2 Theological Ethnography

In order to perform this task, PTE makes use of qualitative research methods, specifically ethnography. Ethnography is the preferred choice because it values the insider perspective and does not immediately shift attention to the general, big ideas, but keeps an open eye for the particularity and uniqueness of situations.[68] It is therefore fit to discover *lived* and *local* knowledge.[69] The knowledge ethnographic research provides is ideographic in nature, as in other forms of qualitative research. In describing the specific nature of ethnographic research, Julie Scott-Jones and Sal Watt pinpoint seven core values of ethnography: participation, immersion, reflection, thick description, active participative ethics, empowerment, understanding.[70] These values themselves already demonstrate how much attention is given to the voices of the participants. What is also clear is that the person of the researcher has great influence. In ethnographic approaches, this influence is not denied or downplayed. Rather, it is made explicit and the value of reflection on this influence is at the heart of ethnographic research. Important methods of such reflection include participant observations, interviews with individuals and/or groups (focus group interviews), and analysis of texts and documents.[71] Hans Schaeffer has identified four elements that explain why ethnographic methods have come to be used frequently in theological and practical theological research:[72]

1. Current developments in epistemology across the sciences, but also specifically in theology, have shown how limited and con-

---

To conclude, PTE can be understood as a critical theological, reflective sub-discipline of practical theology, specifically aimed at understanding the life of the church in all its complexity and interconnectedness and at the promotion of faithful practice.

Church.
[68]Scharen and Vigen, *Ethnography as Theology*, pp. 16–17.
[69]P. Ward, *Perspectives*, p. 9.
[70]Scott-Jones and Watt, *Ethnography*, pp. 7–10.
[71]O'Reilly, *Ethnographic Methods*; Robben and Sluka, *Ethnographic Fieldwork*; Robson, *Real World Research*.
[72]Schaeffer, "Theologie en etnografie".

textual knowledge is. Hence, the particular and unique have come to be revalued.

2. Much theological research cannot be performed if the researcher 'brackets' his or her own convictions and formation by the tradition. Ethnographic research makes it possible to do positioned research and demands attention for reflection on this positionality.

3. This positionality makes it possible to reflect on discrepancies between script and performance because the theological script has its place in the research as part of the researcher's position and formation.

4. Since theology has its place in the research there is also room for normativity, making it possible to formulate constructive proposals.

The ethnographic approach is not neutral, nor is any other form of academic inquiry. Referring to Gadamer, John Swinton argues that all research is in some way biased. Hence, he argues, it is important to account explicitly for one's own positionality and epistemic assumptions. For Swinton, for example, this means that a theistic epistemology that values revelation allows ethnography to be attentive to the work of the Holy Spirit in the Church. Swinton calls this a *sanctified* ethnography.[73] We recognize the rule of *conversion* here, as we encountered it on page 65. Nicholas Healy, too, argued for a specifically *ecclesiological* ethnography, next to theologically informed approaches to history and sociology.[74] As we described it in section 3.4.1, the theological nature of ethnography is especially relevant when describing the life of the church.

3.4.3 Summary

This research project can be understood as a form of *practical theological ecclesiology* in which *theological ethnography* is employed to discern what is actually going on at the level of one concrete congregation in order to contribute to the bigger question of how the church

---

[73]Swinton, "Where Is Your Church?", pp. 80–91.
[74]Healy, *Church, World, and the Christian Life*, pp. 169, 184.

is called to act in this time. The theological component here is the fact that the researcher's theological convictions are not bracketed, but made explicit, as in the above. The final section of this chapter will be more practical in nature, and will describe the methods and how I have employed them.

3.5 Practice Theory — Research Methods

3.5.1 Research Model

The research model as it is shown on page 73 gives insight into the structure and execution of this research in a single glance. At the heart of this study is the reality of Hart van Vathorst and the Ontmoetingskerk. The case study includes three components: (1) an empirical part, (2) exploration of the context, and (3) a literature study to explore and take into account theory on ecclesiology and inclusion.

1. The empirical part consists in the creation of a balanced research design that enables us to answer the project's research questions. We have chosen to approach this project as a single case study (see 3.5.2), using the methods of participant observation (see 3.5.3), interviews (see 3.5.4), and document study. The data collected through these methods was consequently stored and analyzed (see 3.5.5). The main goal of this empirical data collection was to get as complete and valid an image of the reality in Vathorst as possible (see 3.5.6 and 3.5.7).

2. The study of the context took shape in the tracing of the societal and ecclesial developments that are of interest to the project on the global (macro), national/denominational (meso), and local (micro) levels. This was done through the collection of relevant newspaper articles and the reading of relevant sociological reports. The results of this context study have been woven into the presentation of the empirical data (most explicitly in chapter 4).

3. The literature study was conducted for a double purpose: to better understand what is going on through the development of a

theoretical framework (see chapter 2), and to facilitate a discussion between relevant literature and the new perspectives developed through the case study. This discussion will take place in chapter 7.

3.5.2 Single Case Study Research

In *The Sage Handbook of Qualitative Research*, Bent Flyvbjerg argues that statistical methods must be supplemented with case studies in order to understand situations in depth and to explore new hypotheses and research questions.[75] Colin Robson defines case studies as "a strategy for doing research which involves an empirical investigation of a particular contemporary phenomenon within its real-life context using multiple sources of evidence."[76] He observes that although the outcomes of case studies have been used widely (because, so he argues, *local* knowledge is the kind of knowledge that actually transforms), the method itself has been subjected to extensive methodological criticism. Flyvbjerg writes that this is mainly due to a misunderstanding of what case studies actually do.[77] He then formulates a number of different purposes for case study research, and consequently identifies various approaches for the selection of cases. These approaches can be divided into two main classes: *random selection* and *information-oriented selection*. The second approach is meant "to maximize the utility of information from small samples and single cases. Cases are selected on the basis of expectations about their information content".[78] For the present project, the selection was clearly informationbased, in the expectation that the Hart van Vathorst and Ontmoetingskerk case as a unique phenomenon will shed new light on the matter of inclusion and ecclesiology. In this sense, in Flyvbjerg's terms, the selected case can be seen as an 'extreme' or 'deviant' case due to its uniqueness. In more concrete terms, it means that one can hardly imagine there to be *no* interesting developments (whether positive or negative) in terms of inclusive practice in Vathorst, because the boundary conditions seem to be extraordinarily suited to such developments.

---

[75] Flyvbjerg, "Case Study", p. 314.
[76] Robson, *Real World Research*, p. 136.
[77] Flyvbjerg, "Case Study", p. 302.
[78] Ibid., p. 307.

3.5. Practice Theory — Research Methods

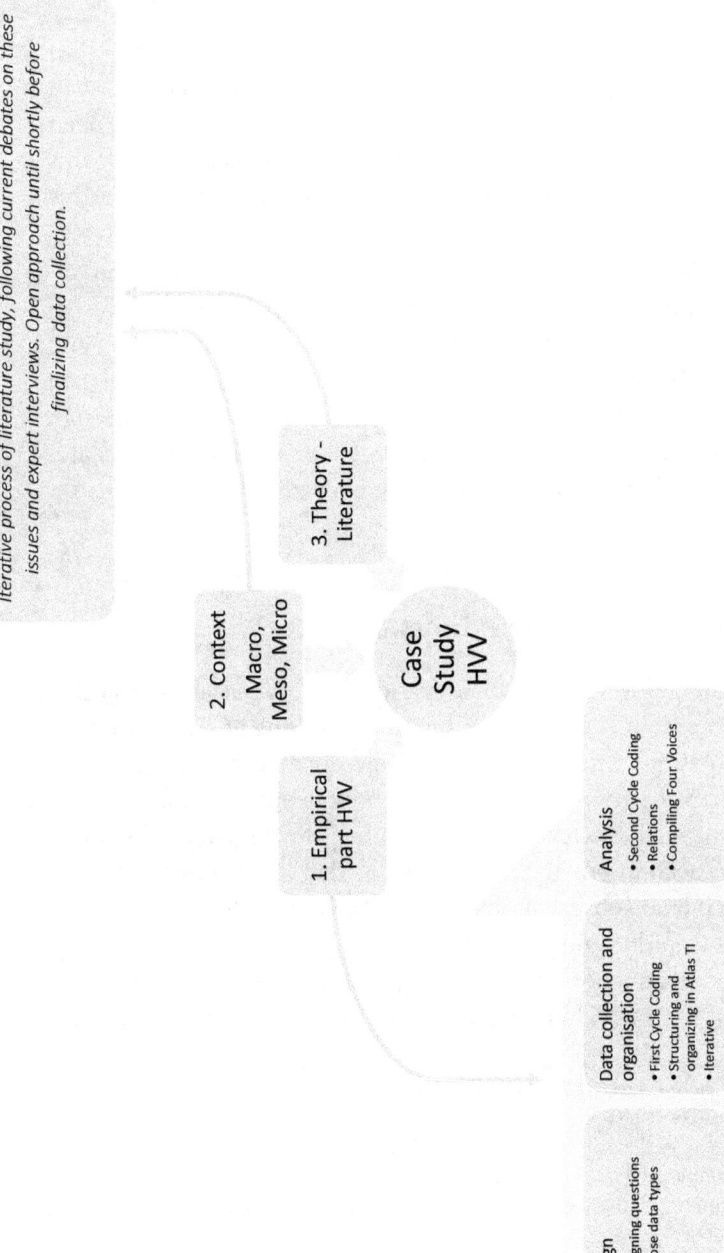

Figure 3.2: Research model

Hence, for our research goals and questions, a single case study can be expected to yield fruitful results. No other, directly comparable cases were available, meaning that it would have been difficult to select several other cases. Additionally, even if two or three cases had been available for selection, that sample size would still not have been large enough to allow for generalization in a classical sense. For this reason, we selected a single case study, enabling the researcher to give it undivided attention.[79]

The case is explored in an ethnographic way using participant observations, interviews, and document study. The following two section will first give closer attention to the methods of observation and interviews. The method of document study was applied in order to enrich the Hart van Vathorst picture and to add reliability through data type triangulation (cf. 3.5.6). Here documents like vision statements and public communications were collected and treated as research data.[80]

3.5.3 Participant Observations

A big advantage of including observations in this research project is their directness. Instead of only hearing opinions about and reflections on situations through interviews and document study, observations open up the prereflective level of how people act and speak in the situation itself.[81] Observations also help to discover non-verbal patterns in social interaction.[82] This means that it is necessary for our research to include observations if indeed we aim to discover all of the four voices from Helen Cameron's model (see fig (cf. fig 1.1 on page 15). Observations will be particularly helpful in describing the operant voice of theology, but also in its function as a *supportive method*

---

[79] Giving a rich description for one case is a very time-consuming task, which is why more authors choose to limit themselves to a single one; e.g. Brouwer, *Geloven in gemeenschap*; Cartledge, *Testimony in the Spirit*; Ideström, "Implicit Ecclesiology"; Williams, *Community in a Black Pentecostal Church*; Hay, *Negotiating Conviviality*.

[80] In this paragraph, there is limited room for elaborating on the role of single case studies in practical theology. I have done so in much greater detail in Tamminga, "Gids in een onbekende stad".

[81] Robson, *Real World Research*, p. 316.

[82] Ammerman et al., *Studying Congregations*, p. 203.

3.5. Practice Theory — Research Methods

to give richer descriptions of the other voices.[83]

Observations are a classical method in most sciences, but in qualitative research, observation has shifted from a maximally bias-free, replicable, and verifiable approach to a more participatory style.[84] As Emerson, Fretz, and Shaw have observed, in qualitative research it is not possible for the researcher to be a 'fly on the wall', nor is it desirable to restrict oneself to video recordings alone or other forms of distanced observation, since every recording results in reduction.[85]

In this study, too, observations were performed in a participatory way. Most observations took place in church services or other public events. During these public meetings, I was present in what Emerson calls a *participating-to-write-style*, meaning that I took quick notes during the actual meeting which I then worked out in detail within 24 hours.[86] Sometimes I took observation notes while watching video recordings of church services, for example when one of the respondents pointed out to me that something interesting had happened during one of those services. At less public events, such as committee meetings, I did not record many notes during the meeting itself, but only tried to remember a number of keywords, which I then worked out immediately after the meeting. I opted for this style so as not to disturb the natural flow of the meeting by disclosing my presence as a researcher all too explicitly.

Observations were mostly carried out in unstructured form, the main open question being: what is going on?[87] Due to the iterative nature of the research, I did unravel certain important themes on the go and in some cases decided to focus on these themes (e.g. the role of the preacher, the roles that were given in services to people with disabilities, the communication between people with and without disabilities in informal settings). When I did so, I mentioned in the field notes what my specific area of interest for that observation had been.

Between March 2016 and September 2018, I conducted 23 observations of church services, and 5 observations of committee meetings and other events, aside from also 'hanging out' in and around HVV for

---

[83]Robson, *Real World Research*, p. 317.
[84]Angrosino and Rosenberg, "Observations on Observation", pp. 467–477.
[85]Emerson, Fretz, and Shaw, *Writing Ethnographic Fieldnotes*.
[86]Ibid.
[87]Robson, *Real World Research*, p. 317.

other appointments.

3.5.4 Interviews

Semi-structured individual interviews formed an important source of data for this project.[88] The interviews were specially designed to discover the espoused voice and, for the minister, the formal voice. Next to informal conversations that were conducted during observations or on a spontaneous basis, an interview protocol was designed centering around the two main themes of ecclesiology and inclusion. Four groups within and around the congregation were asked to respond to six questions spread over three main categories:

1. Ecclesiology, center-focused
   (a) How does the respondent speak about the core tasks of the church?
   (b) How do they connect these ideals to what is going on in their own congregation?

2. Inclusion
   (a) (a) How does the respondent think that people with disabilities should be able to participate in communities?
   (b) How do they link this ideal to what is going on in their own congregation?

3. Ecclesiology, outwardly focused
   (a) How does the respondent perceive the role of the church in society?
   (b) How do they link this ideal to what is going on in their own congregation?

The choice to not explicitly connect topics 1 and 3 to the themes of inclusion or disability was a conscious one, allowing me to see whether the respondents would make this connection of themselves. Whenever respondents did not make this connection in their answer to ques-

---

[88] Cf. Robson, *Real World Research*, pp. 297–280

3.5. Practice Theory — Research Methods

tion 3a, I asked them to make that connection after taking note of the fact that they had not made it themselves.

While the questions were rephrased for each group, in terms of content the questions for all groups came down to the same thing. The following four groups were interviewed:

1. Regular church visitors – residents (A): This group includes people with intellectual disabilities. For these people, I consulted with their care professionals to determine the best way for conducting the interview.[89]

2. Regular church visitors – non-residents (B): This group consists of members of the church who do not live in Hart van Vathorst (HVV), but do attend church there.

3. Church leadership (C).

4. Representatives of all the 'stakeholders' in HVV (regardless of age/gender: representing larger groups) (D).

The individual interviews can be categorized as in the table below. The total number of interviewees approached thirty, which also happens to be the number mentioned by congregational studies specialist Nancy Ammerman as a fitting one to achieve a saturated picture of what is going on in a medium-large congregation.[90] All participants were randomly selected within their age and gender categories. All gave permission for their participation, on the basis of informed consent and the condition of anonymity. For participants under the age of 18, permission was also obtained from their parent/s.

Following the analysis of all the data, this analysis was presented in a number of different academic and non-academic contexts, including presentations to which people from HVV were invited and were present by way of member checking.[91]

---

[89]Cf. Schuurman, Speet, and Kersten, *Onderzoek Met Mensen Met Een Verstandelijke Beperking*.
[90]Ammerman et al., *Studying Congregations*, p. 205.
[91]Cf. Robson, *Real World Research*, p. 158. Academic contexts included the Summer Institute on Theology and Disability, the Ecclesiology and Ethnography conference in Durham, UK, a conference on Joy and Disability at Aberdeen University, the Societas Liturgica, and the Netherlands School for Advanced Studies in Theology and

Group	M 13-19	F 13-19	M 20-39	F 20-39	M 40-65	F 40-65	M >65	F >65	total
A	0	0	1	1	1	1	1	1	6
B	1	3	2	2	2	2	2	2	16
C	–	–	–	–	2	–	1	–	3
D	–	–	–	–	3	–	–	–	3
								total	28

Figure 3.3: Overview of Interviewees

3.5.5 Data Analysis

All data collected with the above methods were imported into Atlas.ti and categorized into document families for analysis in groups (e.g. only interview transcripts) or as a whole (all data combined).[92] During the first cycle, the documents were coded using provisional coding, structural coding, and attribute coding.[93] The main approach to the analysis can best be characterized as grounded theory in the sense that codes arise from interaction with the empirical data and that the objective is to develop new perspectives on theories about church and inclusion based on these data. This study does not represent a textbook example of grounded theory as described by its founders (Glazer and Strauss), but, as Robson argues, grounded theory can also be used as a general approach, is characterized by the inductive values mentioned above.[94]

After the initial coding phase, 12 code groups were identified by means of axial coding.[95] Codes could fall under more than one of these groups, but all belonged to at least one group. From these 12 groups, visual networks were created in Atlas.ti. In these networks, codes were linked to one another so as to gain an overview of the content

---

Religion. Non-academic contexts included a number of presentations for practitioners in the field of disability care, as well as some presentations for the leadership of HVV-partners. Church members of the Ontmoetingskerk were explicitly invited to one of these presentations.

[92] Even though this is only the organization phase and not the analysis itself yet, organization does have an influence on outcomes, which is why Ammerman sees organization as a 'prelude' to analysis; Ammerman et al., *Studying Congregations*, pp. 229–233.

[93] Saldaña, *Coding Manual*.

[94] Robson, *Real World Research*, p. 467.

[95] Cf. ibid., p. 149. The code groups are listed in appendix A.

3.5. Practice Theory — Research Methods

of the data and the relations between the different subjects these data covered. This resulted in 11[96] networks, which in turn became the basis for chapters 4, 5, and 6.

3.5.6 Validity and Reliability

Before conducting this research, I took training in both qualitative interviewing techniques and qualitative analysis.[97] Validity and reliability were further boosted by different types of triangulation, including data triangulation (comparing pieces of data with each other), data type triangulation (including different types of data like documents written by respondents, interview transcripts, and field notes), and methodological triangulation (including different methods, in this case interviews, observations, and document study).

It is impossible to generalize this single case study in a 'hard' statistical sense. Some authors have argued that it is not the task of qualitative research to provide generalizable theories. However, Swinton and Mowat suggest that a level of *resonance* can still be achieved by thick descriptions of situations with which people in other situations may *identify*. Such recognition of ideographic knowledge can work in a transformative way and thus, if not generalizable, still have relevance outside the immediate context of the situation.[98] In this research project "the goal is to use a concrete and delimited situation to better understand the broader social processes which structure it, and how they are mediated by the specifics of the situation".[99]

3.5.7 Limitations

The present project aims to discover ideographic, local knowledge. This implies an important limitation in terms of its contextual nature. The subject of our research is specific in a number of ways: it

---

[96] One of the code groups was a 'rest'-group gathering codes that were relevant only as background information, such as information about the respondent's age and gender. Hence, we did not create a network out of this group, but used the codes only to trace this information back as needed.

[97] Certificates in Qualitative Analysis and Qualitative Interviewing from Evers Research & Training.

[98] Swinton and Mowat, *Practical Theology and Qualitative Research*, pp. 46–47.

[99] J. Sim, cited in ibid., p. 46.

is a Western-European, Dutch phenomenon, the theological tradition is Reformed, and also the geographical and social contexts are quite specific. In spite of the connections which will be drawn to broader discussions, it is important to note how context-bound the research actually is.

Of a similarly limited nature is the connection to theory and existing debates; the performance of practical ecclesiological research brings a lot of interesting questions to the fore. Not all of them can be answered. Although I wanted to be as inductive as possible in my treatment of the data, oftentimes I had to choose not to engage certain questions in order to prevent myself from losing track of the study's main question. This point will become most relevant in chapter 7.

A final limitation that must be mentioned here concerns the inclusive nature of this research project itself. Although I did my best to have all voices heard, I realize that there are limits to my ability to do so. This research presents my interpretation, which I hope to be a justifiable one, of other people's voices. However, as Henk de Roest observes, 'epistemic violence' cannot be ruled out in ethnographic research; as a researcher, I have "the power of representation".[100]

---

[100] De Roest, *Collaborative Practical Theology*, p. 272.

Chapter 4

Four Perspectives on the Ontmoetingskerk

4.1 Introduction

The aim of this chapter is to sketch an overview of ecclesial life in the Ontmoetingskerk. We will use the *Four Perspectives* of Rein Brouwer (et al.) (see 4.2) to structure this overview. Chapters 5 and 6 will zoom in on, respectively, the Ontmoetingskerk's *ecclesial practices* and the interaction between existing members of the Ontmoetingskerk and new members who live in Hart van Vathorst. The current chapter serves as a backdrop for these more specific chapters. It is, in its own right, a thick description in ethnographic style providing important directions for answering our main research question as well as several of the subquestions (specifically the first five) as described in section 1.4. As such, the present chapter represents a congregational studies approach to the Ontmoetingskerk.

This chapter will present a large part of the fieldwork carried out in the Ontmoetingskerk; the overview offered here is based mainly on the self-representation of the people in Vathorst. We will use all types of data acquired in the ethnographic fieldwork. This includes participant observations, qualitative interviews, and document study of documents produced by the congregation or by the organization linked to it. We will also use other sources, such as newspaper or magazine articles, that relate to the Ontmoetingskerk, Hart van Vathorst, or Vathorst in general, as a means to describe the Ontmoetingskerk's interaction with its context. These external sources are secondary, and serve to support the story as it is found in HVV itself.

In what follows, we will first describe the background and use of Brouwer's *Four Perspectives* (4.2). We will then present our material using this structure (4.3-4.6), before closing this chapter with a summary (4.7).

4.2 Four Perspectives on Faith Communities

As described in the section on data analysis (3.5.5), we treated the data resulting from our fieldwork in an inductive manner. We wanted to be as open as possible to the lived reality of the Ontmoetingskerk. For this reason, we decided not to use a preconceived model for the analysis and interpretation of the data. However, for the sake of presentation and conversation, the data must indeed be structured. Following the initial rounds of coding, we created groups of codes that belonged naturally together. What stood out is that a number of these groups resembled a basic structure from the field of congregational studies. This structure, which consists of four perspectives on faith communities, has been presented very concisely in the work of Dutch theologian Rein Brouwer.[1] Brouwer's proposal resembles similar, and perhaps better-known proposals from Nancy Ammerman and Helen Cameron.[2] All three use a number of 'perspectives' or 'interpretative frames' to capture the reality of faith communities. Their perspectives can be compared as follows:

Ammerman's proposal is very similar to that of Brouwer, with two differences. First, Ammerman speaks of context in terms of *ecology*. Ecology is a term that draws our attention to the direct environment of a local church, which is only one aspect of its context. For the presentation of our data, we require a broader conception of context which includes larger societal dynamics and debates and even the congregation's historical context. Secondly, Ammerman categorizes the historical dimension of congregational life under the perspective of process. This perspective is absent in Cameron and Brouwer. But as

---

[1] Brouwer et al., *Levend lichaam*.
[2] Ammerman et al., *Studying Congregations*; Cameron, *Studying Local Churches*.

4.2. Four Perspectives on Faith Communities

Ammerman	Cameron	Brouwer et al.
Ecology	Global and local context	Context
–	Worship and action of the local church	–
Culture and Identity	–	Identity and culture
Process	–	–
Resources	Resources and people	Structure and resources
Leadership	Power	Leadership

Figure 4.1: A comparison of the perspectives in three congregational studies approaches.

a matter of fact, the historical aspect need not be seen as a separate perspective, but rather constitutes an aspect of the other perspectives. Context, identity, structures, and leadership all have a historical or process side to them. While Brouwer's and Ammerman's proposals are largely similar, there are more significant differences when compared to Cameron's. She not only uses the perspectives shown in the table, but also applies four disciplines to each perspective: anthropology, sociology, organizational studies, and theology. What also stands out apart from this methodological difference is that she does not mention identity and culture as a separate perspective, presumably because they will inevitably surface in one of the other perspectives when a theological method is applied. Cameron demands attention for the local church's worship and activity, which of course represents an important aspect of ecclesial life. We have decided to cover this aspect of the Ontmoetingskerk in a separate chapter (5). Cameron also differs from Brouwer and Ammerman in the formulation of her third perspective, where she helpfully includes not only resources (and structures), but also people. Lastly, whereas Brouwer and Ammerman speak about leadership, Cameron frames this perspective in terms of power. While power dynamics are obviously at work in leadership, the use of the language of power focuses on only one aspect - even if an admittedly important one! - of leadership. In light of the above evaluation of the differences between the three models, we opted to use Brouwer's terminology. It is a fairly 'neutral' structure, but at the same time produces a complete picture. It leaves lots of room for the data itself, and does not frame this data beforehand. In line with our inductive methodology, we have used it as a formal structure, and not as an interpretation of the data.

4.3 Context

The first perspective on the Ontmoetingskerk is that of context, and is divided into three subperspectives. We will first describe the micro context, which is constituted by the geographical area of the Ontmoetingskerk's location. What does this area look like and what kind of interaction is there between the Ontmoetingskerk and its micro context? From there, we will turn to investigate the meso context. Brouwer speaks about the meso context primarily in terms of supralocal structures.[3] For the Ontmoetingskerk, this means we will focus primarily on the denomination of which it is a part. How does the Ontmoetingskerk relate to its traditional and ecclesial context of being a Reformed church? Lastly, we will turn our attention to the macro context: how does the Ontmoetingskerk relate to the larger national context of Dutch society as well as to international trends?

4.3.1 Micro Context

Vathorst

Reflecting on his neighborhood, Henk[4] remarked: "When people ask me, 'Where do you live?' I say I live in Vathorst. Although I should actually say I live in Amersfoort."[5] Two main highways separate the newly built suburb of Vathorst from the rest of Amersfoort, a medium sized city of about 150.000 inhabitants in the center of the Nether-

---

[3] Brouwer et al., *Levend lichaam*, p. 52.
[4] Names in this chapter and the following chapters are not the real respondents' names; exceptions are pastor Joost Smit and Bzzzonder president Michiel van Rennes. During the research there was only one pastor working in the Ontmoetingskerk, making it impossible to grant him anonymity. The pastor gave his consent for this choice. Similar reasons led to the decision to use Michiel van Rennes's real name, for which he also gave his consent.
[5] *Interview with C1, 2018-02-21, D75*. Dutch original: "Als ze mij vragen: waar woon je? Zeg ik ook: in Vathorst. Ik moet eigenlijk zeggen: in Amersfoort." D75 refers to the document in the dataset as it is stored in the analysis software Atlas.ti. All quotations from the dataset will be accompanied by a reference to the document number in Atlas.ti

4.3. Context

lands.⁶ Not a day goes by without these highways being mentioned in traffic reports on Dutch national radio. Many people pass Vathorst on their way to work, or else they live there and travel to work elsewhere. Vathorst is a sizable suburb of some 25.000 people, and is still growing.⁷ Almost 35% of the population is under 19 years old, which is a significantly higher percentage compared to other parts of Amersfoort. It is also a rather wealthy suburb; in 2015, the average household income in Vathorst was €49.563, significantly higher than the €41.800 for Amersfoort as a whole. These numbers do not tell the whole story, however. Behind the high incomes lies a life of working long hours outside of Vathorst. Oftentimes, both parents have demanding careers, leaving marriages at risk, so that Vathorst has earned itself the moniker of the 'national divorce capital'.⁸ Wilco, a resident of Vathorst who does not attend church, reflected on his life in Vathorst in an interview with a leading newspaper in the Netherlands:

> Getting married at a young age, buying an expensive house, an expensive car (Audi A6), working hard to afford these things, having children, neglecting your marriage, couples therapy and still getting divorced three years later - that's the prototype of a young Vathorster.⁹

In the same interview, Wilco described Vathorst as a place where many people are selfish, pursuing their careers. Vathorst, he stated, is a place without history. All Vathorsters over 20 years of age share one common experience: they have moved here from somewhere else,

---

⁶Vathorst is a so-called Vinex-neighborhood, part of a building project supported by the Dutch government. Marten van der Meulen has written a doctoral dissertation on churches and civil society in such neighborhoods; Van der Meulen, *Vroom in de Vinex*.

⁷The statistics in this section are taken from the website *Amersfoort in Numbers*, which is hosted by the city government; *Amersfoort in Cijfers*. These statistics were last accessed on January 16, 2019.

⁸Vathorst competes with the city of Amsterdam for this dubious distinction. There is no doubt that the divorces in Vathorst have a large impact, since they involve many more children than they do in Amsterdam. Koelewijn and Remie, "Vinex-verdriet"; Remie, "Scheidingshoofdstad"; Hitzert, *Relatieontbinding in Vinex-Wijken*.

⁹Koelewijn and Remie, "Vinex-verdriet". Dutch original: "jong trouwen, een duur huis kopen, een dure auto (Audi A6), hard werken om het te kunnen betalen, een kind krijgen, je huwelijk verwaarlozen, relatietherapie en na drie jaar toch scheiden. „Het prototype van de jonge Vathorster.""

they are not 'from here'. The construction of the first houses started in 2001. What Vathorst needs is places where people feel known and secure, so Wilco concluded. But such places are rare in Vathorst. Public places include a railway station, some cafés and restaurants, a small shopping center, and a number of schools. The initial planning for this suburb included no plans for a church building, which has historically been at the center of every typical Dutch town or village. But, as we will see in greater detail below, HVV still ended up being right in the center of the suburb, close to the main shopping street.

Faith Communities in Vathorst

There is a small number of faith communities in Vathorst: one Roman Catholic parish, two charismatic-evangelical communities, and three other Protestant congregations ranging from a more 'mainstream Protestant' church (Veenkerk) to more orthodox or evangelical churches (Kruispunt, lit. 'Crosspoint' in English; and the Ontmoetingskerk). Most of these faith communities meet in schools or rent a space elsewhere. The Roman Catholic parish, for example, meets in an older church in Hooglanderveen, a small village that has been annexed to Vathorst. In this respect, the opening of Hart van Vathorst in March 2016 represented a special moment in the history of Vathorst. Due to the economic crisis of the preceding years, a construction site next to the shopping center that had been reserved for a grocery store or other shop became available.[10] When this lot was attributed to Hart van Vathorst for a church building and meeting place, HVV took on a central place within the Vathorst geography, even though most respondents stated that they do not find the building very recognizable as a church from the outside.[11] Reactions to the building's unrecognizable nature as a church differ. While some regret it and would prefer for the church to have a more prominent presence in their neighborhood, others feel it represents a way to raise the curiosity of fellow Vathorsters about what is happening there without scaring them off, as it were, with a building that looks too much like a church. Frits, who works for one of the disability service providers in Hart van Vathorst, sees the building's central location as a kind of

---

[10] *Online post, 2018-02-05, D74.*
[11] E.g. *interviews with C1 (D75), C2 (D78), B4 (D81), B5 (D82), B14 (D94).*

4.3. Context

victory:

> From what I understand, the municipality did not want a church building on this site, so it was not allowed to look too much like a church. Apparently, the development plans did not allow for a church building here, or maybe they did not find such a building fitting in the center of town. And yet it's right there! I think that's cool! (laughs)[12]

The Ontmoetingskerk (about 800 members) is one of the largest congregations in Vathorst, along with Kruispunt (about 1200 members). In November 2017, Kruispunt opened its own building, which is much more recognizable as a church than Hart van Vathorst is. There is a large cross on the roof, and its location near the railway station and main highway means that many people can see it while passing in trains or cars. Kruispunt is a young and vibrant congregation, representing a cooperation between three different Protestant denominations. It is quite well known both locally and even nationally. The Ontmoetingskerk and Kruispunt cooperate in a number of activities for the neighborhood, like the Alpha Course.

Interaction with the Neighborhood

In listing some of the changes he had noticed since the Ontmoetingskerk moved to its new building and became a part of Hart van Vathorst, young church member Niels remarked:

> I notice guests popping in much more often. It has a much more central place in the neighborhood. I think many people think like: Why not take a look inside? That results in some small talk with the pastor and so on. Of course, that's pretty cool. But I don't know if... I feel... It's not fully clear to everyone here in Vathorst that there is a church there. I think it's kind of an indeterminate

---

[12] *Interview with E1, 2018-02-26, D79*. Dutch original: "Wat ik heb begrepen [is] dat de gemeente Amersfoort eigenlijk op deze locatie helemaal geen kerk wilde, dus het mocht ook niet teveel eruit zien als kerk. Want blijkbaar was het bestemmingsplan er niet voor, of misschien vonden ze het helemaal niet passen meer in een stadscentrum,

building. And that is also the reason why people take a look inside. You can also get a meal there, very smart, it attracts people.[13]

In his reflections, Niels mentioned several ways in which the Ontmoetingskerk interacts with the Vathorst neighborhood. The fact that the church is a part of Hart van Vathorst makes people curious, resulting in walk-in guests. From there, it is entirely possible for them to run into pastor Joost Smit, who works in the building most of the time and has made interaction with people from the neighborhood an important part of his work. There is therefore a curiosity as to what is going on in this 'indeterminate' building; there is a pastor who has made reaching out to newcomers a top priority; and, lastly, there is food.

When he speaks of meals, Niels is probably referring to the restaurant at the heart of the building where many HVV residents work. But there is also another way in which communal meals are drawing people to the building. Once a month,[14] the Ontmoetingskerk holds a free meal for anyone who wants to come. They have called this: Vathorst around the table. These meals are one of the ways in which people from the neighborhood can be associated with the church, albeit without membership. In the tradition from which the Ontmoetingskerk stems, church membership is typically framed in 'binary' terms: either you are a member, or else you are not. But during one of the church services I observed, it struck me that the flowers in the front of the church, which are normally given to a church member in difficult circumstances, were designated for a woman with a serious illness who regularly visits Vathorst around the table, but is not a church mem-

---

en toch zit het er. Dat vind ik wel tof (lacht)."

[13] *Interview with B5, 2018-02-28, D81.* Dutch original: "Volgens mij lopen er steeds vaker gewoon gasten binnen ofzo. [...] Het zit veel [...] centraler. Ik denk dat veel meer mensen denken van: he, laten we even naar binnen lopen. Dan krijg je een praatje enzo met de dominee. Dat is natuurlijk wel top. Dus ja, de groei wordt natuurlijk ook veel groter nu, omdat mensen zo'n kerk natuurlijk ook echt als hun kerk gaan zien. Maar ik weet nog niet of... volgens mij... het is nog niet helemaal voor iedereen duidelijk hier in Vathorst dat daar een kerk zit. Volgens mij is het een beetje een vaag gebouw. En dat is ook de reden dat mensen er soms in gaan. Je kan er ook eten, heel slim, trek je mensen aan."

[14] In 2019, the frequency of these meals was increased to twice a month.

4.3. Context

ber.[15] Another time, pastor Smit invited the new neighborhood police officer to attend a service, introduced her to the congregation, prayed for her work in the neighborhood, and then gave her the flowers at the end of the service.[16] It is therefore clear that people in Vathorst can be associated with the Ontmoetingskerk in more ways than simply membership or non-membership. In recognition of this, the church has also introduced a new, 'formal' category of *friends of the congregation*. These friends are part of the community and are invited to join so-called *Encounter Groups*. The members of these groups get together regularly to support one another and to share their lives. The 'friends' category is formal recognition of the various ways in which people associate themselves in practice with the congregation; otherwise stated, on this point the operant theology has informed the formal theology.

Although the HVV building is not very recognizable as a church in the neighborhood, some people from the neighborhood do recognize it as a religious building. At one point, the congregation arranged for a prayer room to be accessed from the building's central hall. An artist from the congregation was then asked to design the room as a space where church members as well as neighborhood people or HVV employees could come to pray. As guiding principles for her design, the artist chose three gifts of God to humanity: creation (signified in natural colors, pictures of trees), the Word (signified in an open and illustrated Bible on a reading desk), and Jesus (signified in a cross with various symbolic references to Jesus' life).[17] During one church service I observed, pastor Joost Smit shared a story of the way this prayer room was used by people from the neighborhood. In my fieldnotes, I wrote the following:

> Joost recounts how recently, on a Sunday after the service, he had seen some people he didn't know enter the church. He had started a conversation with them. It turned out they were looking for a place to light a candle. Their son had told them this was a church as he had attended his

---

[15] *Fieldnotes 2017-10-29, D67.*

[16] *Online post, 2018-04-22, D99.*

[17] The artist described this during the church service in which the prayer room was officially opened. *Fieldnotes 2017-11-05, D68.*

school's musical here and noticed the cross in front of the sanctuary. Joost took them to the prayer room and lit a candle with them, spoke about life and even prayed.[18]

Church members reflect on this interaction between neighborhood and congregation in diverse ways. Some are afraid that over-investment in people from the neighborhood leaves too little attention for the lives and concerns of the church's own members. Hannah, a senior member of the congregation who has been a Christian her entire life, reflected in this way on the greetings pronounced at the beginning of the service:

> Hannah: "For the congregation itself, I always think, well: Am I in some strange church? We are often not explicitly addressed."
>
> Interviewer: "Ok, it's not something I've really noticed…"
>
> Hannah: "Well, maybe I'm exaggerating now… But in any case, the congregation is not put in the first place."
>
> Interviewer: "So, in fact, you are saying: If you look at how the services are led, sometimes it seems as if it is more about the guests than the congregation itself…"
>
> Hannah: "Yes."[19]

Yet there are other church members who feel that much work remains to be done when it comes to neighborhood interaction. Marja, a working mother who moved to Vathorst from a big city a few years ago, remarked:

> My view is: If you have a building like this in a place like this… I would want us to be much more like a neighborhood center where everybody is welcome, a sociable place

---

[18] *Fieldnotes 2017-11-05, D68.*

[19] *Interview with B3, 2018-02-27, D80.* Dutch Original: "R: voor de gemeente vind ik altijd toch wat, ja: waar zit ik nu. Zit ik in een vreemde kerk? We worden vaak ook eigenlijk niet aangesproken: de gasten, de vrienden en de gemeente niet meer… I: Ok, nou dat is me niet opgevallen… R: Nou, misschien overdrijf ik ook. Maar in ieder geval niet in eerste instantie als gemeente. I: Dus het gaat eigenlijk over, u zegt

4.3. Context

that attracts people. And also that we would look more for how we can connect with the issues in this neighborhood. If we take divorce as an example... Let's start a support group for people who are facing problems in their marriage, or... I don't know... But: Use your building and your place in the neighborhood. [...] I believe in being there for people in a very practical sense, being a kind of safe haven where there is togetherness and warmth.[20]

Summary of the Micro Context

It is clear that there is a lot of awareness in the Ontmoetingskerk of its micro context. Not everybody agrees about the extent to which the neighborhood ought to be shaping how things are done in church. Some perceive attention for the micro context as a threat to other things they find important for what it means to be church. Others wish the church would be more intentional in assuming its place in the center of Vathorst. Yet almost all respondents understand that being church in Vathorst is very different from being church in any other given place. Micro contexts have their own unique questions to ask that need careful listening and wise answering, honoring both the needs of the context and the needs of the congregation's own members.[21] In the case of Vathorst, these questions center for the most part around the high pressure of demanding careers combined with family life and a newly-built living environment in which meaningful places of meeting and togetherness are scarce.

---

eigenlijk van: het lijkt soms wel alsof het meer om de gasten draait in de manier waarop de dienst wordt geleid dan om de gemeente zelf... R: Ja."

[20] *Interview with B2, 2018-02-22, D67.* Dutch original: "Ik denk: dit gebouw in deze plek, ik zou willen dat we nog veel meer als een soort buurtcentrum waar iedereen welkom is, wat een gezellige plek is wat iedereen aantrekt zouden gaan functioneren en ook wel nog meer kijken naar wat sluit er aan bij, he, de dingen in deze wijk als dat echtscheiding is, eh, ga een soort praatgroep starten voor mensen met huwelijksproblemen, weet ik veel, maar maak iets meer gebruik van je gebouw en de plek in deze wijk. [...] Ik denk meer in de zin van, ehm, praktisch er zijn voor mensen, een soort veilige haven waar gezelligheid is en warmte..."

[21] See the recent volume Bass, Cahalan, et al., *Christian Practical Wisdom* for a deeper discussion of the nature of this 'wisdom'.

4.3.2   Meso Context

The RCL

The meso context refers to the level between the direct micro context as described above and the broader societal trends and other dimensions of the macro context that will be addressed in the next section. For the Ontmoetingskerk, the most influential aspect of that meso context is its relationship to the denomination to which it belongs, namely the Gereformeerde Kerken vrijgemaakt (Reformed Churches Liberated, RCL for short).[22] The RCL is one of the smaller reformed denominations in the Netherlands, consisting of about 115.000 members and some 265 local congregations of varying size.[23] It is typically considered an orthodox Reformed church.[24] To understand this denomination's identity, it is necessary, as in so many other cases, to consider its formation. The RCL is a relatively young denomination, with origins in a church schism that occurred in 1944. The debates in that time of war centered around more-or-less two main issues: there was deep theological disagreement over the themes of baptism and covenant, and fierce debate over matters of church polity. The background to these debates is too complex for the present section to delve into in full detail, but suffice it to say that the entire history of the RCL is rife with church schisms. Before 1944, the churches that ended up becoming the RCL had been part of the Reformed church that itself was already the result of a secession from the national Protestant Church in 1834. After 1944, another major schism occurred in the RCL in 1967. On this occasion, a group of church members and pastors left the RCL for church political reasons similar to those that had earlier played a role, during the 1940s. These members and pastors were seeking greater openness and diversity, and conceivably held different views on what the schism of 1944 had been all about. The 1967 schism left

---

[22] In this section, we are looking specifically at the meso context of the Ontmoetingskerk as a congregation. The RCL also relates to HVV as a whole, as two of the care providers involved have RCL backgrounds, as discussed on page 98. However, we are restricting our attention here to the ecclesial meso context, leaving other elements out in this section for reasons of space and, more importantly, because no other elements surfaced in our data that could be considered as meso context.

[23] *GKv Website*.

[24] Van Bekkum, "Verlangen naar tastbare genade", p. 133.

4.3. Context

deep marks in the RCL churches.[25] And, even in recent years, a number of small groups have yet again left the RCL to form new denominations over disagreements with developments in the RCL.

Nevertheless, by now there is also much that has changed. The churches that were formed following the split of 1967 are now in contact with the RCL again. So too there are many RCL members who would not be able to tell you exactly what their ecclesial roots are. This new situation has been described by RCL theologians Stefan Paas and Hans Schaeffer as the reconstructing of Reformed identity.[26] Yet in spite of these developments, the history of the RCL, including its origins, are still of influence on church life and individual spirituality. In a study on RCL spirituality, Koert van Bekkum observed a strong desire for tangible grace, as he put it. Within the RCL tradition, there has been a lot of emphasis on the objective value of God's covenantal promises, the importance of sound, biblical doctrine, and on a church that has the task of guarding both. These objective emphases seem to have led to a decreased presence of the more subjective elements of the Christian faith, or even to a spiritual deficit. The longing for these elements, however, is ever present in the RCL as can be observed from the many forms of spiritual practice that exist within RCL churches today, as well as in the classical activist mindset of RCL believers which has been linked to the neocalvinist theological tradition that has been so influential in it. According to Van Bekkum, hiding behind these newly developing spiritual practices (such as the use of contemporary worship in the liturgy) and remaining activist traits in RCL spirituality is a desire to discover God's active and tangible grace in this world.[27]

Various Ways of Relating to the RCL in the Ontmoetingskerk

This brief introduction to the RCL makes a complete description unnecessary.[28] What does remain relevant, however, is to consider how the Ontmoetingskerk as an RCL congregation relates to the broader denomination. Hannah reflected on this relation, saying: "I am not just

---

[25]Siebe, "Tussen wereldkerk en ware kerk".
[26]Paas and Schaeffer, "Reconstructing Reformed Identity". See also De Jonge, Wijma, and Schaeffer, *Chocoladereep of -hagelslag?*
[27]Van Bekkum, "Verlangen naar tastbare genade".
[28]For more on the history of the RCL, one can refer to the following (Dutch) literature: Deddens and Te Velde, *Vrijmaking - Wederkeer*; Jongeling, De Vries, and Douma,

a member of the church in Vathorst, I am simply an RCL member. That [sense of membership in a broader denomination] is disappearing, of course, because we are all changing a bit. That sometimes complicates matters."[29] The topic Hannah's comments raise is an important one. The fieldwork showed considerable variety in the way people conceived of their congregation's relationship to the national denomination. Some were worried about the loosening connection between RCL churches, leading to increasing differences in liturgical practice as well as matters of doctrine. Mr. and Mrs. Wortman, two elderly members of the congregation, offered the following reflection on the many changes they were witnessing:

> Mr. Wortman: "If I consider the speed at which things happen nowadays, I in all honesty have to admit: we can't keep up. But the other side to that is: we are not happy with these developments. Right? We can remember back to when they allowed 10 new hymns for use in the liturgy, and that took them 10 years, so to speak. That's not normal either, I agree. But now they strike a deal on issues like this and it's done in no time. [...]"
>
> Mrs. Wortman: "Yes, things are becoming much freer. People no longer do what has been agreed upon. For example, the songs; we sing less and less Psalms..."[30]

Mr. and Mrs. Wortman were not just concerned about the liturgical changes. As a matter of fact, they shared how they had recently

---

Het vuur blijft branden; R. Kuiper and Bouwman, *Vuur en vlam: Aspecten van het vrijgemaakt-gereformeerde leven 1944-1969*; Douma, *Om de ware oecumene*; Douma, *Hoe gaan wij verder?*

[29] *Interview with B3, 2018-02-27, D80.* Dutch original: "Ik ben niet alleen lid van de kerk in Vathorst, ik ben gewoon lid van de gereformeerde kerk vrijgemaakt. Dat is natuurlijk aan het verdwijnen want we zijn allemaal een beetje anders aan het worden. En dan wordt het moeilijk soms."

[30] *Interview with A1, 2018-05-01, D101.* Dutch Original: "R: Maar als je ziet, ook het tempo waarin veel dingen nu gebeuren, dan moet ik eerlijk wezen: kunnen wij niet bijfietsen. Maar de andere kant is ook: je bent er niet gelukkig mee. He. Wij hebben het tijdperk meegemaakt dat er 10 gezangen bij kwamen, daar hebben ze 10 jaar over gedaan zogezegd. Dat is ook niet normaal, dat ben ik helemaal met je eens. Maar nu is het handjeklap en het is gebeurd. [...] R-V: Ja, het wordt allemaal wat vrijer. Er

4.3. Context

enjoyed a concert in church with very loud contemporary worship music. But they valued the RCL tradition with its strong emphasis on sound biblical doctrine and were afraid that this tradition is waning. Mr. Wortman also represents a good example of the classical activist RCL spirituality. He served as an elder for a good part of his life, devoting himself to the establishment of Reformed elementary schools and getting involved in all kinds of debates. Like Mr. and Mrs. Wortman, Tjalling expressed reservations about the shape of ecclesial life in the Ontmoetingskerk. A resident of HVV, Tjalling used to love going to church when he was younger. Nowadays, however, he no longer attends church services in the Ontmoetingskerk because he finds them way too hectic. Tjalling was in fact quite outspoken in his criticism:

> I don't go to church here anymore because my ear can't handle it. I can't bear the singing. Having a conversation in church during coffee time is not a problem. But as soon as they start to sing, I go completely crazy, completely hysterical, totally mad. It makes me tired and sad, it makes me angry, I start to shout. [...] So I find the singing really annoying. It annoys me so much that I start to curse. [...] I feel it's no longer a real church service. It's almost like a festival. [...] Just sing in a normal and quiet voice in church, play the organ, listen to a long sermon. That's what I like. [...] I just miss church as it used to be.

---

wordt niet meer gedaan wat afgesproken is. En met liederen gaat het steeds minder psalmen... "

[31] *Hervormd* is the name of another denomination which Tjalling had earlier identified as being old fashioned, but may actually be a bit "too oldfashioned" for him.

[32] *Interview with A6, 2018-07-23, D111.* Dutch Original: "Ik ga hier niet meer naar de kerk omdat mijn oor het niet meer aan kan. Ik kan niet tegen zingen. Praten in de kerk bij de koffie enzo is niet erg. Maar zo gauw als ze gaan zingen dan wordt ik helemaal gek, helemaal hysterisch, helemaal doorgedraaid. Wordt ik moe en verdrietig, word ik boos, ga ik schreeuwen. [...] Dus het zingen vind ik heel erg irritant. Zo irritant dat ik gewoon echt zit te vloeken [...] Ik vind het geen echte kerkdienst meer. Het lijkt net een festival ofzo. [...] Ga [in de kerk] gewoon normaal rustig zingen en ga gewoon orgel spelen. Gewoon een lange preek. Dan vind ik het mooi. [...] Ik mis gewoon vroeger de kerk. [...] Vroeger was het echt gezellig en leuk. En rustig. [...] Net pak aan. Dat was echt vroeger he. Vroeger was het echt streng. Ja, vrijgemaakt streng, dus niet Hervormd, maar streng vrijgemaakt. Dat vond ik leuk. En nu is het echt gewoon allemaal modern en... Ik vind het jammer."

> [...] It used to be sociable and nice. And quiet. [...] Wearing your best suit. That's how it used to be. It used to be really strict. Right - RCL-strict, not Hervormd-strict.[31] Strict RCL. That's what I liked. But now everything is modern and... It's something I regret.[32]

In other parts of the interview, Tjalling reflected on how his mental health issues were at the root of some of the problems he was experiencing with church. But his sentiment remained clear nonetheless; there are many things that have changed, and they have not been for the better. Tjalling regretted that the Ontmoetingskerk, like many other RCL churches, has shifted away from the type of RCL church he knew when he was younger. For him, the RCL tradition is very meaningful.

Whereas Mr. and Mrs. Wortman and Tjalling expressed their reservations about recent developments in the RCL and wished things would be like they were in the past when RCL churches were more or less homogeneous, others applauded the renewed and less strict relationship that the Ontmoetingskerk has with the RCL tradition. To them the Reformed tradition felt like a straitjacket. A church member named Ada noted, for example, that the RCL tradition often felt like a "burden" to her, as if life was to be lived within certain set "boundaries". She and her husband had lived most of their lives within these boundaries without a problem, until her husband's burnout made them feel increasingly unfree. She added that the presence of a diverse group of people with and without disabilities in the Ontmoetingskerk was one of the key factors challenging the traditional boundaries which for her characterized the RCL tradition as she knew it:

> That is what we enjoy in this whole HVV-thing. Whether you do or don't have the ability to speak, whether you have a degree in whatever or spend your days shredding paper - you are welcome as you are, and to God you are all equal. [...] Sometimes you might think that you have to do things differently, or know things better, or be able to do things better... But none of that matters. It's about God. He comes to you, and that's it. [33]

---

[33] *Interview with B7, 2018-03-07, D84.* Dutch Original: "En dat vinden we het mooie

4.3. Context

Church member and elder Henk came with a similar reflection:

> What I personally learn really deeply from our newer church members, the residents, is how purely, truly, and authentically they confess their faith, and how they have the courage to talk about that in a very simple, but very authentic manner. It makes me think: Look at me, with all my Reformed doctrine and rules and laws and this and that... I'm not saying that's not important. But what it's really all about... That is what I learn from someone with Down syndrome, or people with dementia, people who are suffering brokenness. [... There is so much] faith and spirit to be found there, that is so contagious. At least it is for me, and I hope the same will be true for [other] church members.[34]

For Henk and Ada, a downside of the RCL Reformed heritage is its apparent focus on outward appearances, on 'getting the doctrine right' and 'staying in line'. To their mind, such an approach to faith risks missing what faith is really all about. Both Henk and Ada therefore expressed their happiness about their congregation's changing relationship to the Reformed tradition, although this did not mean in any way that they want to get rid of this tradition altogether, because they also acknowledged its strengths.

Such responses to the Ontmoetingskerk's loosening relationship to the broader denomination, whether that loss was lamented (as was true for Mr. and Mrs. Wortman and Tjalling) or applauded (as in the

---

ook aan de Hart van Vathorst-toestand, of je nou niet kan praten, of je nou afgestudeerd ben in weet ik veel wat of dat je alleen maar papier versnippert de hele dag, je mag er gewoon zijn en voor God ben je hetzelfde. [...] Denk je wel eens: ja je moet het toch wel anders doen, of weten, of kunnen. Maar dat is het dus helemaal niet, het is God, die komt bij jou en dat is het."

[34] *Interview with C1, 2018-02-21, D75.* Dutch Original: "Wat ik persoonlijk heel erg leer van de nieuwe kerkleden, de bewoners, dat ze zo puur, echt en authentiek hun geloof durven te belijden en, ja gewoon daarover durven te praten op een hele eenvoudige, maar zo'n echte manier. Dat ik denk: daar kom ik aan met al mijn gereformeerde dogmatiek en regeltjes en wetjes en zusjes en datjes. Ik zeg niet dat het niet belangrijk. Maar waar het nu echt om gaat, dat leer ik van de Downer, van dementerenden, van de mensen die te maken hebben met gebrokenheid. [...Er zit] zoveel geloof en geestkracht in, zo aanstekelijk, voor mij althans en ik hoop dat dat

case of Ada and Henk), manifested themselves mostly among participants in the 3rd and 4th age categories (> 40, cf. 3.5.4). Younger participants seemed to confirm Hannah's view that the old sense of denominational membership is diminishing by the simple fact that they hardly ever mentioned it. For them, the Ontmoetingskerk's participation in the RCL denomination seldom represented a primary motivation for becoming or staying members of this congregation. While parents often played an important role for this younger age group in choosing a church, respondents also mentioned social contacts with friends as an important aspect of feeling at home in the Ontmoetingskerk. Most of the respondents in this age group who had made an active decision to join the Ontmoetingskerk mentioned reasons pertaining to the congregation itself, and sometimes its involvement with HVV, rather than its connection with the RCL.

Remaining Influence of the RCL on the Ontmoetingskerk

This seemingly diminishing sense of connection to the national denomination amongst younger church members does not mean, however, that the role of the RCL has disappeared from local church life in Vathorst altogether. Both of the caregiving partners in HVV (Accolade and Sprank) have RCL backgrounds, though they do nowadays have broader identities and provide care to many people who are not members of any church. Although HVV did not begin as a Reformed initiative at all (in fact, one of the project's most prominent pioneers is an evangelical-charismatic Christian), in an unexpected move one RCL church and two disability service providers with RCL roots stepped up to the plate in offering themselves as partners. Other partners were indeed invited, but did not initially take up the challenge. This seems to reflect something of the neocalvinist RCL spirituality described by Koert van Bekkum. The RCL has historically combined a more or less conservative vision on matters of faith with an active engagement in society. One could say that the increased attention for the micro context (see 4.3.1) has brought about shifts in the relationship to the meso context, giving the Ontmoetingskerk more of a local color. Church member Frederik, who had previously had firsthand experience with the planting of new RCL churches in two newly built Dutch cities, re-

---

voor de kerkleden ook steeds meer gaat worden."

4.3. Context

marked how different things were in Vathorst. It used to be quite simple to plant a new RCL church, as everybody had more or less the same ideas on what a church should be like. But in Vathorst, it became very clear that times had changed. This was not just going to be the RCL church of Vathorst, but a congregation in its own right and with its own local color, relating to the neighborhood of Vathorst.[35] So while the relationship between the national denomination and the local congregation has indeed changed and even still seems to be in transition, it has not disappeared or become irrelevant. In fact, when the RCL was looking for a congregation to represent it at the national synod (an ecumenical initiative of various Dutch protestant denominations) they delegated the Ontmoetingskerk with its unique story.[36] Within the RCL ecclesial context, multiple articles were written about the Ontmoetingskerk as an initiative for other RCL churches to learn from.[37] Some students from the RCL seminary also wrote papers or theses on the Ontmoetingskerk with the same objective.[38] So too Hans Schaeffer, one of the seminary's professors, wrote an article about HVV.[39] These examples show how the national denomination continued to stay involved at the local level. Conversely, the leadership in the Ontmoetingskerk continued to stress the importance of not letting go of one's roots. Interestingly enough, the diversification resulting from HVV as mentioned by Henk and Ada as having the potential to overcome certain traits of RCL ecclesial life was also mentioned by pastor Joost Smit as a way to stay rooted in this tradition:

> I feel that those people who live in the group for advanced dementia have their contribution to make too – like, the gospel did not start with us. So you sing a song from the 1930's, or even older... So they place history before our very eyes. They help us with that.[40]

---

[35] *Interview with B6, 2018-03-02, D83.*
[36] *Conversation with C3, 2018-11-09, D32.*
[37] E.g. Luiten, "Unieke samenwerking"; Tamminga, "Een beetje kerk is inclusief"; Ter Horst, "Een beetje Vathorst in het Engelse zuiden"; *Blog about plans for HVV*.
[38] E.g. (unpublished) bachelor theses by Ruben Beijl (D2), who also wrote his master thesis on HVV at the VU University in Amsterdam, and Christiaan Kanis (D3); or an essay written in the context of a master-level seminar on public theology written by Ronald Elzinga, Jan Hooiveld, Pim Poortinga, and Chiel Vleesenbeek (D24).
[39] Schaeffer, "Hospitable Church".

Summary of the Meso Context

The most relevant part of the meso context is the denomination to which the Ontmoetingskerk belongs, namely the RCL. The RCL is an orthodox Reformed church that has historically placed much emphasis on sound doctrine and objective biblical truths, fed by a longing for "tangible grace" (as Koert van Bekkum put it). This longing for realized forms of the gospel in everyday life could still be found in the genes of the Ontmoetingskerk, even if its relationship to the national denomination clearly was in transition, as it has been in other local RCL churches. Today, one could say, the micro context plays a bigger part in the life of the congregation than it used to, while the meso context is not as directly influential as it once was. This creates more space for local congregations to discern how to respond to their calling in their own micro context. Church members evaluate this space in different ways. Some experienced it as a relief and a regained freedom, but others were also nervous about the future because of the great ensuing responsibilities. The process of transition is still ongoing, but it seems that the church's leadership, while taking the freedom to adapt congregational life to the direct environment, is intentional about staying rooted in its tradition and connected to its denomination.

4.3.3 Macro Context

The Concreteness of the Macro Context

Apart from its direct geographic micro context and its relationship to the meso context, the Ontmoetingskerk is influenced also by the larger dynamics of its macro context.[41] The Ontmoetingskerk has also tried to respond to this macro context. Since a full account of the macro context is not possible because it would have to include the 21st century Western world as a whole and the Netherlands in particular, we have chosen to focus on the elements that emerged explicitly from

---

[40] *Interview with C3, 2018-03-13, D88.* Dutch original: "Ik vind dus dat de mensen van de gesloten groep PG, dat die ook inbreng hebben van: het evangelie is niet bij ons begonnen, kijk maar, je doet een lied uit de jaren '30 of nog ouder... Dus in die zin zetten ze ook de historie voor ons neer, daar helpen ze ons bij."

[41] The body of this subsection was previously published as Tamminga, "Countering Ableism".

4.3. Context

the data. The macro context is not just an abstract and distant reality. Within the context of this study, for example, the macro context is encountered when political figures from the local authorities or the national government visit HVV and reflect on their experiences in the media. Their interest for and reflection on this project teaches us a lot about how HVV and the Ontmoetingskerk are situated within the larger macro context.

When HVV officially opened its doors with a public celebration on September 30, 2016, Amersfoort's mayor Lucas Bolsius was present to conduct the official opening ceremony.[42] When asked to reflect on the values driving this project, the mayor clearly avoided religious language and spoke about the universal human need for connection to others.[43] Yet the project clearly did leave an impression on him, for when he later hosted king Willem Alexander of the Netherlands for a visit to the city of Amersfoort, he referred to HVV and invited one of its founders to share something about the unique role of the church both within HVV and in the wider community.[44] More political attention for HVV came in the form of a visit by secretary of state Hugo de Jonge, charged with responsibility for the healthcare portfolio. He visited HVV and spoke extensively about his visit in talk shows and interviews.[45] After his visit, De Jonge also posted the following on his Facebook page: "Everything in Hart van Vathorst is as normal as can be, and exactly that is what makes it so very special."[46] When he launched a campaign to recruit new healthcare workers, he referred to his experiences of the way care and communal living are structured in HVV, and used the picture of one of the professionals working there as one of the faces for the campaign.[47]

These examples of the attention devoted to HVV by the mayor, secretary of state, and king, the subsequent media exposure, as well as the attested impression their experiences with HVV left on them, show how this political attention is not just nice for PR purposes, so to speak.

---

[42] "Complex in gebruik".
[43] *Fieldnotes 2016-09-30, D27*.
[44] Van der Graaf and Dijkstra, "Heden en geschiedenis in Eemland".
[45] Meijer, "Trots in verpleeghuizen".
[46] *Online post, 2018-01-29, D72*. Dutch original: "Alles is hier in Hart van Vathorst zo gewoon mogelijk en juist dat maakt het zo enorm bijzonder."
[47] *Online post, 2018-02-05, D74*.

They also give us insight into the way HVV is situated within larger dynamics in Dutch society relating to the structure of society, healthcare, and political reflection on the strength of communities. When we study the interactions between HVV and the macro context in greater depth, we can conclude that HVV seems in some ways to *following the grain* of certain societal dynamics. In a sense, the mayor and the secretary of state showed themselves very happy with what is going on in Vathorst, because it proves their point about the structure of healthcare, for example. There are other aspects of the project, however, that *go against the grain*, leading to uneasiness or avoidance. In the following paragraphs we will discuss some of the ways in which HVV naturally fits within the macro context and at the same time seems also to be a counter movement to aspects of this same macro context.

Going With the Grain

HVV fits very well in the societal developments that we described as a *turn to inclusion* in section 2.2. When the HVV partners wrote their vision statement, they explicitly connected their plans to developments in Dutch society:

> Healthcare in the Netherlands is going through a sea of change. The classical welfare state is depleted and the government is taking a step back in many areas. Care providers are facing great challenges. They have to change the way they work, and do it for less money. The role of civic society, too, is receiving much attention. How do Christians respond, now that the government is placing much of its responsibility back with networks in society? In Amersfoort-Vathorst, we want to realize a new way of living together: *Extraordinarily Considerate*.[48] As a church, a daycare center for children, and two care providers, we have found each other in the desire to combine encounters, growth, faith, and communal life. We dream of a place in this neighborhood where everyone is welcome and every talent is seen and honored. In this

---

[48]The working title for the project was *Buitengewoon Zorgzaam*, which translates as extraordinarily considerate. The name was later changed to Hart van Vathorst.

4.3. Context

place our residents, fellow Vathorsters, volunteers, and professionals live and work together, seeking new ways of mutual care.[49]

It comes as no surprise that the representatives of both local and national governments mentioned in this vision statement have been quite enthusiastic about this part of HVV's vision. It seems to follow the line of policy and developments in Dutch society that resonate with developments in many other Western countries. The vision statement highlights the responsibility of citizens to shape the good life together, leaving ample room for individual initiatives. In the media, HVV was mentioned as one such initiative among others.[50] Secretary of state De Jonge called HVV "an example of how it can be done, because there are multiple forms that work. At its root, it is all about giving each other more attention and time. For people in care homes, too, normal life should continue as much as possible."[51]

Hvv follows the trend of developments in the macro context with its focus on personal attention and locality. It clearly presents itself as one possible solution for challenges that have arisen in the context of the transition from a classical welfare state to a participation society, and is recognized as such. It also employs the language of inclusion that is used by politicians in the Netherlands and internationally as an

---

[49] *Vision statement HVV, 2014-04-01, D1.* Dutch Original: "In Nederland vindt een aardverschuiving plaats in de zorg. De klassieke verzorgingsstaat is uitgeput en de overheid trekt zich op veel terreinen terug. Aanbieders van zorg staan voor grote uitdagingen. Zij moeten anders gaan werken voor veel minder geld. Ook de rol van de kerk op het maatschappelijk middenveld staat in de belangstelling. Wat doen christenen nu de overheid veel van haar verantwoordelijkheid teruglegt bij de netwerken in de samenleving? In Amersfoort-Vathorst willen wij een nieuwe vorm van samenleven realiseren: Buitengewoon Zorgzaam. Als kerk, een kinderdagverblijf en twee zorgorganisaties vinden wij elkaar in het verlangen om ontmoeten, groeien, geloven en samenleven met elkaar te verbinden. Wij dromen van een plek in de wijk waar iedereen welkom is en waar elk talent gezien en gewaardeerd wordt. Op deze plek leven en werken bewoners, wijkgenoten, vrijwilligers en professionals samen en zoeken zij nieuwe wegen in het zorgen voor elkaar."

[50] E.g. in the daily talk show *1 Vandaag, 2017-04-14, D47* and in late night news show *Nieuwsuur, 2018-12-19, D113*.

[51] Meijer, "Trots in verpleeghuizen". Dutch original: "een voorbeeld van hoe het kán, want er zijn veel verschillende vormen die werken. Ten diepste gaat het daarbij om meer aandacht en tijd voor elkaar. Ook voor mensen in een verpleeghuis moet het gewone leven zoveel mogelijk doorgaan."

ideological drive behind this transition.[52]

Going Against the Grain

However, it is precisely in its understanding of what inclusive communal life really means that HVV is also bucking the trend of developments in the macro context. Governmental legislation, for example, meant that a number of elements in the original plans could not be realized, like the development of a swimming pool for residents and others in the neighborhood. Because HVV's building was co-financed by a social housing organization that rents its space out to the care providers, the plans for the pool had to be abandoned due to legislation forbidding such organizations from investing in anything other than living space.[53] This legal issue had an impact on some of the developers' original plans for HVV; the pool had been envisioned as a place of creative encounters, being both a place for neighborhood people to swim and a place for residents to receive physical therapy and exercise. Legislation also continues to stand in the way of some of the forms of cooperation and inclusive communal life envisioned by the partners. For example, the daycare center would like to be able to visit the elderly residents with dementia. Such visits would provide a chance for the 'grandfathers and grandmothers' to read stories to the children, and to do all kinds of activities together. At one moment, the children and residents with dementia even danced together when the children were invited to join when the residents were visited by a musician.[54] It is these kinds of interactions that HVV wants to enable, from its conviction that they are wholesome for all involved. Such interactions would also seem to rhyme well with the government's notions concerning an *inclusive society*. However, safety regulations make it difficult if not impossible for such interaction to be arranged legally, since legislation requires the doors between the daycare facilities and the residents' living space to remain locked.

The above examples above may seem quite minor. But legislation is not the only level on which the practices of HVV sometimes go against the grain. In fact, the conflicts on that level seem to be symp-

---

[52] see 2.2.
[53] Meijer, "Trots in verpleeghuizen".
[54] *Online post, 2018-07-18, D108.*

4.3. Context

tomatic of the deeper question as to whether the values that drive society and politics really are compatible with inclusion, and what inclusion actually means. Above we noted how the theologian Luke Bretherton demanded attention for the dubious relationship between neoliberal political systems and inclusion language.[55] In Vathorst, this dubious relationship can be witnessed firsthand. Elements of Western society that work to exclude groups of people are often explicitly present there: the prioritizing of rationality, the valuing of people in terms of economic worth, and the high demands for productivity and success. These aspects all exclude people with intellectual disabilities and to a large degree also disadvantage people with physical disabilities. However, as is often said in the Ontmoetingskerk, these elements are actually unhealthy for all human beings, regardless of disabilities. In this sense, HVV is going against the grain of the macro context.

At the same time, there is a kind of duality in how HVV, and the Ontmoetingskerk as a church in particular, relate to these elements of the macro context. On the one hand, they explicitly lay out alternative values. For example, instead of living for economic worth, people are valued because they are made in the image of God. Such a statement can be heard repeatedly in sermons in the Ontmoetingskerk, but it is also part of the daily experience of some church members. Sam, for example, said in his own words that he finds more fulfillment in discovering all that he can learn from a single resident in HVV than he does in his monthly bonus at work.[56] At the same time, it is clear that the Ontmoetingskerk is not a safe haven immune to surrounding culture. For example, my observations of committee meetings and other more public events in HVV often included notes on how much the setting reminded me of corporate culture, complete with expensive cars, tailormade suits, and an environment of seeing and being seen.[57]

An unsettling but clear example of this duality is found in a traumatic event for HVV and the congregation. One of the residents, who was not a Christian but had an important place in the life of HVV and also regularly visited church services, decided to commit euthanasia. She felt her traumatic brain injury had ruined her life to such an extent that she no longer found it valuable enough to live. Her death came as

---

[55] Bretherton, *Christianity and Contemporary Politics*.
[56] *Interview with B13, 2018-04-03, D93*.
[57] *Fieldnotes 2016-09-30, D27; 2016-11-27, D34; 2017-01-23, D39*.

a shock to many, especially the other residents. In this unexpected situation, people were clearly in search of language that fit the situation. On the one hand, some people felt that she had made a brave decision, choosing to take matters into her own hands. This sentiment fits well with what is commonly accepted in the Netherlands. However, the formal and normative theologies of the Ontmoetingskerk point clearly in a very different direction, understanding life as a gift that should be received as such. Members of the leadership were also concerned about what an explicit approval of this resident's choice might mean for other residents who were, medically speaking, worse off than this resident had been. For reasons of privacy, I cannot delve more deeply into this example. Yet it clearly shows how values that are commonly accepted in the macro context have an impact in HVV, even if its own values are very different. There is no hard border between the church (or a Christian community like HVV) and the world. This observation shows that there clearly is a difference between the normative and formal theologies and the espoused theology. In the example, the espoused theology seemed to be influenced heavily by the macro context and its appreciation of individual autonomy. There can thus be apparent inconsistencies in the espoused theology: on the one hand, approval and even near-praise for the decision to commit euthanasia, and, on the other hand, opposition from an ethical stance.[58]

There have also been situations in which HVV, the Ontmoetingskerk, and individual members clearly spoke with one voice against developments in the macro context. A clear example is the interaction with debates surrounding prenatal testing for Down syndrome and the consequent abortion of babies testing positively, which has become a widely accepted practice in the Netherlands as in other parts of Western Europe. The Dutch philosopher Marcel Zuijderland recently wrote a book in which he argued that, given the current availability of prenatal tests, it is irresponsible to allow the birth of babies with severe disabilities, given that their life is not profitable for society in economic terms. Among these severe disabilities he also lists Down syndrome.[59] Zuijderland's book was met with criticism, amongst others from the mother of one of the residents of HVV with

---

[58] *Fieldnotes 2018-03-11, D87; Interview with C3, 2018-02-12, D88.*
[59] Zuijderland, *Gentest of Geen Test?*; Van Soest, "Mensverbetering".

4.3. Context

Down syndrome. In an open letter published in a newspaper, she wrote how hard it is for her as a parent to have to justify her son's existence. Noting the examples of Denmark and Iceland where virtually no babies with Down syndrome are born anymore, she sketched out how it has become increasingly self-evident to test and abort, leaving parents with the feeling that they have to justify their 'choice' to have their baby born. About her son she writes:

> Our son does not smoke, he does not use drugs, he rides his bike or uses public transportation. He does not curse, nor does he discriminate. He doesn't post rude tweets. He is not a hacker and does not create insulting vlogs. He doesn't have dollar signs in his eyes. He has good teeth and never had to wear dental braces. He's never been hospitalized. He gives us loads of love and made us more beautiful people.[60]

The mother's piece was picked up and posted on HVV's official facebook page as well as on pastor Joost Smit's personal page. Many people from HVV responded with approval and encouragement. When Smit preached on the sixth commandment (*thou shalt not kill*) a few months later, he invited that mother to the front to interview her about the experiences that had led her to write the open letter.[61]

This clear and undisputed stance opposing the apparent normality of aborting children with Down syndrome shows how HVV is clearly going against the grain of the macro context in certain respects. On this issue, people involved in HVV found each other in a common conviction, shaped by the Gospel. Undoubtedly, this is the deepest reason why HVV goes against the grain of the macro context in certain areas. It is also the reason that the politicians we introduced at the beginning of our description of the macro context sometimes experience unease with the church's precise role in HVV. The Netherlands are a highly

---

[60] Wolff, "Waarom mijn Down-zoon er is?" Dutch original: "Onze zoon rookt niet, hij gebruikt geen drugs, hij rijdt op de fiets of met het openbaar vervoer. Hij vloekt niet en discrimineert niet. Hij stuurt geen grove tweets de lucht in. Hij is geen hacker of treitervlogger en hij heeft geen dollartekens in zijn ogen. Hij heeft een goed gebit zonder gaatjes en heeft nooit een beugel hoeven dragen. Nog nooit in het ziekenhuis gelegen. Hij geeft ons bakken vol liefde en heeft van ons mooiere mensen gemaakt."

[61] *Observation notes 2017-11-12, D69*.

secularized country, as a recent study by the Netherlands Institute for Social Research confirms, only 31% of the Dutch population consider themselves members of some kind of religious community. This number is also declining quickly. The reduced religious involvement also causes distrust towards religious organizations and declining knowledge and understanding of religious traditions. But the report at the same time shows how religious organizations are at the moment indispensable for civic society, as 48% of committed church members regularly do volunteer work, compared to 28% of the average population.[62] There is a clear issue here: On the one hand, churches are needed for their social capital. On the other hand, their potential in terms of numbers and understanding by outsiders, including those in the government, is declining. This issue became more directly relevant to HVV towards the end of my data collection period, as a nonChristian organization joined HVV as a partner to manage the restaurant which is a part of the building and a workplace for many residents, as well as a meeting space for people in the neighborhood. This organization's participation brings to the fore the tensions that come with working out of a specifically Christian motivation. This tension is not just felt in relation to the context, but also becomes a reality that must be dealt with in everyday decision making in HVV.[63]

Summary of the Macro Context

Hvv fits its macro context naturally in many ways: It is in line with societal trends of valuing the power of local communities over state-organized support. It also intentionally connects its practices to these trends, for example by its use of the terminology of inclusion. At the same time, HVV goes against the grain of elements of the macro context on a number of levels. At the root, this tension between macro context and HVV can be explained by pointing to HVV's explicitly Christian motivation in a highly secularized context.

---

[62] De Hart and Van Houwelingen, *Christenen in Nederland*.
[63] *Conversation with Joost Smit, 2019-01-28, D116.*

4.4 Identity & Culture

In our description of the way HVV and the Ontmoetingskerk relate to their contexts, we have already seen much of their identity. In this section, we want to give a fuller account of who HVV and the Ontmoetingskerk understand themselves to be. In this section, we make a distinction between HVV as a whole and the Ontmoetingskerk in particular. The aim of this study is to learn from HVV, and specifically to focus in on the church's role within the project. For this description, it is important both to note how the HVV partners think about the project as a whole and how the church as an independent project partner with its own history and identity takes up its place in this project. One of the questions is whether this separation can really be made. From our data, it is clear that participants had very different thoughts on the matter. Some saw HVV as one of the 'activities' of the Ontmoetingskerk, while others were more inclined to refer to the Ontmoetingskerk as 'HVV's church'. In the first case, 'HVV belongs to the church', while in the second case, 'the church belongs to HVV'. Given this diversity in descriptions of the relationship between the Ontmoetingskerk and HVV, we have chosen to treat them separately here, notwithstanding the significant overlap, specifically in how HVV as a whole and the Ontmoetingskerk in particular reflect theologically about living together in a community with people with and without disabilities.

4.4.1 Hart van Vathorst: Sharing Life

Rethinking Residential Care in HVV

As we observed in section 4.3.3, HVV positions itself explicitly against the backdrop of developments in Dutch society and healthcare. The HVV founders noted how 'caring for' has become increasingly differentiated in separate areas of professionalism. Michiel van Rennes, one of the leaders of one of HVV's partners, reflected on that in an interview:

> I see, in the end, that social work, care, caring for children, and education all overlap. Imagine I were to organize an event in cooperation with the church. During

the event, the elderly residents would be sitting together with some of the children, and the elderly residents would share something about the past. And suppose one of the attendees was in a wheelchair. Such an event could be called 'social work' because you are bringing these people together and the elderly residents might be lonely. So you'd call it social work. It's education because the elderly people are teaching the children. It's care because one of the attendees needs an injection after half an hour. But in the end it's just sitting together around this table... And in the Netherlands these are four separate boxes.[64]

Against this trend, HVV attempted to design a more holistic approach to residential care. Partners with significantly differing areas of expertise (e.g. children's daycare, brain trauma, advanced dementia) started sharing the same roof and had the intention of also working together wherever possible. In practice, this did not always work out as well as they would have wanted (see 4.5), but there are many examples of where things did work out. For example, the partners work together in organizing a number of activities for residents, while HVV provides work placements for residents of the various partners. Besides this organizational response to the noted differentiation in healthcare, the project's initiators also found it important to apply a holistic approach to the care for individual residents, extending from purely 'medical' care to attention for social and religious aspects. Hvv provides ample opportunities for this due to the presence of a church community. This makes it very easy to organize spiritual support for residents, for example. The Ontmoetingskerk has designated one of its elders exclusively to the visitation of HVV residents. Pastor Joost Smit, too, is very approachable. As a religious residential care provider, partner

---

[64]*Interview with E2, 2018-04-18, D97.*Dutch Original: "Ik zie ook dat uiteindelijk welzijnswerk, zorg, kinderopvang, onderwijs, die gaan geloof ik over elkaar heen. Stel: ik organiseer vanuit de kerk een ochtend waar ouderen en kinderen bij elkaar zitten, waarin de ouderen wat over geschiedenis vertellen aan de kinderen en waar toevallig ook iemand even heen moet die in een rolstoel zit. Dat is misschien wel welzijnswerk omdat de ouderen en de kinderen bij elkaar zijn en omdat de ouderen misschien wel wat eenzaam zijn. Dan noem je dat welzijnswerk. Het is onderwijs omdat die ouderen die kinderen wat leren. Het is zorg omdat er toevallig iemand zit een spuitje nodig heeft na een half uur. Maar het is uiteindelijk gewoon dat je aan

4.4. Identity & Culture

Accolade also has its own chaplain working in HVV, albeit during limited hours due to his placement at a number of other locations as well. The chaplain's tasks include the organizing of a weekly morning Bible study for people with dementia along with pastoral support for Accolade's residents. The extra support offered by the church is a relevant addition to his work. Its participation in HVV also gives residents the opportunity to function in a social group other than the people they live with. Most residents are members of the Ontmoetingskerk, but even if they are not, they still often join social activities hosted by the church.

Another way in which HVV has sought to contribute to the development of residential care in the Netherlands is the facilitation of contact with the neighborhood of Vathorst. The Netherlands, as well as many other countries, have seen a shift over the years from segregated care for people with disabilities in institutions outside of society to more inclusive approaches.[65] Hvv embodies this shift as many of the residents came from other, more remote locations and are now for the first time experiencing life in a 'regular' neighborhood. For them, the ability to shop or go out to eat at a restaurant easily is very meaningful. Hvv explicitly attempts to stimulate interaction between residents and neighborhood, for example in the restaurant located in the central hall, since such interaction does not happen automatically even with a location that is as central as that of HVV.

Ideals and Idealism in HVV

Hvv's vision statement includes four central key words: encountering, growing, believing, and living together. These word frequently pop up in conversations about the mission of HVV. As the project continues to develop, the understanding of these key ideals may undergo change, but they remain at the heart of the project. Interestingly, none of them focus on the 'recipients' of care. They all aim at the community as a whole, and even the micro context of Vathorst as a neighborhood. The underlying conviction is that these four things are generally beneficial and do not fall into the category of 'special needs'. Hvv has high ideals in this regard; it does not just aim to be

---

deze tafel met elkaar zit. En in Nederland zijn dat vier verschillende hokjes."

[65] Cf. Van Loon and Steglich-Lentz, *Geloven in inclusie*.

healthcare providers, but rather a place where life is shared and where people support one another in mutual growth.

Among the key words, the term believing is very explicitly religious. During recent discussions with the new, non-Christian partner in charge of the restaurant, this keyword was indeed debated, but as of yet it is still a part of HVV's central vision. In its vision statement, HVV clearly positions itself as a religious, even explicitly Christian community. That was already obvious from the first part of the statement we discussed in section 4.3.3, but it is even more explicit in the section that follows it:

> For us as initiators of this project, our faith in Jesus Christ plays an important role. Jesus teaches us to serve one another. On the way to God's kingdom, He is searching for what is considered lost or weak, and in those places he shows His power and love. With Him, human accomplishments or successes are not decisive for status or appreciation. Jesus invites you to look after one another in His kingdom and bid everyone welcome. In HVV, we want to follow Jesus in this respect and embody that in our life together. We do not want to confine that to residents or church members, but our goal is to get all inhabitants of Vathorst involved.[66]

Hvv therefore has far-reaching ideals about communal life and about rethinking health care. These ideals are clearly rooted in the Christian faith. However, the identity and culture in HVV are not shaped by ideals alone, but just as much by the complexities encountered in daily life. Respondents in HVV had a clear understanding of how ideals, with all their inspirational force, could also become sources of

---

[66] *Vision statement HVV, 2014-04-01, D1.* Dutch Original: "Voor ons als initiatiefnemers speelt het geloof in Jezus Christus een belangrijke rol. Jezus leert ons om elkaar te dienen. Op weg naar Gods koninkrijk zoekt Hij wat als verloren of zwak beschouwd wordt en juist op die plekken laat Hij zijn kracht en liefde zien. Menselijke prestaties of successen zijn bij Hem niet beslissend voor aanzien of waardering. Jezus nodigt je zo uit om in zijn koninkrijk om te zien naar elkaar en iedereen welkom te heten. Wij willen in Buitengewoon Zorgzaam Jezus daarin volgen en dat praktisch laten zien in het samenleven. We willen dat niet beperken tot bewoners of kerkleden, maar alle inwoners van Vathorst daarin betrekken."

4.4. Identity & Culture

exclusion. They reflected on societal ideals of autonomy and competitiveness that have served to exclude people with disabilities, but also turned a critical eye to their own ideals. Frits, who works for one of the care providers in HVV, remarked: "No system is perfect. And that's why I find it so amazing that a new world is coming (laughs)..."[67] This kind of spiritual down-to-earth mentality is typical for the culture I encountered in HVV. Hvv's mentality in relation to its vision and convictions could best be described as eschatological idealism. People work hard to realize a more inclusive way of living together, but are also aware that the ultimate society is not of this world, but of a world that is yet to come.

4.4.2 The Ontmoetingskerk: Discovering Christ

A Traditional Reformed Church

When it comes to a description of the Ontmoetingskerk's identity and culture, the first thing that stands out is that, despite its uniqueness and changed relationship to the RCL, it in many ways still is a typical, traditional RCL church (cf. 4.3.2). Notwithstanding the changing attitudes towards this tradition that we encountered earlier, a number of elements still justify calling the Ontmoetingskerk a typical Reformed church. What stands out first of all is the focus on the Bible and the liturgical centrality of the sermon as an explanation of the Bible. This can be readily observed in any given church service in the Ontmoetingskerk, and was widely attested by church members during interviews. Even if some of the church members shared a concern that the preaching was becoming more 'superficial' or too 'human-centered', their concerns as such prove the point that they consider Bible-based preaching one of the most important things about church. When I asked Mrs. Hollenberg, who has advanced dementia and had great difficulties answering my far too complex questions, what she thought to be the most important thing about church, she immediately answered: "To hear God's word [...] That's what it's all about. And to live accordingly."[68] Pastor Smit also sees the preaching of the

---

[67] *Interview with E1, 2018-02-26, D79.* Dutch original: "Er is geen enkel systeem dat perfect is hoor. En daarom vind ik het ook zo lekker dat er straks een nieuwe wereld komt (lacht)..."

[68] *Interview with A3, 2018-06-28, D104.* Dutch original: "Nou, om Gods woord te

Gospel as his primary task.[69]

Next to a traditional vision on the Bible as God's word, we also encounter a classical Reformed conception of sin and salvation in the Ontmoetingskerk. Believers see themselves as sinners in need of grace. This is one way in which the equality between church members is highlighted; everyone, regardless of ability, stands in need of grace. Most church members understand salvation primarily in terms of forgiveness of sins by God, although interaction with the secular context questions what this actually entails. This latter point emerges from remarks made by Ada, reflecting on the difficulties of sharing one's faith with non-believers:

> Sometimes faith isn't that easy... That you surrender yourself to a God who cares for you and had His Son nailed to the cross and now your sins are forgiven... well... I don't want to reflect on that, man... sin and grace... If you're raised with all that, it's a piece of cake. But if you come from the outside, it's downright crazy.[70]

Accordingly, the Ontmoetingskerk can be described as a classical Reformed church. Its style of worship may be a bit more modern than it is for the average RCL church, with occasional musical accompaniment by a band and a significant selection of contemporary worship music. But on the whole, as church member Henk once put it, the Ontmoetingskerk fits "within the climate of what is conventional within the bandwidth of Reformed churches."[71] Apart from the specific context, there are two things that stand out when we compare the Ontmoetingskerk with other, similar churches. One is its focus on *connecting faith and life*, and the other is how it sees itself as a *welcoming congregation*. We will explore these themes in the following subsections.

---

horen. [...] Daar gaat het om. En dat je daar ook naar leeft."

[69] *Interview with C3, 2018-03-12, D88.*

[70] *Interview with B7, 2018-03-07, D84.* Dutch original: "soms [...] is geloven is niet zo makkelijk hoor... Dat je... je overgeeft aan een God die voor jou zorgt, die zijn eigen Zoon aan het kruis heeft laten spijkeren en nou zijn je zonden vergeven, zooo... Daar wil ik het helemaal niet over hebben joh, zonde, genade. Als je daar mee opgevoed bent dan is het gesneden koek. Maar als je van buiten komt is het: koekoek."

[71] *Interview with C1, 2018-02-21, D75.* Dutch original: "in het klimaat wat binnen de bandbreedte van de gereformeerde kerken gebruikelijk is."

4.4. Identity & Culture

Connecting Faith and Life

One thing that really comes to the fore in observing the Ontmoetingskerk is the amount of emphasis on linking faith with experience. This should come as no surprise if we take into account the prominent place that experience has in our current culture, which is the Ontmoetingskerk's macro context. We might also see a link here with the meso context and with Koert van Bekkum's description of the RCL as a denomination that has always been seeking 'tangible grace' (cf. 4.3.2). This desire for experiencing faith is visible on the level of individual church members as well as the leadership. During a meeting for small group leaders that I observed, five themes requiring attention in the congregation were discussed. The first three were personal liturgy (practicing one's faith in places other than the organized worship service), the dedication of all of life, and spiritual practices.[72] These themes all clearly connect faith to daily life and experience. When I asked elder Henk what he thought to be the church's most important task, he used the word discipleship, which he explained as "following Christ in the place where He puts you."[73] Pastor Smit, too, often demands attention for the presence of God in all of life. During services, he often creates room for personal testimonies or prayer requests. The underlying reason for this practice is to help church members to see how faith is not just something for Sunday worship services, but encompasses all of life. There are some church members who are afraid that the role of faith in the lives of church members is diminishing. They feel that people lack the language to share their spiritual lives, and that they can only "talk about their vacations"[74], or "chitchat"[75] during small group meetings.

In the fact of this loosening connection between faith and life and the growing inability to share one's spiritual life, the church's leadership has sought to pay attention to elements like discipleship and practices of naming God's presence and activity (e.g. testimonies and prayer requests), as we saw above. Central to these efforts is the element of *discovering, discernment*, or *seeing properly*; it is about looking

---

[72] *Fieldnotes 2017-09-18, D63.*
[73] *Interview with C1, 2018-02-21, D75.*
[74] *Interview with B3, 2018-02-27, D80.*
[75] *Interview with B4, 2018-02-28, D81.*

at life with an open eye for God's presence, discovering His gifts, and discovering His presence in others. Strikingly, the presence of a sizable group of people with disabilities plays an important part in this discovery. Many HVV residents were often quite direct in linking their everyday experiences to their faith. Simone, for example, expressed how she felt God's presence in HVV:

> I once said - this was before I lived here and when I was going through a hard time, I really wanted to go to Jesus, I mean, I still do, but back then I really wanted to do it, I almost did it for myself... And I said: Now I can live in the house of God. I haven't been picked up yet [to go to heaven], but I will be living in the house of God. That's how I saw it.[76]

For Simone, the fact that she is living under the same roof as the church means she shares her house with God. She feels His presence in her life and in the other residents, she says. Simone's mom shared Simone's story during a church service once, causing emotional responses from church members.[77] The ability to link faith directly to experience and everyday life is something many people find difficult. Examples like Simone's help church members realize how easy it can sometimes be to acknowledge God's activity in life. Ada, for example, reflected on how some of the HVV residents sometimes take the opportunity to raise rather 'mundane' prayer requests. This inspires her to be more attentive to how God is related to even the small things in life. Ada said:

> They just let it go. Like children. It's all just a lot easier. I was riding my bike with a granddaughter and she saw a beautiful sky in the evening. Her response was: Look, the Lord God is painting again. You wonder how they think such thoughts... But it was beautiful and it really struck

---

[76] *Interview with A5, 2018-06-28, D106.* Dutch Original: "Ik heb vroeger gezegd, toen ik hier nog niet woonde en toen ik het nog zo moeilijk had, want ik wilde altijd naar de Here Jezus toe, nog steeds wel maar toen wilde ik het echt graag doen, toen deed ik het ook bijna zelf... En toen zei ik: ik mag wonen in het huis van God. Ik word nog niet opgehaald, maar ik ga wel in het huis van God wonen. Zo zag ik dat."

[77] *Fieldnotes 2016-04-17, D13.*

me. That you just see it, observe it.[78]

Connecting faith and life is a challenge for the Ontmoetingskerk, felt by leadership and church members alike. In this respect, the HVV residents seem to be important teachers for the congregation. This does, however, require them also to be acknowledged as teachers, which is indeed not always the case. As church member Sam once put it, "I think there are a lot of people who do not see [the contribution of the residents]."[79] According to Sam, one only begins to see things in a different light after truly encountering the other person as a valuable human being. In his case, this happened when he began making music together with one of the residents after being pushed into it by another church member. Meaningful connection between faith and life seems to be about a double change of perspective: seeing the world as God's world, and seeing each other as valuable human beings from whom one can learn, regardless of (dis)abilities. These two renewed ways of seeing can then strengthen each other: By seeing the other as part of God's world, one values the other person more highly and is willing to learn. By learning from the other's spiritual life, one gains a deeper understanding of the world as God's world.

A Welcoming Congregation

A second characteristic of the Ontmoetingskerk's identity and culture that stands out is its self-presentation as a welcoming congregation. This is done on three levels: First, the Ontmoetingskerk strives to welcome its own members as much as possible out of its conviction that Christ gives unity, even in a group as diverse as its own. Secondly, this unity has an *inclusive character*, as it questions so-called self-evident boundaries between people of different social status, age, ability, etc. Thirdly, the welcome also extends to people who are not (or not yet) part of the Ontmoetingskerk. This three-layered welcoming character

---

[78] *Interview with B7, 2018-03-07, D84.* Dutch Original: "ze laten het gewoon los. Net als kinderen, dat gaat gewoon veel makkelijker. Ik was met een kleinkind aan het fietsen en die ziet hier 's avonds een mooie lucht, zegt ze: o, de Here God is weer aan het schilderen. Ja, hoe bedenk je het. Ik bedenk het zelf niet. Maar het was wel mooi. En dat vind ik fijn, dat je dat ziet, dat je dat waarneemt."

[79] *Interview with B13, 2018-04-03, D93.* Dutch original: "Ik denk dat er mensen zijn die dat niet zien ja."

of the Ontmoetingskerk will now be briefly explored.

First, we will look at the unity in diversity as a ground for mutual welcoming in the Ontmoetingskerk. For pastor Smit, the essence of the church is located precisely in this unity:

> To me, the essence is to receive unity from Christ. That means coming together beneath the Cross again and again to find renewal, to find acceptance of others and yourself. So it's a kind of unity that start with receiving, that would be the essence for me.[80]

Coming together beneath the Cross, as pastor Smit says, is of course a spiritual expression, but it also refers concretely to a cross on the wall behind the podium in the sanctuary. This cross is made from pieces of glass varying in size and shape, symbolizing the unity in diversity in the Cross. Pastor Smit often uses this image when he speaks about the congregation. As we saw in section 4.3.1, it can be a challenge to receive such unity in Vathorst because people are very diverse in their backgrounds and often have little in the way of a historical connection to the neighborhood and church. The Ontmoetingskerk is a sizable congregation of about 900 members which gathers in two different services on Sunday mornings, making it even more difficult to experience unity. Nonetheless, the Ontmoetingskerk strives for embodied unity in the congregation, for example by the use of Encounter Groups, which are small groups to which everyone in the congregation belongs. Despite these efforts, not all church members really experience this unity. One such person is Ms. Wiertz, who lives in HVV: "Sometimes, I get the feeling that I am not really being seen."[81] This remains a difficult challenge for the Ontmoetingskerk. As Willem, a church member without a Christian background who started going to church after he met his wife a few years ago, commented: people who are "assertive enough" will probably feel welcome soon enough,

---

[80] *Interview with C3, 2018-03-12, D88.* Dutch Original: "Voor mij is de essentie dat je samen de eenheid ontvangt van Christus. Dus dat je elke keer onder het kruis samenkomt, onder het kruis vernieuwing vindt, onder het kruis aanvaarding van de ander, van jezelf... ehm. Dus eenheid die begint met ontvangen, dat zou voor mij de kern zijn."

[81] *Interview with A4, 2018-06-28, D105.* Dutch original: "Soms heb ik ook wel eens een beetje dat ik dan denk dat ik niet gezien wordt ofzo... "

4.4. Identity & Culture

but if you are not assertive, it is entirely possible for you to go home unnoticed.[82]

Secondly, the diversity in the Ontmoetingskerk is broader and more obvious than it is in the average congregation due to the presence of a sizable group of people with various disabilities. Unity in diversity therefore requires extra intentionality; people with disabilities are often not seen as valuable members of the congregation, but rather as recipients of the community's care. The Ontmoetingskerk strives to be an *inclusive congregation* in honoring the contributions of *all* its members. The residents of HVV are supposed to be part of the *unity*, not a separate category. In the next two chapters we will look at how this inclusion shapes the practices of the Ontmoetingskerk (chapter 5) and consider the extent to which the inclusive vision and practice actually lead to meaningful encounters (chapter 6). For the present section, it is important to note the inclusive vision of the Ontmoetingskerk as a second layer of its welcoming character.

The third layer of being a welcoming congregation lies in the Ontmoetingskerk's relationship to the Vathorst neighborhood. In section 4.3.1, we already explored how much this interaction shapes congregational life in the Ontmoetingskerk.

The attention to being open and welcoming also shines through in the metaphors people use when they talk about church. They use metaphors like the church as an inn, or a home, or a family, or a body with many different members, whose contributions are all valuable. What I did not encounter was the metaphor of the church as a temple, for example, or as a gathering of a select group of chosen believers. It is clear that most church members and leaders think of the Ontmoetingskerk as an open and welcoming congregation. This openness shapes their practices in many ways, as in the option of becoming a 'friend' of the congregation mentioned above. The church has relatively low 'thresholds'. All the same, some church members still question this openness, wondering whether it really is as open as people claim. They point, for example, to the Ontmoetingskerk's orthodox position on homosexuality: how inclusive and open are we really?[83] Or, like church member Marja, they simply point to the fact that in

---

[82] *Interview with B11, 2018-03-16, D90.*
[83] *Fieldnotes 2016-03-27, D9.*

practice most church members do not really reach out to newcomers: "If you're completely new, nobody will talk to you."[84] Yet others, as we saw in section 4.3.1, feel that the congregation's openness towards newcomers has excessive influence on its own life.

4.4.3 Ongoing Reflection: An Emerging Theology of Inclusion

Hvv and the Ontmoetingskerk stepped out on unfamiliar terrain when they embarked on the project. A small group of interested people started reading *Living Gently in a Violent World* by Jean Vanier and Stanley Hauerwas to begin thinking through the themes of disability and community.[85] But as was observed by elder Henk, who has been heavily involved in the project from the start:

> The reflection on vision was mostly internally oriented and wasn't really a factor of importance. You could construct beautiful models and make wonderful plans, but as long as they are not implemented... As long as the project wasn't operational, it wasn't really a factor of importance. And when it became a reality, we were like: what do vision and mission matter? We were completely taken up by the question of how we can be inclusive as a church. How can we... They sit next to us and that's a bit scary... They're sitting next to me and make noises and movements, and can I even talk to them? How should I do that? And am I allowed to help them get back to their rooms after church, or am I not allowed to push their wheelchairs? Things like that. Very practical. And that pushed vision and mission into the background. Of course it played a role, because we had our slogans of encountering, growing, believing, and another one that I can't remember right now. We had all that. But again: practice remained obstinate.[86]

---

[84]*Interview with B1, 2018-02-22, D76*. Dutch original:"Als je helemaal nieuw bent dan gaat niemand zomaar tegen jou praten."
[85]Hauerwas and Vanier, *Living Gently in a Violent World*.
[86]*Interview with C1, 2018-02-21, D75*. Dutch original: "Dat visietraject was voornamelijk intern en voor een hele kleine groep en het leefde niet. Want je kon hele

4.4. Identity & Culture

Henk's description gives us interesting insight into the way theological reflection functions in HVV, and presumably in many projects carried out by churches. Theological reflection only becomes relevant to people when they feel that their reality demands such reflection. But, as Henk recognizes, without adequate prior reflection, important questions may remain unanswered, causing difficulties in practice. The balance is a difficult one to attain, since one cannot force an entire congregation to find a certain abstract theological topic interesting. Yet when a congregation embarks on a project like HVV, it runs into very real and meaningful *theological* questions 'on the go'. Difficult questions that the Ontmoetingskerk has encountered include questions about the nature of disability, the nature of Christian community, and the borders of the church.

By dealing with these questions, a kind of 'espoused theology of disability inclusion' arose over the course of the research. This espoused theology is multifaceted and calls for further reflection, as we will discuss it in chapter 7. One important question concerned the framing of disability as primarily a 'given' or a social construct.

Whenever disability was seen as a 'given', a biological 'fact', it was often framed primarily as part of the brokenness of creation and hence a result of sin. While none of the respondents posited a direct relationship between a person's individual sin and disability as a punishment by God for that sin, there still was a rather strong sentiment that there would be no impairment in a sinless world. In this line of thinking, people find motivation for interaction with others with disabilities primarily using the language of 'caring', although this does not exclude the possibility of also learning from each other. For ex-

---

mooie modellen opzetten en hele mooie plannen maken, maar zolang het niet geëffectueerd kon worden, zolang het niet operationeel was leefde het niet. En toen het wel ging leven, toen hadden we zoiets van wat is nou eigenlijk visie en missie. We hadden onze handen er vol aan om te kijken van: hoe kun je nou inclusief kerk-zijn? Hoe kunnen we ze nou... Ze komen bij ons zitten in de kerk, nou da's een beetje eng... He, ze zitten naast me en ze maken geluid en ze maken bewegingen en mag ik ze wel aanspreken, hoe moet ik ze aanspreken, mag ik wel met een rolstoel de kerk uitlopen, mag ik dat niet, nou al dat soort dingen, ook heel praktisch, kwamen op ons af. En daarmee kwam visie en missie eigenlijk helemaal naar de achtergrond toe. Het speelde natuurlijk wel een rol, want we hadden wel onze slogans van samen ontmoeten, samen groeien, samen geloven en samen, eh, nou nog eentje, ik weet niet meer zo gauw welke dat is. Dat hadden we wel allemaal. Maar nogmaals: in de praktijk was het wel weerbarstig."

ample, respondents said that they were learning to deal with this brokenness without losing their faith, or living in complete dependency. Most respondents who fit into this category would recognize a deep equality between people with and without disabilities in the Imago Dei. But regardless of this equality, a *charity perspective* in which the superior cares for the inferior often remained unquestioned.[87] In other words, the disability (or impairment) is perceived to be the real problem, now we just need to deal with it the best we can. The language employed by many of these respondents revealed a clear dichotomy between 'us' and 'them'. Although I did not personally hear anybody say that disabilities need to be healed or cured, that could be seen as a logical consequence of this line of reasoning. This was also how some people experienced it, among them Martin, who lives in HVV and is a member of the Ontmoetingskerk. When I interviewed Martin, his epilepsy had left him with very little energy:

> I feel that the Devil still has a lot of influence. Yes, he lets people get sick. And I find that hard. I hear all these stories. Like my sister, she went to this charismatic festival, which took place past weekend. And people were just healed from their diseases right there, on the spot. I find that hard, that it doesn't happen to everybody... Yes, that I would be completely fit by tomorrow, or yesterday.[88]

Other participants perceived disability to a greater or lesser extent as a social construct, and drew connections between people with disabilities and other marginalized groups, such as foreigners or people with different sexual orientations. Inclusion was then understood as a larger phenomenon, pertaining to all groups facing social exclusion, and people with disabilities became just one 'example' of such a

---

[87] I wrote on this charity perspective in Tamminga, "De evangelische paradox van geven en ontvangen: Risico en kracht van diaconale barmhartigheid belicht vanuit een theologie van beperking".

[88] *Interview with A2, 2018-05-31, D103*. Dutch original: "Ik zie het als dat de Duivel nog steeds heel veel de hand in dingen heeft, ja, dat die mensen laat ziek worden. En dat vind ik wel moeilijk ja. ... Ja. Ik hoor zoveel verhalen, mijn zus is naar opwekking geweest, dat was ook afgelopen weekend. En daar zijn gewoon mensen live genezen van hun ziekten. Ja, en dat... Dat vind ik moeilijk, dat dat niet bij iedereen... Ja, dat ik morgen of gisteren helemaal fit was of wat dan ook..."

4.4. Identity & Culture

group, or, as one participant framed it, they could function as a 'crowbar' to enable the inclusion of people with disabilities as well as other groups.[89] In this perspective, the central problem to be dealt with is not the disability or impairment, but the community as a whole. Respondents who fit in this category asked questions like: what do we consider success to be in our community, and how healthy is that? Or they observed how 'unsafe' the church often was for expressing and sharing one's faith in all authenticity. In these issues, the presence of people with disabilities helped them to recognize problems in their community or in their own lives, and sometimes also helped them to find solutions to these problems. A clear example can be found in what church member Sam recounted in his interview. He felt that the Ontmoetingskerk often lacked safety and authenticity, and that this absence affected the spiritual growth of church members. What he saw was a different kind of openness and security in HVV's residential groups:

> To be honest, I also won't be one of the first to raise my hand for a prayer request because I find it hard to express myself at such moments. But well, if you felt 100% safe, you would do it. So let me say that I don't apparently feel 100% safe. Because you are in a group. And in any group there is always someone behind you shooting an arrow at you, yes... Maybe in the residential groups you don't have that, maybe that's just it... That could be...[90]

As a professional theologian, pastor Joost Smit represents the formal voice. He was clearly more inclined towards the second approach we sketched above. In his sermons or other forms of communication, he sometimes included life stories from some of the HVV residents to question the values driving people in Vathorst. He specifically

---

[89] *Fieldnotes 2016-03-27, D9.*

[90] *Interview with B13, 2018-04-03, D93.* Dutch original: "...ik sta zelf ook niet vooraan hoor, met een gebedspunt, want ik vind het lastig om dan uit mijn woorden te komen. Maar goed, als je je 100% veilig zou voelen dan zou je het wel doen. Dus, laat ik dat zeggen, ik voel me dan dus niet 100% veilig. Omdat je dus in een groep - en waar heb je dat niet he, in elke groep is er altijd iemand die vanachter met een pijl op je schiet, ja... Misschien hier op de woongroepen heb je dat niet, misschien is dat het, dat zou kunnen..."

requested attention for the *gifts* that each member of the body contributes, including those with disabilities. He was also quite creative in discovering those gifts:

> God has given everyone their own face and talent. Where it gets interesting is when we begin to discover those and don't focus on disabilities or target groups. For example, we have Mark in our midst. He has the most contagious laughter in the congregation. So when it's time to celebrate, he'll lead us in the gift of roaring with laughter. Or take a look at Laura. She always takes a front seat when we baptize a baby. And after the service, she gives free hugs to the preacher. And why do they live with us? Let me think... Mark has cerebral palsy and Laura has Down syndrome. But who really cares? In our church, we've formally closed the debate on 'the disabled'.[91]

Pastor Smit's 'formal voice' seems to have inspired large parts of the espoused voice of the Ontmoetingskerk. At the same time, the espoused voice is not unequivocal and is still developing for many people in the congregation. As elder Henk already noted, for most people in the Ontmoetingskerk a theological vision on HVV has not been a top priority.

4.4.4 Summary of Identity & Culture

This exploration of the identity and culture of HVV as a whole and of the Ontmoetingskerk in particular can be summarized as follows. Hvv sees itself as a unique project responding to societal challenges, and is clearly rooted in a Christian understanding of care and community. The Ontmoetingskerk can be described as a traditional, orthodox

---

[91] *Column by Joost Smit, 2017-07-09, D57.* Dutch original: "Iedereen heeft van God een eigen gezicht en dito talent gekregen. Interessant wordt het pas als we dat samen ontdekken en niet angstvallig te focussen op beperking of doelgroep. Zo hebben wij Mark in ons midden. Hij heeft de meest aanstekelijke lach van de hele gemeente. Dus als er wat te vieren valt, gaat hij ons voor in de gave van de schatering. Of neem Laura. Zij staat vooraan als een baby gedoopt wordt. En na de dienst geeft zij een free hug aan de voorganger. En waarom wonen ze ook als weer bij ons. Even nadenken.... Mark is spastisch en Laura heeft het syndroom van Down. Maar wat maakt dat uit?

Reformed church in many ways, with notable attention for the connection between faith and everyday life and a vision that clearly aims at being welcoming and open. Both HVV and the Ontmoetingskerk have had many lessons to learn since they embarked on the project. A basic understanding of cooperating and inclusive, communal life that shaped the original vision statement is gradually evolving into a more developed vision. This process is still ongoing, and with our study we hope to make our own contribution as well, particularly in the final chapter (chapter chapter 7).

4.5 Structure & Resources

A third perspective on HVV is the perspective of structure and resources. Whereas the first two perspectives demanded our attention for ideas and concepts, this third perspective is much more 'material' in nature, evaluating how ideas and concepts are embodied in concrete structures and identifying the resources available for this embodiment. We will first look at the organizational elements of HVV (section 4.5.1), and then seek special attention for the *people* involved in HVV (section 4.5.2). In this separate attention we are seeking for the people, we take our lead from Cameron (cf. 4.2). For when we speak of churches, the people are an important 'resource', and they cannot just be swapped for other people, as in other organizations.

4.5.1 Organization

A Tour Through HVV

From the outside, HVV looks like a block of houses. It occupies about 5000 m^2 and is built to look from the outside like a number of separate houses, with facades in different styles. Facing the building, the section on the left hand side was purchased by the church. The rest of it was bought by Amersfoort's social housing cooperative de Alliantie, and has been rented out to Bzzzonder (an inclusive daycare center for children), Accolade (a care provider which uses this location to house people with dementia and major brain trauma), and Sprank (a care provider which houses people with intellectual and sometimes multi-

---

Het debat over 'de' gehandicapten in de kerk hebben wij hier voor gesloten verklaard."

ple disabilities at this location). Other building patrons include a hairdresser, an entrepreneur who manages HVV's restaurant, a midwife practice, and a dentist. The former two have close ties with HVV, the latter two for the most part just rent a space in the building without any further ties.

On entering the building through the main entrance, we come to the central hall where the restaurant is located. Throughout the week, Vathorsters can be spotted there getting a cup of coffee or lunch. If we sit down, Rita, Connie, or another HVV resident will come and take our order. In the evenings, you can run into church members who get together in the restaurant before a meeting, or else just come and sit here for an evening as 'hosts', offering residents and guests the opportunity for some small talk or a game. On Sundays, the central hall is crowded with people getting coffee before or after one of the morning services. The central hall therefore functions as the most important informal meeting space in HVV.

If we turn through one of the big doors on the left, we enter the sanctuary. This hall, offering seating for up to 450 people, looks a bit like a theater with a large podium and an impressive sound system and multimedia devices, but is still recognizable as a church due to the big cross on the wall behind the podium and the church organ. Other typical liturgical items include a table with a plate and cup symbolizing the Lord's Supper, a baptismal font, as well as a small pulpit. On the podium a number of instruments can also be found, including a concert piano and sometimes also other instruments like drums. Unlike the cross and organ, which are fixed, all of these items can be easily removed from the podium, making it possible to use the space for a variety of activities. Schools use it for their musicals, musicians for their concerts, and organizations for their meetings. The walls are white, the chairs are green, and for the rest there is little color. This is the result of a conscious decision to create an environment offering little in the way of distraction for people who are susceptible to easy distraction. The podium includes a ramp, making it accessible for people in wheelchairs so that they can perform such liturgical tasks as the Scripture readings. The chairs have been grouped into three main sections, with the aisles leaving enough room to maneuver a wheelchair through or to park a walker. The middle aisle is extra wide, and this is where most people using wheelchairs sit during worship services.

4.5. Structure & Resources

The sanctuary also includes a balcony, providing extra seating. From the balcony, one can also enter the church offices on the second floor. This is where pastor Joost Smit's office can be found. The second floor also contains a number of rooms that are used for catechism classes or committee meetings. During daytime, these spaces are used by the building's other users or rented out to third parties. The floors above the church hall and offices include a number of apartments for HVV residents. Most, but not all, receive care from either Accolade or Sprank.

Going back down to the first floor, we walk out of the sanctuary and back into the restaurant. On our left hand side, we find the prayer room described on page 89 above. As we cross the restaurant (which is quite a challenge on busy Sunday mornings, especially if you use a wheelchair or walker), we pass a terrace on our left. On reaching the other side of the restaurant, we can turn to Bzzzonder's space on the left, where parents drop off their children in the morning and pick them up in the afternoon. The rooms here are designed to be as 'homely' as possible. The same area also includes the midwife practice. If we continue straight ahead, we enter a very long hallway with only one door on the right hand side, leading to the hairdresser; HVV residents do not have to go outside to get a haircut. The original idea was for this hallway to have many more doors opening up to the other businesses renting space in HVV. However, the other building patrons had no interest in such doors, as they did not feel a real connection with HVV and only wanted to rent space in the building. If we turn right, we can take the elevator up, where we can find the apartments of HVV residents who receive care from Accolade and Sprank. On Sundays following the service, people with wheelchairs and walkers line up in front of the elevator to go back home. Some of them live independently in an apartment, with some support from professionals. Others live together as a group. Some residents with advanced dementia live in a closed ward. However, the architecture of this section has been shaped in such a way that residents do not feel 'confined'. Wide meandering hallways and lots of windows suggest that there is freedom to move about, to leave, and to come back home. This ward is close to the rooftop playground used by the children from the daycare center, making for a close connection between the people living in this section (most of whom are elderly) and the children of Bzzzonder. The first floor includes a number of workshops where some HVV residents and others come to work during daytime to make candles, wood carvings, or other crafts. Their products are sold in a small store downstairs, which can be seen from a balcony on this floor overlooking the central hall and the lively activity in the restaurant.

If we leave the building by the main door through which we came in and turn right, we find ourselves in Vathorst's shopping street. Here residents can go shopping, have a drink in a café, or get something to eat in one of the nearby restaurants.

Cooperation in HVV

The different users of HVV's building have already been identified above. As we saw in previous sections, HVV sees itself as a whole, with its own vision. However, HVV is at the same time also a cooperation project involving organizations with their own interests and methods, as well as complex legislation demanding compliance. The balance between cooperation and independence is yet to be found. The cooperating partners meet officially during so-called *hartoverleggen* (Heart Consultations). In these meetings, they discuss practical issues regarding their use of the building, but also strive to talk on a more fundamental level about the direction for things in HVV to go. Frits, who works for one of the partners, noted how this latter element of direction is becoming a more prominent one in the cooperation. An example he mentioned is the question raised during one of these Heart Consultations of how new employees could really become HVV employees, and not just employees of one of the partners:

> Couldn't we offer [these new employees] a program focusing on the question of what HVV is all about? What happens at our organization is that new employees go to the main office and are initiated to the DNA of our organization. What we want to do here, is to add the Hart van Vathorst-DNA. So those things are now being discussed in the Heart Consultations as well, I really appreciate that, you know: moving from loose screws to thinking about vision, so to speak. How can we take up things communally? I've noticed that this past year we've been really

4.5. Structure & Resources

> focused on each organization finding its own place. And, well, you started something new here, so the focus was quite internally oriented. But now there is slowly some space to seek more cooperation, how are we going to do things together. That is a good development.[92]

Frits's remarks about the initial difficulties in creating cooperation are further underlined by an example from HVV's organizational history. In 2017, HVV recruited a *Heart Manager* who was charged with responsibility for the combined work of Sprank and Accolade within HVV. However, soon after this Heart Manager started to do his work, it became clear that the level of cooperation between the two organizations was not yet at a level where it would be feasible for a single manager to manage both organizations, especially with a view to their cooperation within the larger HVV project. Sprank and Accolade therefore went back to their old model, with each organization being managed separately. One of the managers, Mr. Bakker, recognized the need for further steps on the level of management and policy to finetune cooperation between the partners:

> I really like the concept. What they started, based on their vision about how to be HVV, is beautiful. But the vision was written with a pioneer mindset. And after two years, we can see that the pioneering phase has kind of reached its end. So it is time to set things in stone, like: how are we going to do things together? So that things aren't being fought out on the work floor, while they should actually be attuned on the level of policy.[93]

---

[92] *Interview with E1, 2018-02-26, D79.* Dutch original: "Zouden we die een programmaatje kunnen aanbieden: wat is nou Hart van Vathorst? Wat bij [..] gebeurt is dat je, iedereen die nieuw in dienst komt gaat naar het hoofdkantoor en je krijgt daar vooral je [...]-DNA mee. Wat we dan hier willen doen is vooral het Hart van Vathorst-DNA eraan toevoegen. Dat gebeurt nu ook in het Hartoverleg, dus dat vind ik tof weet je wel: van de schroefjes naar een stukje beleid zeg maar. Hoe gaan we nu een aantal dingen gezamenlijk oppakken. En wat ik merk is dat we afgelopen jaar heel erg gefocust waren op: elke organisatie moest ook wel z'n eigen plek nog vinden en, nou ja, je bent hier gestart dus ook best wel intern gericht. Nu komt er langzaam ook ruimte om elkaar op te zoeken, he hoe gaan we dingen samen doen en dat is een mooie ontwikkeling."

[93] *Interview with E3, 2018-04-18, D98.* Dutch original: "Ik vind het concept heel erg

The Ontmoetingskerk differs from the other partners in the sense that it has no commercial interests; it is able to finance its activities and its part of the building with member contributions. The position of the Ontmoetingskerk is therefore less complex. Its representatives participate in the Heart Consultations, but the congregation is structured is independently from those meetings. Apart from the sharing of space, HVV's greatest impact on the Ontmoetingskerk *at the level of organizational structure* relates to the time pastor Smit spends at HVV and to the fact that one of elders has been designated specifically to HVV. For the rest, the congregation's structure is like that of other classical Reformed congregations: there is a church council which leads the congregation, while many tasks are delegated to committees. But an important structural change took place when the congregation decided to adopt the small group system. In these Ontmoetingsgroepen (Encounter Groups), in which all members including HVV residents are expected to participate, members share their lives and encourage one another. The groups are intended to take over most of the pastoral duties that elders used to do, as the number of people willing to serve as elders has been on the decline. Our intention here is not to evaluate this system, but just to note it as an important aspect of the structure of the Ontmoetingskerk. In section 5.5, we will discuss how communal life in the Ontmoetingskerk, including this system of Encounter Groups, functions with a specific interest in the inclusion of people with disabilities. The Ontmoetingskerk follows a broader trend in RCL churches to move to a small-group structure.[94]

4.5.2 People

We are devoting a separate subsection to one specific type of 'resource' for the Ontmoetingskerk: its members, the people who make up this congregation. Church members represent both 'demand' and 'supply' in the church. Churches try to adapt their life to what the people in

---

mooi. Waar men mee gestart is vanuit de visie hoe men Hart van Vathorst wil zijn is ook mooi, maar het is echt een pioniersgedachte. En je komt nu naar twee jaar er wel achter dat het pionieren er een beetje af is. En dan moet je eigenlijk meer gaan borgen en vastzetten van: hoe gaan we nou met z'n allen doen? Zodat niet op de werkvloer dingen uitgevochten worden terwijl eigenlijk het beleid meer op elkaar afgestemd moet zijn."

[94]See Modderman, *Kerk (in) Delen*.

and around the church *desire*, but they are at the same time limited by what those same people can contribute. This is particularly so in a presbyterial-synodal denomination like the RCL where ecclesial life happens primarily at the local level. On the whole, a big shift can be detected with regard to 'people' in Vathorst. Not only are there many more people due to a growth in numbers, but there is also much greater diversity among them. This diversity extends beyond the two groups of those 'with' and 'without' disabilities, as if 'the disabled' are now part of a congregation that used to be 'normal'. Such a dichotomy is much too simple as a description of the people of the Ontmoetingskerk. This is so first of all because the difference between having and not having a disability has proved to be very complicated in real life. The presence of the HVV residents has offered a more adequate view on the range of abilities already found in the Ontmoetingskerk all along. The language of the Ontmoetingskerk is much more one of being *temporarily able-bodied*, according to the realization that sooner or later in life, every human being is going to be disabled to some degree. Secondly, the dichotomy could make it seem like the residents of HVV are a uniform group. They most certainly are not. Their conditions vary widely, from dementia, to mental health issues, and Down syndrome. Thirdly, the increased diversity is not just limited to disabilities, but can also be seen in such other themes as theological positions or previous church experiences. Fourthly, there has also been a growing diversity in 'social status', although the Ontmoetingskerk can on the whole still be described as a church composed of people with average incomes and from the social majority. This is a result of its geographical location in the neighborhood of Vathorst (cf. 4.3.1). There is a high percentage of people with successful professional careers. On the one hand, this provides the church with opportunities. For example, when a critical situation presents itself, a team of lawyers, communication specialists, and other professionals can be quickly formed.[95] On the other hand, this high level of professionalism can also leave its mark on the atmosphere in church, as I noted on page 105 when I described my experiences during some meetings I attended.

In view of the vision of HVV, an important question that we will discuss in chapter 6 is whether people actually experience the diver-

---

[95] *Conversation with C3, 2018-10-15, D112*

sity we have described or just remain in their own safe subgroups. As teenage church member Niels remarked, the high level of professionalism and its impact on the church's atmosphere might actually impede the experience of unity in diversity:

> Well, of course there are people that annoy me. Just people who are really rich and kind of show off. [...] There are a lot of them around here [...] They just really show: look how good I am, look how often I attend church. That's how I look at it. I might be completely off here, but it's just something that annoys me. [...] I also feel that with those show-offs, many groups are starting to form. And you get those kinds of groups that can really tear the church apart. You just literally see one group of people here, another one there, another one there...[96]

4.5.3 Summary of Structure & Resources

We have described the HVV building and seen how it is used by a variety of patrons. The cooperation between these different users is still developing, but quite complex. The short history of HVV shows how difficult cooperation can be between organizations with diverse and sometimes possibly competing interests and their own diverse working methods. Nonetheless, those in leadership have recognized the need for more cooperation, and are working to realize it. In this cooperation, the position of the church is slightly less complex, as its interests are not on the same territory as those of the other partners, who need to run successful businesses and comply with complex legislation. Nonetheless, apart from other levels of influence, participation in HVV has certain consequences for the way ecclesial life in the Ontmoetingskerk is *structured*, primarily in terms of the pastoral capacity

---

[96] *Interview with B5, 2018-02-28, D82* Dutch original: "Ja, ik heb natuurlijk wel mensen waaraan ik me gewoon irriteer. Gewoon mensen die dan heel rijk zijn en die dan gewoon een beetje patserig daar rond gaan lopen. [...] Jazeker, die zijn er wel veel [...] ze laten echt gewoon zien: kijk hoe goed ik ben, kijk hoe vaak ik in de dienst kom. Dat is hoe ik er naar kijk, misschien helemaal fout. Het is gewoon iets waar ik me aan irriteer. [...] ik denk ook doordat patserige mensen... er ontstaan heel veel groepjes zeg maar. En je krijgt groepjes waardoor je zeg maar, de kerk echt uit elkaar getrokken gaat worden. Je ziet echt gewoon ook dat: groepje mensen, groepje

of pastor Joost Smit and one specially designated elder, as well as in the shared use of building space. In terms of people as resources, the Ontmoetingskerk has large potential in terms of professional capacity. However, some people fear that this potential may also be a downside if this professionalism leaves too deep a mark on the church's atmosphere.

4.6 Leadership

The role of leadership is a crucial one in a project like HVV. As we saw in section 4.4, the move from an abstract and theoretical vision statement to renewed practice does not pass in self-evident fashion. Leaders play an important role in this transition.

4.6.1 Leadership in HVV

Leadership takes different shapes in the organizations involved. Sprank and Accolade are part of bigger organizations, meaning that those who hold final responsibility are remote from HVV itself. The organizations' managers at HVV have to deal with decisions that are made at higher levels, and in some cases have added responsibilities outside of HVV. Both Sprank and Accolade have seen quite some personnel changes in terms of leadership. Most of the people originally involved are no longer working at HVV. One of the managers noted that he had already become one of the 'veterans' after just one year of working at HVV.[97] As Mr. Bakker noted in a quotation already cited above, this follows partly from the fact that HVV is no longer in a 'pioneering' phase and therefore requires other forms of leadership. But as was illustrated in the failed attempt to implement a shared 'heart manager' and in the desire expressed for more fine-tuned cooperation, the situation is not experienced as ideal.

Circumstances are somewhat different for Bzzzonder, as its president Michiel was deeply involved in the HVV initiative and in the creation of its vision. While he remains regularly involved, he also oversees a number of other Bzzzonder locations. Michiel's direct motiva-

---

mensen, groepje mensen."
[97] *Interview with E1, 2018-02-26, D79.*

tion for creating an 'inclusive' daycare center for children of all abilities lies in his own experience of what it's like to have to bring your children to different daycare centers every morning because some are supposedly 'different' and 'need care'. Michiel is therefore intrinsically motivated to implement and develop HVV's vision. He also realizes that he is moving somewhat faster than some of the other partners involved. This can be seen, for example, when he reflected on the role language plays in the realization of HVV's inclusive vision. For him, this is a very relevant issue, although he thought it to be less so for some of the other partners:

> If [my daughter, who has a disability] were to come and work here, in my estimation, she would be a *colleague*, and even if she only pealed potatoes all day, that is still a contribution... And it would also be fine with me if she were to play all day long, but that still doesn't make here a 'client', it would make her a fellow resident of this house. Colleagues, fellow residents... That will really change the perception. If you don't use those [other] words and start to call each other 'colleague' or 'fellow resident', that really makes a difference. If I were to call you 'client' all the time, you would begin to think: I just feel myself getting smaller and smaller. And I would begin to feel: Oh boy, I'd better go and help you, because I now am responsible for you in some way.[98]

4.6.2   Leadership in the Ontmoetingskerk

In the church the leadership has been structured very differently compared to what we saw at Sprank, Accolade, and Bzzzonder. As has already been noted in section 4.5, the Ontmoetingskerk is led officially by the church council. With specific regard to its participation in the

---

[98] *Interview with E2, 2018-04-18, D98.* Dutch original: "Als [...] hier komt werken dan is ze wat mij betreft ook een collega en al is ze alleen maar bezig om de piepers te jassen, het is een bijdrage aan... En ze mag voor mij ook heerlijk zitten puzzelen ergens, maar dat maakt haar nog steeds geen cliënt dat maakt haar een medebewoner. Collega's, medebewoners... Dat gaat echt die perceptie veranderen. Als je die woorden niet gebruikt en je gaat het collega noemen of medebewoners dat is echt wat anders. Als ik [...] jou elke keer maar cliënt [zou] noemen dan zou jij denken: hé, ik

4.6. Leadership

larger HVV project, the role of a small number of individuals stands out. As we saw before, not the entire congregation was all that involved in the earlier stages of the process. In this respect, the most visible and undoubtedly most prominent role was played by pastor Joost Smit. It was also with a view to the initial stages that the church called him to be its pastor. In an interview, Smit himself reflected:

> When I came here, there was a lot of division on themes like transition or consolidation, and, well, how do we deal with other churches, how do we deal with other Christians... That was number 1. And I think that I can play a connecting role in these matters. [...] The second thing that really triggered me was the beautiful plan they had, a beautiful (idea for a) building, a church that would be organically woven together with other partners in the center of Vathorst, while I also thought: Have you really thought about the vision behind all this? What it means to be in church together, and the impact that will have on church services? There hadn't been much in the way of reflection on such themes. So I was not called with the intention of 'giving a final push towards inclusivity', because this reflection had yet to start.[99]

Leading this reflection together with a small group of other men and women became one of the core aspects of pastor Smit's work in the Ontmoetingskerk. His approach was multi-faceted. His conviction is that people, himself included, learn by doing and reflecting. So as soon as he moved to Vathorst, he started doing volunteer work in a group home for people with disabilities, so as to learn by doing. He also attempted to get other church members involved in this way, for example by trying to make something of the new HVV constellation visible prior to the actual opening of the building in inviting future residents to church services of the congregation, for example. Pastor Smit referred to this approach in terms of 'organic growth'; instead of drawing out a complete plan covering every detail, he just tries to ex-

---

voel mezelf langzaam aan wegzakken en ik heb het gevoel: help, ik moet jou nu wel gaan helpen want ik ben wel een beetje verantwoordelijk voor jou nu."

periment with small steps towards the realization of the vision. One example is the small albeit necessary adaptations in the practice of the Lord's Supper so as to enable some of HVV's residents to participate. While we will look at this case in greater detail in section 5.2, for now we can already note that it was pastor Smit who clearly took the lead in these adaptations, backed by the church council. He did so by experimenting with different ways of celebration and learning on the go, while also listening to the voices and complaints of people in the congregation. This approach differs clearly from what one would normally expect in an RCL church (cf. 4.3.2). Its tradition has typically been more about first 'getting the theory right' and then implementing it in practice. But, specifically in view of this congregation's unique nature as part of HVV, Smit deliberately chose to do things the other way around:

> [The absence of a fully worked out vision at the start] has been a kind of blessing for us because true inclusion of course means doing things together. So that means you really begin to do things when you're together, rather than working out all kinds of plans in Vathorst for people who will come and live with us later. So in that sense the saying "more haste, less speed" really applied to this project.[100]

---

[99] *Interview with C3, 2018-11-09, D32* Dutch original: "Toen ik hierheen kwam was er best wel veel verdeeldheid in de gemeente over andere themas, van: verandering of consolidatie, nou, hoe ga je om met... ehm... andere kerken, hoe ga je om met andere christenen... Dus dat was 1. En ik denk van mijzelf dat ik daarin een verbindende rol kan spelen... [...] En het tweede wat mij heel sterk triggerde was dat er een mooie plan lag, een mooi gebouw, een kerk die organisch verweven was met andere partijen op een plek in het centrum van Vathorst en dat ik wel dacht van: nou, volgens mij hebben jullie over de visie daarachter, van wat het dan betekent om met elkaar in een kerk te zitten en wat de impact dan ook op je diensten... Daar was nog niet heel veel over nagedacht. Dus ik ben niet beroepen met, van: he, kom ons nog een klein zetje geven rond inclusiviteit, want het was nog een redelijk groen weiland wat dat betreft."

[100] *Interview with C3, 2018-11-09, D32* Dutch original: "[...] heeft ook een bepaalde, eh, zegenrijke werking gehad omdat je dus - bij ware inclusiviteit hoort natuurlijk ook dat je het met elkaar gaat doen, dus dat je het ook pas gaat doen op het moment dat je bij elkaar bent en niet dat je hier in Vathorst allerlei dingen gaat bedenken voor mensen die er bij komen wonen. Dus in die zin was ook het 'haast u langzaam', dat

4.6. Leadership

It is clear that pastor Smit assumed a central role in leading the congregation to be a part of HVV; in all the initiatives and experiments, he kept the oversight and sought to learn from previous experiences by bringing about a process of reflection. Overseeing the developments in Vathorst over the past years, the role of pastor Smit can hardly be overstated. At the same time, his predominant role can be a point of concern. Both pastor Smit himself and others were very much aware of the possible dangers: What if he were to leave? Is the vision really shared by a wider group of people that can continue what has been started? Another downside was mentioned by multiple respondents during the interviews; the fact that pastor Smit devotes much of his time to HVV means that he has less attention to give to other responsibilities. This moved the church to hire a second professional theologian, whose primary focus is the young people in church. While this move and the concern for the youth in the Ontmoetingskerk are both very understandable, they also reveal something of the way church members view the relationship between their congregation and HVV. Apparently, they are still really two separate things. This is a point that will be taken up further in chapter 7.

4.6.3 Summary of Leadership

The perspective of leadership has shown us how crucial leadership is in a project like HVV. The different partners showed themselves to have very different forms of leadership. Some leaders were more intrinsically interested in the inclusive ideals of HVV, while others had less opportunities to concern themselves with that side of the project, as they formed parts of larger organizations and needed their time to 'run their business'. Considering the stage at which HVV currently finds itself, this is an area of concern; the leaders themselves acknowledge that it will be necessary to fine-tune cooperation in HVV to secure a successful future. The church's leadership is of its own kind, as the central role of pastor Joost Smit stands out in it. His work has been of great influence for the direction taken by the developments in HVV. But, as many participants note, overdependence on a single person also creates a situation of vulnerability.

---

was ook iets wat hier gewoon echt wel bij paste."

4.7 Summary

In this chapter, we have become acquainted with life at HVV and the Ontmoetingskerk by looking at this reality from four perspectives, taking our lead from Rein Brouwer et al. The data acquired during empirical research have been our guide in this exploration. The first perspective - that of context - showed us how HVV and the Ontmoetingskerk are woven into a number of different contexts:

- The micro context of the neighborhood of Vathorst with its financial welfare combined with a competitive and demanding environment.

- The meso context of the RCL denomination to which the Ontmoetingskerk belongs remains a factor of influence even if the relationship is clearly in transition.

- The macro context, which is not just an abstract reality but becomes concrete in interaction with local and national governments, whose view of HVV is marked by a duality between appreciation for social engagement and increasing uneasiness with its faith dimensions due to the growing secularization in the Netherlands.

The perspective of identity and culture helped us explore the vision of HVV and how it works out in practice. We specifically noted the deeply Christian aspects of this vision, as well as the many theological and other questions that remain unanswered for now, pointing to the need for ongoing reflection. The perspective of structure and resources opened our eyes for the concrete forms this vision takes. We explored the building of HVV, the cooperation between the different organizations, the place of the Ontmoetingskerk in all of this, and the composition of the congregation in terms of its members and structures. Finally, the perspective of leadership shed light on the crucial role of leadership in projects like HVV, and showed a variety of leadership styles. It also pointed to some areas of concern for the leadership of the Ontmoetingskerk as well as the other HVV partners.

Chapter 5

Practicing Church in the Ontmoetingskerk

5.1 Introduction

In the previous chapter, we became acquainted with ecclesial life in the Ontmoetingskerk through a congregational studies lens. The current chapter will explore how the *practices* of this congregation are shaped. As we discussed in section 3.3.2, we follow in the line of the work of Alasdair McIntyre and Bass & Dykstra in understanding practices as complex social activities that form people into certain behaviors, while also providing insight into the values or goods internal to these practices. Even if the formal voice in the Ontmoetingskerk is not framed in academic language, it too shows evidence of such a conception of practices. For example, pastor Joost Smit, as a representative of this formal voice, once spoke in a sermon of human acts as *pointing to God*.[1] Human activity in Smit's conception is not neutral, but reveals deeper convictions and shapes them. Therefore, in an evening church service in which the themes of abortion and euthanasia were discussed, pastor Smit encouraged those present not just to engage with these themes on an intellectual level, but rather to develop ways of acting that embody and communicate convictions about the value of life.[2] These examples show that, at least on the level of the formal

---

[1] *Fieldnotes 2017-06-21, D51.*
[2] *Fieldnotes 2017-11-12, D69.*

voice, there is a conception of practices as meaningful human activity which is both an expression of convictions and a formation of these convictions.

The specific question guiding our exploration of the Ontmoetingskerk's practices concerns the way they were influenced by and attuned to the presence of a diverse congregation, including many members with disabilities. What stood out during the open coding of our data and the subsequent analysis (cf. 3.5.5) is that the practices in the data flow naturally into the church's so-called *emphnotae externae* or 'external marks'. Pascal D. Bazzel writes:

> [...] the purpose for which the Church exists is revealed in the *notae ecclesia*, which includes the *notae externae* represented in *koinonia, diakonia, kerygma, martyria*, and *leitourgia*. Surely, the mystery of the Church cannot be framed with these typological categories, yet traditionally they have been recognized as a description of what one finds in the Church.[3]

Originating in the New Testament, the *notae externae* can be understood as fundamental clusters of practices that are embodied in any church. This makes them appropriate for use when giving an ethnographic description of a church community; by describing how the four *notae externae* are embodied in a specific setting, one gains an understanding of the specific shape that elements present in any church take in that setting. This is how Bazzel uses the *notae* in his ethnographic study of two faith communities, from which the above citation comes. There are some variations between the precise *notae externae* included in the lists in ecclesiological literature.[4] We for our part have chosen to adopt Bazzel's proposal loosely, subsuming the *notae* of *martyria* and *kerygma* under the single heading 'martyria'.

As in the previous chapter, the focus here will be on the presentation of the data gathered during the fieldwork. In the following sections, we will discuss *leitourgia*, the liturgical aspect of the church (5.2); *diakonia*, the diaconal aspect of the church (5.3); *martyria*, the

---

[3]Bazzell, *Urban Ecclesiology*, Chapter 6, II, C.
[4]Fackre, *The Church* gives an overview of the use of the *notae* through time (e.g. by the World Council of Churches).

witnessing aspect of the church (5.4); and, lastly, *koinonia*, the communal aspect of the church (5.5). The data collected yielded much more information for the notae of leitourgia and koinonia than for the other two notae, which explains the respective length of these sections. The reason for this difference may well follow from the methods used in the collection of data; many church services were visited for the observations (leitourgia), while interviews centered primarily around the community aspects of being church (koinonia), rather than aspects that can easily be linked to diakonia or martyria. The chapter will end with a summary (5.6).

5.2 Leitourgia

5.2.1 Church Services in the Ontmoetingskerk

In the Ontmoetingskerk, the liturgical aspect of being church is understood in a wider sense than church services alone, comprising also the liturgical aspect of the believers' everyday life (cf. 4.4.2). There is thus attention for other liturgical moments, like the monthly prayer meetings with professionals working in HVV initiated by pastor Smit.[5] So too one might think of the prayer room described in section 4.5.1 and the liturgical activity that takes place there, such as prayer and the lighting of candles. However, the focal point of liturgical action remains the church service. The Ontmoetingskerk hosts two services on Sunday mornings, and another one in the afternoon. Most HVV residents tend to attend the second service in the morning due to the time they need to get ready (cf. 5.2.2). In the data, frequent mention is made of three 'standard' elements of church services: preaching, singing, and sacramental celebrations (specifically, the Lord's Supper).

Preaching

The preaching takes an important place in the Ontmoetingskerk's worship services. We will not explore the general content or detailed homiletical structure of the sermons heard in the Ontmoetingskerk here, but look rather at the position they occupy in the liturgy. The position of the sermon is so central that some church members regard

---

[5] *Conversation notes, 2016-11-09, D32.*

it as the very heart of the church service, or even of church life in general. Mrs. de Vries thus remarked: "I like a good sermon, and if I get one, I for the rest don't really care what we sing, so to speak."[6] In Mrs. de Vries's estimation, the other elements in the liturgy are merely additions to the sermon as the key ingredient. Tjalling, whom we met before in section 4.3.2, expressed a similar opinion on what he finds important about the liturgy: "Just a long sermon, that's what I like." "Just a long sermon, that's what I like."[7] For Hannah, preaching is not only central to the liturgy, but indeed crucial to the life of the congregation as a whole:

> What church is all about? Well, that is something I sometimes miss, because we often put ourselves at the center, and not the Lord. I sometimes find that hard. And for the rest it is wonderful to hear a good message from the minister, to have Scripture explained, and to praise God together.[8]

Preaching is thus seen as the way in which God's word is kept central and communicated. The centrality of the sermon raises the question of the ways in which this central element of the liturgy is accessible to all church members, for example in terms of the kinds of communication used during sermons. Particularly when it is pastor Smit leading the services, the communication in the sermons is often quite personal in nature, with room for anecdotes, personal attention, and the occasional joke. Pastor Smit also uses certain other means of communication, like images on the projector screens, or objects, like flowers. For one morning service, I wrote the following in my fieldnotes:

Preaching is seen as the way in which God's word is kept central and communicated. The centrality of the sermon poses the question

---

[6] *Interview with B15, 2018-04-23, D100.* Dutch original: "Ik houd van een goede preek en dan maakt het mij niet uit wat er naast allemaal gezongen wordt, zeg maar."

[7] *Interview with A6, 2018-07-23, D111.* Dutch original: "Gewoon een lange preek. Dan vind ik het mooi."

[8] *Interview with B3, 2018-02-27, D80.* Dutch original: "Waar draait het om in de kerk? Nou, dat ik wat ik wel eens mis is dat wij inderdaad, wij zetten onszelf vaak centraal in plaats van de Here. Dat vind ik wel eens moeilijk. En verder is het heerlijk om een goed woord te horen van de predikant, de Schrift uitgelegd te krijgen en met elkaar God te loven en te prijzen."

5.2. Leitourgia

in which ways this central element of the liturgy is accessible to all church members, for example in terms of the kinds of communication used during sermons. Specifically when pastor Smit leads the services, the nature of communication in the sermons is often quite personal, with room for anecdotes, personal attention and a joke here and there. Pastor Smit also makes some use of other means of communication, like images on the screens, or objects like flowers, as in one morning service when I wrote down the following in my fieldnotes:

> [Pastor Smit] is talking about the tulips that are on a table on the podium. They are beautiful tulips, he says, but the arrangement is a bit boring. All the tulips are sorted by color and put in separate vases. 'What can we do about that?', he asks. He invites some young people to come forward. One of them is Frans, and the other two are HVV residents. It takes some time before some young people who have already been living in Vathorst for some time come forward. Joost insists, and then some come forward. A girl high fives Frans. They get to it and mix the sorted tulips, creating colorful bouquets. Afterwards, they hand the tulips to first-time visitors.[9]

We will further reflect on the kinds and levels of interaction with HVV residents during church services in section 6.2. For now, we will zoom in specifically on the role of sermons in the Ontmoetingskerk's services and on their shape in relation to the HVV ideals of inclusivity. Despite the level of personal attention and interaction, and notwithstanding the exceptional use of means of communication other than the verbal, the sermons remained largely verbal and often seemed to be aimed at cognition. In the perception of Henk, for example, the level of difficulty is quite high: "[...] Preaching is quite complicated. The sermon is a difficult topic. On that point we are quite traditional. [...] And on that point I think we need to reflect at greater length on what inclusion really means."[10] This observation from Henk is in line

---

[9] *Fieldnotes 2016-03-27, D9.*
[10] *Interview with C1, 2018-02-21, D75.* Dutch original: "[...] preken is best lastig. De preek is best moeilijk. Ja op dat punt zijn we nog vrij traditioneel. [...] en ik denk dat we op dat punt ook nog wel eens wat na moeten denken: wat is nou inclusie?"

with my own impressions of the church services I observed. This can be illustrated, for example, in the following fragment from my fieldnotes: "Sermon on Song of Songs chapter 8. About love that always refers to God. Joost gets straight to the point and makes the odd joke now and then. The atmosphere is informal. But the sermon is still in significant measure aimed at cognition.""[11]

When other ministers preach at the Ontmoetingskerk, this impression becomes even stronger. The reason seems to be that guest preachers have difficulties adapting their style of communication to the diverse audience in front of them. What also stands out is that they often struggle to address the issue of disability, or use ambiguous language for the experience of people with disabilities. This can be seen in my fieldnotes from a service led by a visiting minister who preached on John the Baptist's doubts regarding Jesus' messiahship in Matthew 11 and Jesus's self-representation as the healer of the blind and lame promised by the prophets:

> What strikes me is that the pastor does not address the sensitive fact that the lame are now walking again. He sometimes alludes to it: maybe you feel a prisoner of your disability, etc. But he does not work it out in any detail. Furthermore [...], the sermon is clearly aimed at cognition, at conceptions and images of Jesus. But in my opinion, there are many reasons to communicate on a more emotional level and to seek interaction. After the sermon, we watch a clip on the evangelist Nick Vujicic, who has no arms and legs. The point of the clip can be summarized as follows: God has a plan for your life, even if it's not immediately clear. The clip is played in English, moves quite fast, and is subtitled. I wonder if the people here can understand it.[12]

Singing

Whereas the sermon is for some clearly the most important element of a church service, other interviewees shared that music and singing are very central to their experience of church services. Linda said:

---

[11] *Fieldnotes, 2017-07-06, D56.*
[12] *Fieldnotes, 2017-03-26, D45.*

5.2. Leitourgia

> I always notice a difference when we've had a service accompanied by the band, compared to a regular service, so to speak. These days regular services are no longer just Psalms and classical hymns, there are also newer hymns. But when there's Opwekking and Sela [contemporary worship songs], when the band is playing, it touches me much more than, like, a regular service does. But that's also because I'm really into music.[13]

Like Linda, many other church members (mostly the younger ones) indicate that they would prefer to sing more contemporary worship songs accompanied by a band. Martine was one who suggested such a change in musical practice: "Well, I'd like to sing more Opwekking. [...] Then the band is also playing, which I enjoy very much."[14] As things currently are, services combine many different musical styles to suit the diversity of the congregation, but this has also led to debates on musical preference as well as the textual quality and theological soundness of some of the contemporary worship songs. Moreover, not all styles seem well suited to the building and its acoustics. During many services, I noted that the sanctuary seems to be made for accompaniment by a fully amplified band. With just a piano or organ, you only hear yourself singing and do not really feel part of a larger group singing together.[15] It is quite likely that this acoustic element also plays a role in people's preferences and contributes to the evaluation of some songs as 'old fashioned' and lacking in experiential quality. Conversely, it may be a factor in some members' perception of church being so different from what they are used to, thereby contributing to their sense of liturgical estrangement.

Music allows some residents to participate actively by playing an instrument or singing in the band. An added benefit is the interac-

---

[13] *Interview with B2, 2018-02-26, D77.* Dutch original: "Ik merk altijd wel verschil als er [...] een kerkdienst is geweest met de band er voorin, dan een gewone dienst zeg maar. Een gewone dienst met, ja tegenwoordig zijn het niet meer allemaal psalmen en gezangen, het zijn ook allemaal liedboekliederen tegenwoordig. Maar met Opwekking en Sela enzo dan, als de band speelt dan raakt het me altijd meer dan een gewone dienst zeg maar. Maar dat komt omdat ik ook heel erg van de muziek ben."

[14] *Interview with B10, 2018-03-16, D89.* Dutch original: "Ja, meer opwekking vind ik wel mooi. [...] Dan is de band er ook, dat vind ik mooi."

[15] E.g. *Fieldnotes 2016-11-27, D34; 2017-02-05, D40.*

tion with other band members, for example during rehearsal times. Another way in which music is used to involve people liturgically is the selection every service of one song from a 'golden oldie list'. This list is made up of songs that are well known to most elderly people and enables church members with dementia to participate in the worship, since many of them know these songs by heart. Pastor Smit's impression is that this list is working quite effectively.[16] During one church service I noted how an elderly church member with dementia who had seemed zoned out for most of the service suddenly sang along with the first two lines of 'What a friend we have in Jesus' (in a well known Dutch translation), although he appeared to retreat back into his earlier state thereafter.[17]

Celebrating Sacraments

Most church members I interviewed spoke about the sermon or singing as important aspects of the church's liturgical life. When pastor Smit speaks about the liturgy, he often mentions the Lord's Supper as a central if not constitutive element. In terms of the four voices of theology, there is thus a noteworthy difference here between the espoused voice and the formal voice. In the Ontmoetingskerk, explicit changes have been introduced to the celebration of the sacraments through its participation in HVV. The congregation has become more open and welcoming to people of all abilities, as well as diverse ecclesial backgrounds. In the RCL, two sacraments are celebrated: baptism (infant baptism) and the Lord's Supper or Eucharist. Pastor Smit really does his best to involve all members in the sacramental celebration, as illustrated by the following example from a baptismal service:

> [Baby boy] Bas is baptized. Joost introduces Bas to the congregation. He holds him in his arms and first walks over to the baptismal font with him. Holding him in his arms, he gives a short explanation of baptism. The explanation includes elements from the prescribed liturgical forms, although Joost uses his own words. Afterwards,

---

[16] *Conversation notes, 2017-08-22, D60.*

[17] *Welk een vriend is onze Jezus*, hymn number 150 in the *Joh. de Heer* hymnal; Fieldnotes 2017-10-01, D65.

5.2. Leitourgia

> Joost passes through the aisle to introduce Bas to people who are sitting a bit further back in the sanctuary. Joost holds Bas close to a lady with dementia, who says, "Isn't he a doll?", Joost replies "beautiful, isn't he?", Joost also says: "Mark, this is Bas", or "Evan, this is Bas".[18]

The celebration of the Lord's Supper in the Ontmoetingskerk is particularly interesting for the significant changes it has undergone. The Lord's Supper occupies a very central place in the church experience of Chloë, a member of the Ontmoetingskerk living in HVV. Her experience has been published on a Dutch website for other churches to learn from it:

> I enjoy talking about the Lord's Supper. I feel it is the most beautiful thing in our church. In our church everybody walks to the front. Not everyone, I mean. People who cannot walk are served in their pews. The songs are very beautiful. When I think of the Lord Jesus, I sometimes start to cry during the Lord's Supper. But I don't feel alone. I feel together with other people. And together with God. I find it so beautiful when everybody walks by. You see all those different people. Old people, young people, people in wheelchairs, people you know, people you don't know... But God knows everyone! That fills me with a wonderful feeling. Because you can really taste and feel and because everything goes much slower than the rest of the service, you can really experience it. I feel just like I'm in heaven. I really love that.[19]

While the sermons are normally highly verbal and cognitive, Chloë observed that the Lord's Supper is particularly suited to people who are less verbal; bread and wine can be tasted and felt, and the entire

---

[18] *Observation notes 2017-07-06, D56*. Dutch original: "Bas wordt gedoopt. Joost stelt Bas aan de gemeente voor: hij houdt hem vast en loopt met hem eerst naar het doopvont. Met hem in zijn armen legt hij wat uit over de doop, inhoudelijk zijn dat elementen uit het formulier, maar Joost formuleert het in eigen woorden. Dan loopt Joost naar achter door het brede gangpad om Bas voor te stellen "ook aan de mensen die wat verder achterin zitten". Joost houdt Bas dicht bij een dementerende vrouw, die zegt: "och, wat een poppie", "leuk he", zegt Joost. "Mark, dit is Bas", "Evan, dit is Bas"."

celebration and the movement of people through the building evoke emotions. However, the Ontmoetingskerk has had to adapt its style of celebration in a number of ways to make it possible for HVV residents to participate. These are the focus of the next subsection.

Celebration of the Lord's Supper

The celebration of the Lord's Supper normally begins with some words of explanation by pastor Smit. He does not use the RCL's traditional liturgical forms for this, although he does sometimes take elements from them, and sometimes even literal citations. At a minimum, his explanations always include the socalled words of institution from 1 Cor. 11. He also adds that no one deserves bread and wine, but that Christ invites us nonetheless, out of grace. After a brief explanation, he breaks the bread and pours the wine, speaking the classical words from the liturgical forms: "Take, eat, remember, and believe that the body of our Lord Jesus Christ was given for the complete forgiveness of all our sins." And: "Take, drink, remember, and believe that the precious blood of our Lord Jesus Christ was shed for the complete forgiveness of all our sins."[20] At some point in his explanation, or before the actual celebration begins, pastor Smit mentions that guests are welcome to join, provided that they profess their full dependence on Christ. He adds that those who have not yet come to know Christ may come forward during the celebration to receive a blessing by the laying on of hands.[21] This liturgical practice is rare in other RCL churches. In-

---

[19] *Online Post, 2018-04-12, D96*. Dutch Original: "Ik vertel graag over het heilig avondmaal. Ik vind het het mooiste van de kerk. Bij ons in de kerk gaat iedereen lopen. Niet iedereen bedoel ik. Mensen die niet kunnen lopen worden bediend in hun zitplaats. De liederen zijn heel mooi. Als ik denk aan de Here Jezus dan moet ik soms een beetje huilen bij het heilig avondmaal. Maar ik voel me dan niet alleen. Ik voel me samen met de andere mensen. En ik voel me samen met God. Ik vind het heel mooi als iedereen langs loopt. Je ziet allemaal verschillende mensen. Oudere mensen jonge mensen mensen in een rolstoel mensen die je kent en mensen die je niet kent. Maar God kent iedereen! Dat geeft mij een fijn gevoel. Omdat je het ook echt proeft en voelt en omdat alles veel langzamer gaat dan bijvoorbeeld de rest van de dienst kun je echt goed mee beleven. Ik voel me net alsof ik in de hemel ben. En dat vind ik heel fijn." Web page: *Blog about liturgy in HVV*.

[20] *Fieldnotes 2016-03-25, D8; Video recordings 2016-06-05, D117; 2017-04-14, D118*.

[21] *Fieldnotes 2016-03-25, D8*.

5.2. Leitourgia

terestingly, during two other services in which the Lord's Supper was celebrated, pastor Smit added that those who depend on Christ *and are admitted to the sacraments in their own church* are welcome at the table of the Lord Jesus. Yet he still added that it is possible for people to come forward and receive a blessing instead of the sacrament itself.[22] As such, the celebration of the Lord's Supper is more open in the Ontmoetingskerk than it traditionally is in the RCL, where more formal criteria tend to be in place for participation in the Lord's Supper.[23] The criterion of admission to the Lord's Supper in one's own church as it was mentioned in two services was striking in light of the absence of this element in the other, earlier service. This may have had to do with a number of critical remarks that were made after the first 'open celebration'. Pastor Smit indicated that he had received a few negative comments after that open celebration, although he added that he had also been given much support from the church council and heard many positive comments from church members.[24]

The change from a traditional celebration to a more open one was not meticulously planned, but, in the words of pastor Smit, happened in an organic fashion. It did, however, seem to involve some kind of strategic goal. Reflecting on the Lord's Supper, Smit said: "If you see someone with Down Syndrome coming forward and participating in the celebration, it's hard to be critical."[25] In other words, by the adaptation of liturgical sacramental praxis, people in the congregation are formed in their perception of who is in and who is out.

Following the explanation and invitation, the pastor and a number of elders walk through the church to serve the sacrament to those who are not able or willing to walk or roll to the front of the church to receive bread and wine. They are asked to indicate this preference by raising their hand. In the week leading up to the service, pastor Smit will already have visited people to ask if and how they want to

---

[22] *Video recordings 2016-06-05, D117; 2017-04-14, D118.*

[23] It used to be that only members of other rcl congregations or sister churches were allowed to participate; formally they were also required to present a letter from their own church council stating that they were members in good standing prior to the start of the service. This practice is gradually changing in many rcl congregations, and is a matter of consideration on the denominational level. See Bosman, *Celebrating the Lord's Supper in the Netherlands.*

[24] *Fieldnotes 2016-04-17, D13; Conversation notes 2016-06-06, D19.*

[25] *Conversation notes 2016-06-06, D19.*

receive the sacrament. This is a necessary act of preparation, because not everybody is able to raise his or her hand. Smit is not entirely happy with the way this works at the moment; he cannot visit everybody, and therefore sometimes has to improvise when it comes to a person's participation. Sometimes the care professional attending the service can help out, but this is not always the case.[26] This leads to some hesitation during the service, resulting from the more open style of celebration (since formal criteria are easier to establish). Pastor Smit takes his role in this very seriously, as he has a high view of the sacrament both doctrinally and in terms of what the celebrations mean to people and their families as an important aspect of participation in the life of the church and the practice of one's faith.[27] After the people who wish to remain seated have been served, the elders invite the remaining people to walk to the front of the sanctuary. They are invited row by row. Most of the children remain in their seats, though some parents take their children with them. These children do not receive the sacrament, but they do sometimes receive a blessing. Pastor Smit always first asks the parents if they want this. The HVV residents participate in this as well. Some of them are church members and receive bread and wine, while others receive a blessing. Everything is organized in such a way that people in wheelchairs or requiring assistance can participate; there is sufficient space, level floors, or even alternate routes and helping hands as needed.[28]

In terms of the formal and normative theology, Lord's Supper services typically give a lot of attention to the cross of Christ, to suffering, and to the idea that all people stand in need of aid and grace. In one instance, the prayer following the celebration of the Lord's Supper made specific mention of all who feel that they do not belong or are not needed. The communal celebration of the Lord's Supper may therefore be perceived as a way to counter that reality.[29]

To conclude, the openness of the Lord's Supper celebrations can be seen as an attempt to be as accommodating as possible in making

---

[26] *Fieldnotes 2016-03-25, D8; Conversation notes 2016-06-06, D19; Video recording 2016-06-05, D117.*

[27] *Conversation notes 2016-06-06, D19.*

[28] *Fieldnotes 2016-03-25, D8; Observation notes 2016-05-05, D16; Video recording 2017-04-14, D118.*

[29] *Fieldnotes 2016-03-25, D8.*

5.2. Leitourgia

the sacrament accessible to all, regardless of ability. This is done for the sake of those who need this accessibility, but also with a view to a more general openness in accepting one another as full members of the body of Christ, without first demanding to see formal credentials.

5.2.2 Adaptations in Liturgy?

A tension in the congregation's reflection on church services in the Ontmoetingskerk concerns how 'special' things need to be. Due to existing agreements with its classis, the Ontmoetingskerk sometimes holds church services designed specifically for people with intellectual disabilities, as has become customary in the RCL. This conflicts with its own vision of including everybody in every 'normal' service, instead of catering to specific target groups. It has come to realize, however, that even in those 'special' or 'adapted' services, the inclusion of one group often means the exclusion of another. While having congregants use noise makers is great for some, for others it is a real problem. In practice, the tension between 'all-inclusive' and 'special' or 'adapted' has therefore proved to be a complicated one. As we saw above, the reality of a diverse congregation has led the Ontmoetingskerk to adapt its liturgy in certain areas. Some adaptations are merely practical, but others, like the changes in Lord's Supper celebrations, impact the way church services are conducted. Most respondents, however, did not really feel that church services had undergone major changes. Church member Floris remarked:

> What has changed? The sermon... I don't feel that the sermon is different from the way it used to be. I also don't have the impression that the service as a whole is all that different. So they [the residents of HVV] sit in church and sing along, they participate as much as they can, they sometimes read Scripture from the lectern. Those are things that are different - well, actually, different? ... It

---

[30] *Interview with B14, 2018-04-11, D94.* Dutch original: "Wat is er veranderd? De preek... Ik heb niet de indruk dat de preek anders is dan anders. Ik heb ook niet de indruk dat de dienst als zodanig anders is dan anders. Dus ze zitten in de kerk en zingen mee, voor zover ze kunnen, ze doen mee, voor zover ze kunnen, ze lezen soms vanuit de bijbel achter het spreekgestoelte. Dat zijn dingen die dan anders zijn, of anders... Het zou het zelfde in een andere gemeente geweest zijn, het zijn gewoon

would actually be the same in other congregations; they are just church members. So I don't feel that many things have changed. It is just that [pastor] Joost has the ability to involve those people and I find that a great asset.[30]

To the church members, the regular services apparently do not feel like 'special services'. At the same time, there is a clear difference between the early morning service and the late morning service. In the latter, the ratio of HVV residents is much higher, as many of them need time in the morning to get ready for church. Their presence does make a difference in the way the service goes, both by their own influence on the service (e.g. in performing the Scripture readings, or singing on stage) and by the intentional changes pastor Joost Smit makes in the liturgy, mostly on the level of interaction. Church member Jolanda described how, in her estimation, she has a choice between two very different services every Sunday morning:

> In our church, you have a choice... You can go to the early service, where they are not present. And then there's the second service, where they are always present. So if I don't feel like it, I just go to the early service. [...] Nice and quiet... Everything goes a bit quicker then, too, and I can concentrate much better. Because I do find that difficult if I'm seated next to someone... especially if they are severely disabled, then I get very easily distracted by all the pumps, all those noisy things on their carts... That doesn't work for me.[31]

Jolanda therefore remarked that she is easily distracted by the presence of some people with disabilities. However, many other interviewees observed that they have become used to the unexpected sounds and movements and no longer find them distracting at all. Yet the fact remains that some church members experience a kind of unrest in the Ontmoetingskerk's liturgy. We have seen other examples of that earlier on in this chapter as well as the previous one. This disruption of the liturgical order can be explained by pointing to the presence of a

---

gemeenteleden... Dus ik heb niet de indruk dat er zoveel dingen anders gebeuren dan voorheen. Maar wel dat Joost in staat is om die mensen erbij te betrekken en dat vind

5.2. Leitourgia

number of people who make unexpected noises or movements, but it must also be nuanced. The question is which order is actually being disrupted. This is difficult to answer as the liturgical order in the Ontmoetingskerk, which is not a 'high church' congregation, is not highly scripted. Consequently, 'liturgical sensitivity' is not a hallmark of the congregation as a whole, as the following example from my fieldnotes shows:

> I see and hear people talking to one another. There is enthusiasm about the new building. Children are running around and exploring the sanctuary. The projector shows the following text: "Good Friday, time to experience silence together."[32]

At other moments, it does seem possible to be together in silence. Such moments are not disrupted by HVV residents in any way. On these occasions, the pastor clearly takes a leading role.[33] In view of this, the view that the liturgy of the Ontmoetingskerk has become 'disorderly' as a result of the inclusion of people with disabilities appears to be inadequate or at least incomplete. The reasons for the experience of liturgical incongruity, as in the example from Good Friday, seem to lie at least partly elsewhere, and can apparently be addressed by intentional liturgical leadership. Of course, the presence and participation of people who make unexpected noises does present a challenge for those leading and taking part in the liturgy, but it does not make fruitful liturgy impossible. Rather, it asks for intentional liturgical leadership, as seen in other examples in this chapter. This leadership consists in reflecting on the functions of the different elements of the liturgy

---

ik een heel groot pluspunt."

[31] *Interview with B4, 2018-02-28, D81.* Dutch original: "je hebt een keuze he, bij ons. Je hebt de vroege dienst, dan heb je ze niet. En je hebt de tweede dienst, dan heb je ze altijd. Dus als ik geen zin heb, dan ga ik naar de vroege dienst. [...] Even rustig... Dan gaat ook alles wat sneller en kan ik ook me eigen beter concentreren vooral. Want ik heb er wel moeite mee als ik naast iemand zit, vooral iemand die heel zwaar gehandicapt is, dat ik heel snel afgeleid word door al die pompjes, al die herrie-dingen die ze aan hun karretje hebben zitten. Da's niet voor mij..."

[32] *Fieldnotes 2016-03-25, D8.*

[33] E.g. *fieldnotes 2017-07-06, D56; 2017-10-01, D65.*

and in shaping them in such a way as to be an expression and formation of the faith of the entire congregation. We will return to how this can be done in chapter 7.

The church services in the Ontmoetingskerk are therefore not intentionally 'special', nor are they necessarily disorderly. Nonetheless, there do seem to be two things that characterize how the church services in the Ontmoetingskerk have changed as a result of its participation in HVV: a high level of lay participation in the liturgy, and a more embodied worship. We will discuss these characteristics below.

Participatory Liturgy

In the Ontmoetingskerk, church members participate in the liturgy in more ways than just the 'regular' participation of attending the worship services, singing, listening, etc. This wider liturgical participation manifests itself in a number of liturgical activities: church members do the Scripture readings; a large number of church members is involved in the musical accompaniment due to the variety of musical styles in use; during most services, prayer requests are collected during rather than before the service, as used to be the custom; church members are regularly asked to share testimonies (cf. 5.4) by telling their own story, being interviewed during the service, or having the minister tell their story for them with permission. All these activities involve the participation of members who live in HVV as well. The podium at the front of the sanctuary has been deliberately designed to be wheelchair accessible so that people in wheelchairs can do the Scripture readings, for example.

Respondents offered different evaluations of this liturgical participation. Some understood it as a 'favor' to those who enjoy being on stage. Niels thus remarked:

> Well, I do think, I know that they really enjoy it... But I just want a normal... I enjoy it when they sing, but just once in a while... then it's nice. [...] See, if those people really, really, really, REALLY want to, I'd be fine with them singing a song every time during the offertory.[34]

---

[34] *Interview with B5, 2018-02-28, D82.* Dutch original: "Ja, ik denk, ik weet dat ze het heel leuk vinden... Maar ik wil gewoon het liefst een normale... ik vind het heel

5.2. Leitourgia

Others saw greater liturgical participation of a diverse group of church members as an asset, due to the combination of what is happening in the liturgy and the person performing it. These respondents were appreciative of the greater space that had been created for personal experience and expression in church services. However, most respondents also agreed that it is necessary to maintain a certain standard of 'quality'. Jolanda formulated this concern very clearly. For her, it was unclear what added value the liturgical participation of anyone other than the minister really had:

> He has been trained to [speak in public]. He reads well. No mistakes, most of the time, pastors. Quick, neat, understandable above all. I really think that you can hear a pastor has been trained to do that. People don't realize it, but it's so important when your hearing starts to deteriorate. [...] If somebody else reads; some of them read too fast, others read... well, I don't know, I just can't understand them, not only those disabled people, also the normal people. Not everyone is trained to do it, so I really don't understand why they ever introduced that [practice of having other people do the Scripture reading].[35]

Embodied Liturgy

The Reformed liturgy of the Ontmoetingskerk and its denominational context traditionally does not make much room for the body. The following example from my fieldnotes can serve to illustrate this point:

> During the blessings, I observe body language. There are churches where people assume specific poses when they

---

leuk als ze gaan zingen, maar af en toe... is het leuk. [...] En kijk, als die mensen dat echt echt echt ECHT heel graag willen, dan maakt mij het niet zoveel uit als ze elke keer als de collecte komt een lied zingen."

[35] *Interview with B4, 2018-02-28, D81.* Dutch original: "Hij is er voor opgeleid. Hij leest goed. Zonder fouten, vaak, dominees. Snel, keurig, verstaanbaar vooral. Dat vind ik wel he: een dominee kan je echt merken dat 'ie daarin getraind is. Daar hebben de mensen geen erg in, maar als je slechter gaat horen is dat heel belangrijk. [...] Want als iemand anders leest: sommigen lezen snel, sommigen lezen... ja, weet ik veel, die kan je echt niet verstaan hoor, niet alleen de gehandicapten, ook de gewone

> receive the blessing. Here I do not see much of that. Of course, the pastor does hold up his hands in a blessing pose. A few people hold their hands open in front of them in a receptive pose, some with their eyes closed, others with open eyes. A few residents do this as well. But the vast majority of people just stand up straight without assuming any special pose.[36]

In this area, some developments in the Ontmoetingskerk's liturgy could be noted over the course of this research project. Some are 'scripted', like the laying on hands during blessings, as in our description of the Lord's Supper. Other examples of scripted change towards more embodied forms of worship include liturgical elements using candles or flowers that pastor Smit sometimes introduces to underline special occasions. Besides these intentional and scripted developments, there are also spontaneous developments in which the HVV residents often play an important part. For example, some residents express connection by hugging at special moments during the liturgy,[37] while others lead even the stiffest of church members into something resembling dance by their active participation in the liturgy on stage.[38] Elder Henk similarly described the role of HVV residents in the liturgy in terms of them reminding him to worship in a more embodied way:

> Well, the roles include that they, too, can make music, can sing, can praise and worship God. There is someone here who has Down syndrome who sings very loudly, the louder the better, and with his hands in the air... And it makes me think: what kind of role do you play for me? Praise and worship flow from your heart, from your body, from your whole being. For me, praise and worship come from my mouth, just maybe raising my hands just a little bit, it does come from my heart, and my intellect. But my

---

mensen hoor. Niet iedereen is daarin getraind dus ik snap echt gewoon niet waarom ze dat ooit hebben bedacht."

[36] *Fieldnotes 2017-02-05, D40.*
[37] E.g. *Fieldnotes 2017-04-16, D48.*
[38] *Video recording 2018-03-11.*

5.2. Leitourgia

gut feeling doesn't play a role in that at all. For them it does. It includes emotion, fun, joy.[39]

It does seem that these developments in the direction of more embodied worship have brought about some change in the worship of people in Vathorst, as the following example from my fieldnotes illustrates:

> What strikes me, too, is that a few dozen church members raise their hands or sing along in an otherwise 'embodied' way (holding up their hands in a praying gesture, moving to the music). Earlier, I had noted that this does not happen. Could this be related to the atmosphere set by the band? Or the musical style? Or has something changed?[40]

Changed Experiences of Liturgy

The overall impression that the study of *leitourgia* in the Ontmoetingskerk leaves us with is that the 'soft changes' resulting from the presence and participation of new members with disabilities have been of greater influence on member experience of the church services than the 'formal' and intentional liturgical changes. Henk's experience as recounted above is a clear example, but the point likewise emerges from other examples in both my fieldnotes and the interviews. Ada, for example, cried tears of joy as she reflected on a meaningful moment in a church service in which two HVV residents hugged each other after publicly professing their faith. This moment made her realize that there really is room to be yourself in church, and underlined the significance of the important life choice these two had

---

[39] *Interview with C1, 2018-02-21, D75.* Dutch original: "Ja, de rollen, sowieso om te laten zien dat ze ook muziek kunnen maken, dat ze ook kunnen zingen, dat ze ook God kunnen loven en prijzen. Er zit iemand met het syndroom van Down, die zingt heel hard en hoe mooier hoe harder en die handen omhoog en dan denk ik van: welke rol speel jij nou voor mij? Lofprijzing en aanbidding komt uit je hart, komt uit je lijft, komt uit je hele zijn. Lofprijzing en aanbidding komt bij mij uit de mond, heel misschien een klein beetje mijn handjes optillend en best wel enthousiast zingend, het komt uit mijn hart, het komt ook uit mijn verstand een beetje. Maar mijn buikgevoel dat speelt daar geen rol in. Dat speelt bij hun wel een hele grote rol. Een stuk emotie, een stuk plezier, een stuk blijdschap."

[40] *Fieldnotes 2017-10-01, D65.*

just made by the public profession of their faith.[41] Even pastor Smit shared how his involvement with people with disabilities in church has brought him closer to his emotional life, and how he no longer feels like "a brain on a stick".[42] In this sense, *leitourgia* in Vathorst seems to have become more emotional, joyful, and holistic by virtue of meaningful interactions with a diverse group, including people with disabilities.[43]

While the unscripted or soft changes seem to be decisive factors in these developments, the 'formal' and organized changes are likewise necessary to facilitate the presence and participation of HVV residents. Furthermore, one can ask whether this organizational aspect of liturgical change has gone 'far enough' in the Ontmoetingskerk. We will discuss this issue in chapter 7.

5.2.3 Summary Leitourgia

The *nota* of leitourgia is recognized most clearly in the Ontmoetingskerk's worship services, although other aspects of congregational life likewise form a part of leitourgia. One group of members sees the sermon as the central element of leitourgia. Questions arise concerning the accessible and inclusive shape of leitourgia if the often highly verbal and cognitive sermons take center stage, even though the style of communication in them is sometimes adapted with greater or less success. Another group sees the act of singing together as a key element of leitourgia. Musical styles have elicited some tensions, although it has also become clear that music is well suited as a vehicle for involving and including those that might otherwise feel left out. Yet others, and pastor Joost Smit in particular, see the celebration of the sacraments as a third central aspect of leitourgia. The sacramental celebrations have undergone a number of significant changes in order to facilitate participation for HVV residents and involvement of non-church members. The overall vision is to include everyone in regular worship, rather than just catering to specific target groups. This vision is upheld, with some exceptions. Nonetheless, since its involve-

---

[41] *Interview with B7, 2018-03-07, D84.* -

[42] *Interview with C3, 2018-03-12, D88.*

[43] Tamminga, "Receiving the Gift of Laughter: How Joy Transforms the Life of an Inclusive Congregation".

ment with HVV, the Ontmoetingskerk has seen some developments in worship, which has become more participatory and embodied over the course of our observations. Many respondents experienced these developments as contributing to a more holistic and joyful way of worship.

5.3 Diakonia

5.3.1 Concrete Support and Practical Care

The diaconal aspect of being church has to do with *service*: helping one another in concrete needs. As such, it would seem reasonable to frame HVV as a diaconal project. One might think, then, that in HVV it is those who need help receive help from those who can offer help. However, what emerges very clearly from my analysis is that HVV is not only understood only as a diaconal project, and that even words that could be considered typically diaconal words (such as *sharing* or *caring*) are not used in exclusively diaconal ways, but relate also to the aspect of *koinonia* (cf. 5.5)). Nonetheless, the diaconal aspect of the church is indeed present in the Ontmoetingskerk. As in any church, some church members are in need of concrete assistance. While in many churches a large part of the deacons' work is quite invisible, in the Ontmoetingskerk at least one aspect is decisively noticeable. An example is the pushing of wheelchairs, as deacon Pieter remarked:

> A number of residents need support. They are picked up from their apartments. This is the responsibility of the deacons. I am a deacon myself. In the beginning, we deacons did this a lot. At a certain moment we concluded that it's a task for the congregation as a whole. It can be initiated by the deacons, but they shouldn't have to do it all

---

[44]*Interview with B8, 2018-03-08, D85*. Dutch original: "Er is ook een aantal bewoners die ondersteuning nodig hebben, die worden dan opgehaald. Dat is vanuit de diaconie, ik ben zelf ook diaken, vanuit de diaconie hebben we dat in het begin veel gedaan. Op een gegeven moment hebben we gezegd: dat is ook een taak van de gemeente, dat kan wel geïnitieerd worden door de diakenen maar ze hoeven dat niet helemaal zelf uit te voeren. [...] Het is eigenlijk gewoon in praktische zin wat zorgen voor elkaar."

> by themselves. [...] So in fact it is just a matter of taking care of each other in a practical sense.[44]

Pieter's final words show one way in which diakonia is embodied in HVV; the need for supporting each other, taking care of each other in small and practical ways, is visibly present and cannot be ignored. At the end of every service, church members are reminded of this as they wait in their pews for those who need extra space and time to leave the sanctuary first. I reflected on this moment in the liturgy in my fieldnotes:

> After the blessing everyone waits. [Pastor] Joost explains that we have the custom to wait a moment, asking the guests to take this into account. What follows is a beautiful exodus of wheelchairs and walkers. An elderly woman stops [in the aisle] and a church member asks, "Are you okay? Or are you waiting for someone?" People do look after one another.[45]

Mr. Wortman recognized that this willingness on the part of the congregation to take practical care of one another is indeed noticeable:

> Yes, that's remarkable, the friendliness of the people here, it really stands out to us. If we get ready to leave our seats... You can just fold up this walker... And they fetch it for my wife and get it ready for her. There's always someone willing to do something like that.[46]

5.3.2   Diakonia and Leitourgia

Every church service includes one clearly diaconal liturgical element, namely the offertory. This moment is well suited to the participation of all church members. Some HVV residents help deacons pass the collection baskets, but even if they do not, the collection is an element

---

[45] *Fieldnotes 2017-05-21, D51.*
[46] *Interview with A1, 2018-05-01, D101.* Dutch original: "Ja, grappig ook die behulpzaamheid hier, dat valt ons heel erg op. Als wij dan van onze zitplaats afkomen... Deze rollator kun je zo inklappen he... En dan pakken ze 'm voor mijn vrouw en zetten het meteen even klaar. Er is altijd wel iemand die dat even doet."

5.3. Diakonia

of the liturgy in which everyone can make a contribution. This seems to be a very meaningful aspect of this liturgical element, for example for Rob:

> When it is time for the collection, it seems like we have reached the climax of the service for Rob. By making eye contact, noises, and movements, he communicates to me that I should take the coins from his wheelchair and put them in the collection basket. He then looks at his direct support professional with a satisfied smile.[47]

Remarkable about diakonia in this liturgical shape is its clearly reciprocal nature: everyone is invited to share and give, including those who would normally be perceived mainly as 'receivers' of care.

5.3.3 Diakonia and Koinonia

Following the division of the congregation into small groups, responsibilities that once lay with office bearers (deacons and elders) were placed with the congregation itself. With respect to diakonia, this resulted in some unclarity as to the precise diaconal responsibilities of the small groups. This unclarity came to clear expression during a meeting I observed involving small group leaders and deacons.[48] The ideal upheld by pastor Smit and others in leadership is for diakonia to be a mark of the entire congregation rather than the exclusive responsibility of the deacons.[49] Deacon Joop spoke of some of the ways in which the deacons are trying to make this ideal a reality. He referred to the example of picking up people from their apartments, explaining why they decided to delegate this task to a broader group. For him, it is about sharing mutual responsibilities, but also a way to employ church members' specific areas of expertise:

> We also ask people with a specific medical background. As in: if something happens, that they can act immediately. Because, well, as deacons, you go and pick them

---

[47] *Fieldnotes 2017-12-10, D70.*
[48] *Fieldnotes 2017-01-23, D38.*
[49] *Conversation notes 2017-08-22, D60.*

> up, they are given a place somewhere, but then the deacons go and sit in the front and you won't notice very quickly if something happens...[50]

What stands out in Joop's explanation is the intimate connection between *diakonia* and *koinonia*. By intentionally asking people to look out for one another, people also get in touch with one another. Of course, this contact may not surpass the level of one who helps and one who needs help. But this first step can also spark interest in further contact. That, at least, was the experience of young church member Jolien:

> I sometimes accompany one of the severely disabled members who uses a wheelchair back to his apartment. And people often don't interact with them all that much because, you see, they don't really know how to interact with them. So there is less interaction with him. But I sometimes accompany him back to his apartment upstairs... Yes... He's quite difficult... And it makes me very curious - I don't really know him - I just know him from accompanying him. And I'm curious what he's really like. How you could tell that he understands you and how he responds.[51]

5.3.4 Summary of Diakonia

In the Ontmoetingskerk, diakonia as one aspect of church life is clearly present and visible. There are two areas that evince some change and

---

[50] Interview with B9, 2018-03-09, D86. Dutch original: "En ook mensen zeg maar, die medische achtergrond hebben. Van: stel er gebeurt wat, dat ze wel gelijk kunnen schakelen. Want ja, als diaken, je haalt ze op, ze worden ergens neergezet, maar jij gaat als diakenen zit je voorin en merkt dan niet snel wat daar natuurlijk achter gebeurt..."

[51] Interview with B16, 2018-05-03, D102. Dutch original: "En ik breng ook wel een zwaargehandicapten die in een rolstoel vastzitten. En daar gaan mensen veel minder mee om omdat je ziet: daar weten ze minder goed mee om te gaan. Dus daar is minder contact mee. Maar die breng ik wel eens naar boven... Ja... Hij is heel lastig... Dan ben ik heel benieuwd, ik ken hem helemaal niet, ik ken hem alleen van het soms naar boven brengen. En van hem ben ik benieuwd hoe hij is. Hoe je uit hem kunt zien dat hij je begrijpt en snapt en hoe hij antwoord geeft."

5.4. Martyria

evoke some further reflection: how can diakonia become a mark of the entire congregation instead of just the deacons, and how can the relationship between diakonia and other aspects of the church (most notably koinonia) be protected and strengthened in order to prevent diaconal activity from remaining or becoming nonreciprocal?

5.4 Martyria

The nota of martyria refers to the witnessing practices of the church: how does the church's activity refer and testify to the Gospel? In this section, we will explore this nota with a specific interest in the place that people with disabilities receive in the Ontmoetingskerk's witness practices. These practices were divided into three subgroups relating to preaching and church services, to teaching, and explicitly to mission.

5.4.1 Church Services

We have already discussed church services and the place of sermons in them in section 5.2. Nonetheless, in the current section, we need to note one important characteristic of practices of martyria in the context of church services and sermons in the Ontmoetingskerk: they are often very *personal*, with attention for narrative, anecdotes, and emotional elements. The full complexity of life and faith is in view. This means that there is room to share stories, to laugh together during church services. This can be illustrated with the following example from my fieldnotes:

> Some prayer requests are collected from the congregation. Frank, a resident who uses a wheelchair, recounts how thankful he is for the place he has here. He has really found his place here, he says. He is proud of that place. [Pastor] Joost asks him if he can share the story about the empty wheelchair. Frank does so partly on his own. He had gone out, but his battery died and he was brought back in a police van. People laugh and so does Frank.[52]

---

[52] *Fieldnotes 2016-04-14, D13.*

The attention for the personal and for the full complexity of life also means that there is room in public communication during church services for the less humorous aspects of the lives of concrete people. In an interview, Pastor Smit spoke of this as one of the ways in which he tries to integrate the reality of his diverse congregation in the worship services:

> ...to also name vulnerability and to invite people to name that for themselves as well, either in their hearts or out loud, for example by collecting prayer requests or in the intercessory prayer, mentioning things in all their vulnerability. By talking about things in a certain way, not only factually, but also in terms of asking how this affects a person and how they relate to God in suffering.[53]

In combination with what our earlier exploration of sermons in the Ontmoetingskerk, these examples show us how practices of martyria are not disconnected from the reality of everyday life. Rather, stories from real people embody the content of the church's witness in a way that leaves room for the complexity of human experience ranging from telling funny anecdotes to sharing hard times together. The involvement with HVV has led to a significant broadening of this spectrum of human experiences.

5.4.2 Teaching Practices

Another way in which the Ontmoetingskerk practices martyria is teaching. Most of the activities that could be seen as forms of teaching are aimed at young people, with the exception of a number of short courses, or the Alpha Course, which is aimed at seekers. What stands out after an analysis of the Ontmoetingskerk's teaching practices is that its inclusive vision seems not to have had an effect on these practices. In teaching practices, there is little interaction between people with and without disabilities. There are catechism classes for young people from church and a separate 'bible course' for HVV residents and other people with disabilities from the neighborhood. And even

---

[53] *Interview with C3, 2018-03-12, D88.* Dutch original: "...dat je ook kwetsbaarheid benoemt en mensen daardoor ook uitnodigt het voor zichzelf ook te benoemen, of in hun hart of expliciet, dat je bijvoorbeeld gebedspunten vraagt of in de voorbede, hoe je dingen gewoon in alle kwetsbaarheid naar voren brengt. Door er op een bepaalde manier over te praten, dus niet alleen feitelijk, maar ook: wat doet het met iemand en hoe staat 'ie daarin ook voor God in het lijden."

5.4. Martyria

in that bible course, there is a differentiation based on levels of functioning, as one of the volunteers leading these courses explained: "We try to create groups based on ability, because we have participants with traumatic brain injuries, Down Syndrome, and autism, as well as people who find our methods too simple and can have it adapted to their levels."[54]

Although teaching practices in the Ontmoetingskerk are organized in arguably segregated groups, standard roles are nonetheless questioned and sometimes re-framed. Frederik, a church member and teacher, recounts, for example, how the 'volunteers' who teach the bible course for people with intellectual disabilities were very easy to recruit, and how he is not only a teacher with something to give but also a recipient of much joy:

> Like that bible study group, I derive so much pleasure from it. Just to have something together on a given night every week. Whether you have a disability or not, or however you want to call it... You are just different, but still you are there, together. And you mean something to one another. It's not just that I mean something to them, but they mean a lot to me as well. I find that remarkable. I really find that fantastic. I always say: I have many 'side jobs', but this is the most enjoyable one. At least, if you want to call this a job at all... But it's just the most enjoyable thing to do. I always come home smiling after the bible class. [...] The nice thing about this little project is that when a call was issued for people to do this, there was more supply than demand.[55]

The general picture of segregated teaching practices must also be nuanced with a number of exceptions, such as public profession of faith

---

[54] *Online post, 2017-10-07, D66*. Dutch original: "We delen de mensen zoveel mogelijk in naar hun mogelijkheden, want we hebben deelnemers met een niet aangeboren herseneafwijking, met het syndroom van Down en ASS (autisme) maar ook mensen die deze methode te eenvoudig vinden en dit wordt dan aangepast aan hun niveau." Web page: *Blog about liturgy in HVV*.

[55] *Interview with B6, 2018-03-82 D83*. Dutch original: "Zoals die bijbelstudie doe ik met heel veel plezier. Dat je dus gewoon iets samen hebt op een avond in de week. En of je nou een beperking hebt of niet, hoe je het maar noemt. Je bent gewoon

as the shared goal of much church education. In profession services, both residents of HVV and other members of the congregation make profession of their faith. These services are also prepared in togetherness:

> In a while we'll have our young people who will make profession of faith, the boys and girls, as well as a number of HVV residents. Then we eat together and talk about the songs we would like to sing and their place in the service.[56]

5.4.3 Missional Practices

Another set of practices that embodies the nota of martyria in the Ontmoetingskerk can be labeled missional practices. We have already discussed some of these practices in section 4.3. In section 4.4, we furthermore recognized an important tension in the missional activities of the Ontmoetingskerk: how explicitly should the Christian vision driving HVV and the Ontmoetingskerk be presented in these activities? Many respondents noted the importance of embodied witness over verbal convincing. A young church member called Marieke, for example, expressed her conviction that HVV can be a place where people are challenged to change their perspective on Christians and faith because of the way people live together there:

> I hope they won't think we are some kind of strict church, but that it's a place where people care for one another and talk about faith together, and well, that they see we all belong together, like. Christians sometimes have a negative

---

verschillend, maar je bent er wel, samen. En je betekent ook iets voor elkaar. Niet alleen ik voor hen, maar zij ook voor mij, want ik vind het echt geweldig. Ik vind dat echt geweldig. Ik zeg altijd: ik heb een heleboel van die bijbaantjes he, maar dit is de leukste. Voor zover je van een baantje kan spreken. Maar het is gewoon het leukste om te doen. Ik kom altijd lachend thuis, als ik het gedaan heb. [...] Dat was het leuke van dit projectje, dat toen gevraagd werd om het te gaan doen zeg maar, dat er meer mensen waren dan... er was meer aanbod dan dat er nodig was."

[56] *Interview with C1, 2018-02-21, D75.* Dutch original: "straks hebben we de belijdeniscatechisanten van de kerk, de jongens en meiden en we hebben er een aantal van Hart van Vathorst. Dan gaan we gezamenlijk met ze eten en gezamenlijk afspreken: welke liederen vinden we mooi en hoe gaan we dat inbouwen in de kerkdienst."

5.4. Martyria

image, that they have so many things they're not allowed to do, that they are very strict, and stuff like that. But I hope that this is not what they see, but see the love of God in us.[57]

Some respondents noted how the presence and contributions of people with disabilities play an important role in the Ontmoetingskerk's missional practices. They often linked this to the broad range of human experiences which we discussed in section 5.4.1. Niels, another young church member, formulated another way in which the Ontmoetingskerk's diversity could contribute to its missional character: "I also think that it shows people on the outside: Guys, it doesn't matter who you are, come on in! You are a child of God. That is just something you can communicate very clearly with this project."[58] According to Niels, the inclusion of people with disabilities therefore creates an overall inclusive environment which will also make people feel at home if they feel 'outsiders' for reasons other than (dis)ability. It doesn't matter who you are, everyone is welcome.

5.4.4 Summary of Martyria

Martyria as the witnessing aspect of the church's life manifests itself in a number of sets of practices in the Ontmoetingskerk. There is the witness during church services, which is characterized by attention for and personal sharing of a broad range of human experiences. There are also practices of teaching, which seem to be organized in a more or less segregated way, but still also become opportunities for genuine encounters. And, finally, there are explicitly missional practices in which, according to the respondents, the inclusive vision of HVV and the Ontmoetingskerk as it is embodied plays a vital part.

---

[57] *Interview with B12, 2018-04-03, D92.* Dutch original: "Ik hoop dat ze niet denken dat het een strenge kerk is ofzo, maar dat het juist een plek is waar mensen voor elkaar zorgen en met elkaar over geloof praten en, ja, dat ze wel zien dat we allemaal bij elkaar horen ofzo. Je hebt wel eens een beetje een negatief beeld over christenen, dat ze heel veel dingen niet mogen en streng zijn en allemaal dat soort dingen, maar dat ze dat juist niet zien, maar juist de liefde van God zien in ons."

[58] *Interview with B5, 2018-02-28, D82.* Dutch original: "en ik denk ook dat het ook wel iets is van, dat wij aan anderen mensen er buiten laten zien van: jongens, het maakt ons niet uit wie of wat je bent, kom naar binnen. Je bent gewoon Gods kind."

5.5 Koinonia

Koinonia refers to the communal aspect of the church's life. We will look at some of the ways this communality is embodied in the Ontmoetingskerk, with special attention for the place of people with disabilities in these practices and the influence of the experience of disability on koinonia in Vathorst.

5.5.1 Intentional Connections

As we saw in our explorations of some of the other notae above as well, responsibilities that once rested with office bearers or other 'officials' have largely been handed over to the community as a whole. Pastor Smit described this development as follows: "Indeed, there are special people appointed for pastoral work, but the questions 'how are you?' and 'what is your life with God like?' should be part of the basics, don't you think?"[59] Smit's vision is hence to put more emphasis on koinonia. Of course, this does mean that people need to assume the responsibilities handed to them, which does not always happen. Sometimes they experience a lack of clarity about what is really expected from them. This concern was clearly voiced during a meeting of small group leaders that I attended, for example.[60] A key responsibility for leadership seems to lie in somehow facilitating fruitful practices of koinonia. This is one of the marks of the way pastor Smit works in the congregation; he strives to bring people in touch so that they can support each other. This is shown in the following example from an interview with Willem, a new church member who had no previous experience with church but started attending because of his wife:

> But I also spoke to someone who is not in our Encounter Group, but just one on one... Someone who has a similar background and... [...] Joost suggested that once. He said that was a person with a similar background, and it just worked out.[61]

Dat is gewoon iets wat je daar best wel duidelijk mee maakt."
[59] *Fieldnotes 2017-05-21, D51.*
[60] *Fieldnotes 2017-05-22, D52.*

If koinonia is given a central role in pastoral care, church leadership must enable meaningful connections between people in which spiritual support can actually take place.

5.5.2 Encounter Groups

One of the means intended to facilitate these intentional connections in the Ontmoetingskerk is the Encounter Groups. As church member Floris explains in the following passage from an interview, these groups are a way to embody koinonia or, in his words, mutual love. He places this mutual love alongside God's love as one of the two important things about church, and immediately went on to talk about the Encounter Groups. Floris also noted some difficulties relating to the diminishing role of office bearers in pastoral care now that the system of Encounter Groups had been introduced:

> That you are always nourished to experience God's presence and love. I think that that's important. And also to experience that mutual love with each other. I think that, too, is important. In our church we have Encounter Groups, and all these things have to settle in a bit, you have to get to know each other first. In this area, we had a group of people we knew well, that we had a lot of contact with. Then you got those Encounter Groups, where you have to go through all of that again together and that is a complex process. It doesn't happen over the course of a single year, it takes time. Because you have to trust each other, to know what others are about. What I find difficult is that they assume that people also interact with each other on a pastoral level. I see some problems in that area, I should add. Because when I see the kind of problems that some families, some people, are dealing with and you want to discuss that with them, I think... well, you have no authority. In that sense it's different from

---

[61] *Interview with B11, 2018-03-16, D90.* Dutch original: "Maar ik heb ook met iemand gesproken die gewoon niet bij ons in de Ontmoetingsgroep zit, maar waar je gewoon een op een mee.... Iemand die specifiek een beetje dezelfde achtergrond heeft en wat... [...] Joost heeft daar eens een keer een suggestie over gedaan. Die zei: dat is

> an elder who comes with a certain authority because of his office. I am just a church member, and of course I am a part of the Encounter Group, but I don't have that authority like an elder does. I can't say, "Hey, I'm coming to visit you to discuss this or that…" Of course I could, but people wouldn't accept it.[62]

Other church members, like Hannah, reported that it is not that easy for conversations during Encounter Group meetings to reach a meaningful spiritual level. Hannah made it clear that she understands church membership to be different from just meeting a group of friends. To Hannah, if the conversations in church fail to surpass the level of the mundane, they are meaningless and not worth having:

> Well, take those Encounter Groups, for example, or the neighborhood evenings that we had before… You go to an evening like that, and people only talk about their vacations and stuff… Then I'm like: I don't need to go there. I can find my own friends….[63]

---

iemand met dezelfde achtergrond en dat klikte gewoon."

[62] *Interview with B14, 2018-04-11, D94.* Dutch original: "…dat je steeds weer gevoed wordt om Gods nabijheid en Gods liefde te ervaren. Ik denk dat dat heel belangrijk is, en die liefde ook naar elkaar. Ik denk dat dat ook heel belangrijk is. Als kerk hebben we dan de ontmoetingsgroepen en dat moet allemaal nog een beetje zijn beslag krijgen, je moet elkaar eerst leren kennen. We hadden in deze omgeving een aantal mensen die we goed kenden, waar we veel contact mee hadden. Toen kreeg je die ontmoetingsgroepen, dat moet je allemaal weer opnieuw met elkaar ondervinden en dat is ook weer een proces. Dat is ook niet in een jaar tijd gerealiseerd, daar heb je tijd voor nodig. Want je moet elkaar vertrouwen. Je moet weten wat je aan elkaar hebt. Wat ik een beetje moeilijk vind is dat er van uitgegaan wordt dat je ook pastoraal met elkaar bezig bent en daar zie ik nog wel wat moeite, moet ik zeggen. Want als ik dan zie dat er toch bij bepaalde gezinnen, bepaalde mensen, behoorlijke problemen liggen en je wilt daar met die mensen over praten dan denk ik: kijk, je hebt geen gezag. In de zin van een ouderling die komt met gezag vanwege zijn benoeming. Ik ben gewoon kerklid en natuurlijk zit ik in een ontmoetingsgroep maar ik heb niet een gezagsverhouding zoals een ouderling. Ik kan niet zeggen: joh, ik kom even bij je want dit of dat… Dat kan ik natuurlijk wel doen, maar dat wordt niet geaccepteerd."

[63] *Interview with B3, 2018-02-27, D80.* Dutch original: "Ja, nou neem de ontmoetingsgroepen, de wijkavonden die we vroeger hebben gehad. En dan kom je op zo'n avond en dan wordt er alleen maar over vakantie enzo gesproken. En dan zeg ik: daar hoef ik niet heen. Dan kan ik mijn eigen kennissen uitzoeken…"

5.5. Koinonia

Nonetheless, there are also many examples of people who did note the positive impact of the Encounter Groups on their personal lives and on the life of the congregation as a whole. Church member Pieter spoke of a *general experience of togetherness*, which clearly points to the nota of koinonia. For Pieter, koinonia as it is practiced within the Encounter Groups has a significant impact on his spiritual life:

> Just an overall experience of togetherness, having conversations together. We are now part of an Encounter Group, and can really share things together. Sharing positive things is easy enough, but there is also room to share hardships. It functions like a sounding board. Many people are about our age, because my age group is just very large, there are many people at the same stage of life, so you can just share your experiences... [...] That notion of real mutual encounters is something I recognize very strongly.[64]

The place of HVV residents in these Encounter Groups is a complex issue. On the one hand, from a purely organizational perspective, all residents have their 'home' in one of the groups, as elder Gerrit explains:

> So they are all assigned to an Encounter Group. Every small group leader knows which people from HVV are part of their Encounter Group, so yes: they are always in view. You cannot always make contact with them, but they are always in view.[65]

---

[64] *Interview with B8, 2018-03-08, D85.* Dutch original: "Gewoon algemeen het gevoel van daar samen zijn inderdaad, de gesprekken die je kan hebben met elkaar. We zijn nu in die ontmoetingsgroepen, dat je de dingen met elkaar kan delen. Je leuke dingen met elkaar delen is heel makkelijk, maar ook gewoon je moeiten inderdaad. En zeker dat je een stukje klankbord hebt met, het zijn heel veel van onze leeftijd, de leeftijdsgroep waar ik in zit is gewoon erg groot, heel veel mensen in dezelfde leeftijdsfase, dat je gewoon je ervaringen kan delen... [...] Echt dat elkaar ontmoeten dat zie je toch wel heel sterk terugkomen"

[65] *Interview with C2, 2018-02-26, D78.* Dutch original: "Dus ze zitten echt allemaal wel, allemaal ingedeeld. Elke ontmoetingsgroepsleider weet welke mensen van Hart van Vathorst in zijn ontmoetingsgroep zitten, dus ja: ze zijn altijd in beeld. En dan kun je niet altijd contact met ze hebben, maar altijd in beeld."

Every Encounter Group, and specifically its leader, is asked to figure out fitting ways to include the HVV residents that are part of the group. In practice, the result is a mixed picture of more and less successful practices. Church member Frederik shared the following:

> We have one member in our Encounter Group... You've probably heard that they've assigned a HVV resident to every Encounter Group. And sometimes it works really well, like in the case of my wife's aunt, who is more than 90 years old but doesn't have dementia, she is still very alert. Anyways, she got a place in the building since they had to rent out those rooms... She's a part of an Encounter Group, and well, now and then someone comes to visit her. And you know, like that... But there is another one, and she acts in really unpredictable ways. So you can invite her, and she came once, in the beginning, but she never showed up after that again. [...] She can get angry, very angry. It requires a special approach, which is why you need professionals who tell you to do this or that... That's how it works. You see, a perfectly inclusive society doesn't exist. You always encounter resistance and things like this, which makes it complex. [...] But you also witness how things sometimes go surprisingly well, how it brings you a surprising amount of good, mutually, to them and to us; reciprocity.[66]

In this quotation, Frederik speaks of resistance and 'things like this', referring to the difficult behavior shown by some residents, like the woman in his Encounter Group. These things prevent a 'perfectly inclusive society' from becoming a reality. He points to the need for professionals to offer support in these kinds of situations. This reveals a sense of incapacity on the part of the current small group leaders who, at least in some cases, seem to have encountered difficulties in finding suitable approaches. This does mean that, in some instances and depending on the small group leader or members, questions regarding the participation of HVV residents in Encounter Group activities are not asked or addressed. Assumptions are left unchallenged; it seems to be too difficult to invite a woman who has anger outbursts or

5.5. Koinonia

residents with other challenging behaviors. In some cases, this means that residents have the sense that they are being left out, even if the issues preventing their participation could be solved quite easily. This was the case, for example, for church member and HVV resident Simone:

> But these tings are often planned at 7 in the evening, and I always go to bed around 6:30, or 7. Because I just need a lot of sleep. I will also sleep until 10 the next morning. [...] I sometimes have the sense that people - because they do sometimes invite me [...] but then I can't come - and I think that they might sometimes think: there she goes again with her sleep issues... I find that hard..[67]

During the interview, Simone indicated that she would want to participate in Encounter Groups activities and suggested that it would be helpful for activities to take place on Friday nights, for example, so that she could sleep in on Saturday. But she added that these conversations had not yet taken place with her small group leader.

---

[66] *Interview with B6, 2018-03-02, D83*. Dutch original: "Want wij hebben bijvoorbeeld in onze ontmoetingsgroep... Dat heb je waarschijnlijk ook wel gehoord: elke ontmoetingsgroep heeft ook iemand toegeschoven gekregen vanuit Hart van Vathorst. En soms gaat dat heel goed, bijvoorbeeld een tante van mijn vrouw, die zit ook in Hart van Vathorst, die is over de 90, die is niet dement ofzo, ze is nog heel bij. Maar goed, die heeft daar toch een plekje gekregen, ze moesten die kamers natuurlijk ook kwijt. Zij zit ook bij een ontmoetingsgroep en nou, zo nu en dan gaat er even iemand naar haar toe. En weet je wel, zo... Maar er is er ook eentje, en die is onberekenbaar. Dus die kun je wel uitnodigen, die is een keer geweest in het begin, en daarna eigenlijk nooit meer... [...] Die kan boos worden, heel boos. Dat vergt een heel speciale aanpak. En dan heb je toch professionals die dan zeggen: je moet het zus en zo doen.... Zo gaat dat. Kijk, de volmaakte inclusieve maatschappij die heb je natuurlijk niet. Je hebt altijd te maken met weerstanden en gewoon dit soort dingen, dat is gewoon lastig. [...] En je ziet dat het ook soms verbazend goed gaat, dat je daar verbazend veel aan hebt, over en weer, zij aan ons en wij aan hen. Wederkerigheid."

[67] *Interview with A5, 2018-06-28, D106*. Dutch original: "Maar dan is het vaak om 7 uur 's avonds en ik lig altijd half 7, 7uur in bed. Omdat ik gewoon echt heel veel slaap nodig heb. Ik slaap dan ook tot de volgende ochtend 10 uur ongeveer. [...] Ik heb dan ook wel eens het idee dat mensen, want soms nodigen ze me dan uit [...] maar dan kan ik dan weer niet en dan denk ik wel eens dat ze dan denken van: ja, heb je haar ook weer met 'r slaap hoor. Vind ik wel eens lastig."

5.5.3 Unity or Subgroups?

Social contacts play a vital part in why the younger interviewees enjoy coming to church. Many of them mentioned their friends in church as their primary connection to church. Martine offered an example when she was asked what she values most in church:

> I think, like, the togetherness, I have quite a few friends in church. It's not like I talk about faith with them all the time, but it is nice to have a group of friends in church, and we get together quite often, meet up and just hang out at night. I find that important, to have some people in church that you just talk to and stuff.[68]

The importance of friends raises an ensuing question as to how wide koinonia in the Ontmoetingskerk really is. Is it something that is only embodied in friend-to-friend contacts, therefore excluding by nature those who do not belong to one's particular circle of friends? Does koinonia extend as wide as the congregation? Or does it stretch even beyond its formal borders? On page 132, we saw young church member Niels expressing his concern that people get together in subgroups and therefore do not really experience the togetherness that, to his mind, is so important for being able to learn from one another in church. This concern underlines the significance of the question that we posed in section 5.4.2 regarding the extent to which teaching practices, for example, promote interaction beyond the boundaries of subgroups. Although there are examples of such boundary-crossing interaction, in many cases that interaction does not take place - at least, not yet. This is not only the case for young people, but applies also across the entire congregation. Ada, for example, shared how having coffee following the service often represents a moment to catch up with friends from one's subgroup, rather than an opportunity for newer members to get to know new people:

---

[68] *Interview with B12, 2018-04-03, D92.* Dutch original: "Ik denk toch wel de gezelligheid ofzo, ik heb best wel veel vrienden uit de kerk. Het is niet eens dat ik heel vaak met hun over geloof praat, maar het is wel leuk dat we een soort van vriendengroepje binnen de kerk hebben waar we elkaar gewoon best wel vaak opzoeken, met elkaar afspreken en gewoon gaan chillen 'savonds. Dat vind ik altijd wel belangrijk, dat je mensen in de kerk hebt die je ook gewoon, waar je mee praat en zo." Similar

5.5. Koinonia

> Having coffee after the service... Well, I am critical of that because, if it is kind of cliquish, which it is for many people, then - if you don't know me, you won't approach me. What do we have to do with each other? So we end up standing around with the two of us, and I say to my husband, "The coffee is good, isn't it? But the coffee at home is better, so shall we drink the rest at home?" "Good idea..." And then no one approaches you. But that's not just the case in our church, it's the same everywhere, across the entire country.[69]

It should be noted that Ada's experience is not representative of the experience of everyone, but it is also not unique. The picture is mixed, as I wrote in my fieldnotes after one Sunday morning service: "There is coffee after the service. The situation is as usual: some residents leave immediately, while another group stays for coffee. There does seem to be some interaction."[70] So, while there are indeed examples of boundary-crossing interaction, there are also people who do not or do not yet experience this personally. Noteworthy about practices like teaching as we described them above is that they do not seem to involve such interaction from an organizational perspective. Another example of the danger of subgroups can be found in the difference between the first and second morning services in Vathorst as we described it in section 5.2.2. There too it is possible to choose one's own subgroup. The question of the extent to which organized practices should challenge or, on the contrary, strengthen existing subgroups is an important one and will be discussed in chapter 7.

---

statements in *Interview with B5, 2018-02-28, D82; Interview with B10, 2018-03-16, D89.*

[69] *Interview with B7, 2018-03-07, D84.* Dutch original: "Koffiedrinken na de kerk. Ja, daar ben ik wel eens kritisch over hoor, want als het een ons-kent-ons-situatie is, wat voor een heleboel mensen zo is, dan, als jij mij niet kent kom je ook niet naar mij toe. Wat heb je mij te vertellen? Dus dan sta je daar met zijn tweeën en zeg ik tegen mijn man: lekkere koffie he, maar die van thuis is lekkerder, zullen we maar thuis koffie gaan drinken? Ja goed idee... En dan word je niet aangesproken. Maar dat is niet alleen in deze kerk, dat heb je overal. In het hele land."

[70] *Fieldnotes 2017-07-16, D58.*

5.5.4 Developments in Koinonia

When interviewees were asked to describe things that had changed in the Ontmoetingskerk since its involvement with HVV, many mentioned an increase in social interactions or a growth in experienced community. Jolien noted:

> I have the feeling that things are more sociable now. Because the building is also accessible during the week. And many people are getting involved now, with the Encounter Groups. And you can drink coffee and tea there. So I think more people are more involved with church than they were before. Because now you have a place where you can get together and hold catechism classes, etc. So I think we have become more of a congregation in that sense [...] Well, you go there especially for catechism classes. And that's a very sociable event. And you see other church members there. And people from upstairs [HVV Residents] just come down and join us.[71]

Jolien's experience is shared by many, and 'objectively' one could say that the possibilities for practices of koinonia have greatly increased through the Ontmoetingskerk's involvement in HVV. There is space to use for social activities, there are many courses and meetings, there are informal opportunities for interaction on evenings when activities are hosted in the building, and many more examples could be listed. Nonetheless, there are also people who do not experience koinoinia, and for whom involvement in practices of koinonia remains a difficult question. One such person is Ms. Wiertz, who lives in HVV's group home for people with dementia. In her interview, she recounted how she often felt lonely. It was difficult to determine whether this was still a reality for her, or whether things had changed for the better. The latter is suggested in the quote below, but at other times in the interview one had reason to think that things had only taken a turn

---

[71] *Interview with B16, 2018-05-03, D102.* Dutch original: "Ik heb wel iets meer dat het iets socialer is. Omdat je er ook doordeweeks kan komen. En mensen worden er ook heel veel bij betrokken, nu met die Ontmoetingsgroepen. En je hebt dat je daar koffie kan drinken en thee kan drinken. Ik denk dat zo meer mensen meer doen met de kerk dan ze toen deden. Omdat je nu ook gewoon een plek hebt waar je kan

5.5. Koinonia

for the worse. The constant factor in Ms. Wiertz's account was this sense of loneliness and of not being seen, not feeling part of the community. Such feelings persisted in spite of the fact that she belongs to an Encounter Group, and is in that sense never 'out of view'.

> Ms. Wiertz: Well, how should I put it... When I first moved here, I felt a bit lonely. But well, that has all changed now. [...] Because back then I found it quite difficult. That first period was pretty crucial in fact. But apart from that things are fine here.
>
> Interviewer: And do you get the feeling that you can participate in activities in church? [...] For instance, with the small groups, just to name an example? [...]
>
> Ms. Wiertz: Well, yes, but I've never heard anything about those small groups. They do not have them here, or do they?
>
> Elder Henk: Yes, we talked about that last time, that you don't really have a connection with your small group, and that they don't really reach out to you. You didn't even know who was part of your group, we'll work on that. But that really is a missed opportunity. So she *is* assigned to a small group.
>
> Ms. Wiertz: I haven't noticed at all...[72]

The experience of people like Ms. Wiertz shows how koinonia may have come to occupy a more central place in the Ontmoetingskerk and grown, but is not a reality for everyone involved. This raises the question whether we must acknowledge this to be a sad reality since 'the perfectly inclusive society does not exist', or whether additional steps can be taken. This question will return in chapter 7.

---

samenkomen en catechisatie kan houden en dat soort dingen. Dus ik denk in dat opzicht dat we meer gemeente zijn geworden. [...] Ja, vooral met catechisatie kom je er wel. En dat is wel heel gezellig. En je ziet ook gewoon andere gemeenteleden. Dan komen er mensen van boven, die komen er gewoon gezellig bij zitten."

[72] *Interview with A4, 2018-06-28, D105.* Dutch original: "Ms. Wiertz: Ja, hoe moet

5.5.5 Summary of Koinonia

In this section, we explored koinonia as the communal aspect of church life. We saw that koinonia has been given a more central role in the Ontmoetingskerk. Some aspects of church life, like pastoral care, have undergone changes towards greater responsibility for the community itself, or, in other words, heavier reliance on koinonia. This process is still ongoing, and some areas of concern remain in terms of the clarity regarding responsibilities and the extent to which the entire congregation is 'covered' or certain groups are left out. An important example of this transition as well as its continuing challenges can be found in the system of Encounter Groups. These are designed as an embodiment of koinonia and expected to cover many aspects of church life, including pastoral care. Yet there are also examples of people for whom this system in its current state does not provide sufficient opportunities to connect. On the whole, the Ontmoetingskerk seems to have experienced growth in practices of koinonia since the beginning of its involvement in HVV. Yet it remains possible for people to withdraw into their own, like-minded subgroups. Moreover, these existing subgroups or other issues like practical and sometimes solvable issues related to people's impairments leave some people in HVV and the congregation feeling like they cannot fully participate in the communal life of the Ontmoetingskerk.

5.6 Summary

In this chapter, we have gained an overview of the ways in which key aspects of church life are embodied in the practices of the Ontmoetingskerk. The overview was structured using four of the church's *no-*

---

ik dat zeggen... De eerste periode dat ik hier woonde zeg maar, toen voelde ik me wel een beetje alleen. Maar goed dat is allemaal veranderd. [...] Want het was toen wel, toen vond ik het wel moeilijk. Die eerste periode en die was wel cruciaal eigenlijk. Maar het is hier verder prima. Interviewer: En hebt u het gevoel dat u met alles kunt meedoen wat er in de kerk gebeurt? [...] Met kringen bijvoorbeeld, ik noem maar wat? [...] Ms. Wiertz: Ja, maar daar heb ik nog nooit iets van gehoord. Die zijn er niet? Elder Henk: Jawel, daar hebben we het de vorige keer over gehad he, dat je inderdaad helemaal geen aansluiting had bij de kring, de kring ook niet bij jou, je wist niet eens wie de kring was. Dus daar gaan we aan werken... Maar dat is wel een misser ja. Ze is wel ingedeeld in een kring. R: Daar merk ik niks van..."

5.6. Summary

tae externae (*leitourgia, diakonia, martyria,* and *koinonia*). This structure flowed from our data in an inductive manner, even though it must be noted that two of the notae (leitourgia, koinonia) surfaced much more prominently than the other two did (diakonia, martyria). A particular interest in our explorations was to assess the ways in which the practices in each of those four notae were specifically attuned to HVV's inclusive vision and the presence and participation of people with disabilities.

The discussion of leitourgia showed that liturgy in the Ontmoetingskerk is primarily understood as something that happens in church services. For many people, the sermon is at the heart of this service, though others also mentioned singing and worship as the key element of the church service, while yet another, smaller group pointed to the sacraments. If it is the sermon that takes center stage, the next questions to be raised obviously concern accessibility. For music or singing, creative inclusive practices are quite easily found. The sacraments pose problems of their own, as criteria for participation are quite explicit. Yet they also present an opportunity for practices of leitourgia that involve all the senses, rather than cognition alone. A significant number of interviewees shared how their experience of leitourgia had become more holistic, involving their bodies as well as their minds, through the presence and participation of HVV residents.

With respect to diakonia, there were two main points of reflection: How can the entire congregation rather than just the deacons take ownership of this nota? And what can be done to prevent diakonia from becoming a nonreciprocal practice? Concrete practices of diakonia offer natural and easy ways for inclusion, since diakonia is about the contribution of everyone, big or small.

Martyria was recognized as an aspect of the church's worship services, teaching practices, and missional activities. An important question for each is whether and how full credit is given to the witnessing voice of believers with disabilities. We saw positive examples of this, showing how the inclusion of those voices broadens the range of human experience and hence the possibility of identification for the intended audience of the church's witnessing voice.

Finally, our exploration of the nota of koinonia produced a mixed picture. On the one hand, koinonia has come to occupy a more central in church life, with many examples of its embodiment. On the other hand, organized practices of koinonia did not always challenge or question existing boundaries, which seems to be one reason why some people recounted feeling they could not partake fully or at all in the koinonia of the Ontmoetingskerk.

Chapter 6

Putting Inclusion into Practice

6.1 Introduction

In the previous chapters, we have explored ecclesial life and practice in the Ontmoetingskerk and studied the ways in which this congregation and the broader HVV project strive to be inclusive. In the current chapter, we will zoom in on how the vision for inclusion is embodied in Vathorst. What kind of interactions have come to fruition? And what are the reasons people either participate in these interactions or choose to stay on the sidelines? These two questions will be discussed in sections 6.2, 6.3, and 6.4. Section 6.2 will be largely devoted to an exploration of the *operant* theological voice: what do practices of interaction reveal about the convictions inherent to these practices? Sections 6.3 and 6.4 focus more one the *espoused* voice: how do respondents explicitly reflect on the reasons for their varying participation in interaction with others? We will end this chapter with a summary (6.5).

6.2 Interaction between Residents and Non-residents

In this section, we will study the ways in which HVV-residents and non-residents - people 'with and without disabilities', for lack of a better term - interact and what impact these interactions have. We will first look at interactions in communal gatherings (6.2.1), and then explore interactions on an individual level (6.2.2), before examining some of the ways respondents experience these interactions as beneficial (6.2.3). This section will close with a summary (6.2.4).

6.2.1 Interaction During Communal Gatherings

An important way in which interactions take place is shared participation in communal gatherings. While not all church members maintain individual contact with HVV-residents, they are all part of the interaction that happens during church services, for example. Therefore, this type of interaction is important to explore, even if it does not go as 'deep' as interactions or encounters on the individual level.

Visibility and Presence

Gerrit, an elder and church member, described the presence and visibility of people with disabilities in the Ontmoetingskerk's worship services as an important way to challenge existing social imagery of the good life:

> That is the image that we create in society: everything needs to be good, and if it isn't good... It has to be more and more and more, and better, best, right... [...] And if it isn't, things get really tough. And you see many people who can't handle that. [...] So that's something I would want to change. [...] That is the benefit of HVV, that we *see* it more now. [...] Now you are really confronted, so to

---

[1] *Interview with C2, 2018-02-26, D78.* Dutch original: "Dat beeld creëren we wel in de maatschappij. Alles moet goed zijn en als het niet goed is... Het moet meer meer meer en beter, beter best, he. [...] En als dat niet zo is dan wordt het heel erg lastig. En dan zie je ook veel mensen die daar ook op stukgaan. [...] Dus dat zou ik wel willen veranderen. [...] Dat is wel het voordeel met Hart van Vathorst dat we dat nu meer zien. [...] Maar nu wordt je echt, zal ik maar zeggen, met meerdere mensen geconfronteerd die echt deel uitmaken, een substantieel deel uitmaken van je gemeente. Ja dat betekent dat je er gewoon veel meer mee te maken gaat krijgen, dat je er veel meer dingen van hoort en ziet en dat je zegt: ja, maar daar kun je zoveel voor betekenen in zulke situaties, dat je denkt: wat raar dat dat niet gewoon common sense is in de samenleving dat iedereen dat gewoon kan doen, dat je elkaar helpt."

6.2. Interaction

> speak, with multiple people who are really a substantial part of your congregation... So that means you are just confronted with it that much more, you see much more of it and hear much more and it makes you say, "You can be of so much value in a situation like that." And that makes you think how strange it is that common sense in society doesn't dictate that we can all do that, just help each other.[1]

For Gerrit, the opening of HVV was one of the first occasions where he was 'confronted' with people with disabilities and experienced how this impacted him and others. The experience of another church member, Floris, was very different, although he too stressed the importance of the presence and visibility of people with disabilities in communal gatherings. He did so from an autobiographical perspective, reflecting on his own experiences with his son who during his lifetime had serious impairments:

> Whenever we took him along, we would get the feeling that people weren't comfortable with it at all... To have a child like that in church. And that's what I like about this place: let them be seen! And we see that these people are just as human as the rest of us, even though they have a disability. So what, who doesn't have some kind of disability? We all have our better and lesser qualities. So I enjoy the fact that these people are now given a full place in church and society. [...] A few of the disabled girls do the Scripture readings for the sermon. Well, I just find that beautiful. They can't always read very well, and sometimes they stumble a bit. But I'm like: please, do this. It's, well, it becomes more or less normal, and I think that's a good thing.[2]

---

[2] *Interview with B14, 2018-04-11, D94.* Dutch original: "...als je hem dan meenam dan kreeg je het gevoel van: mensen vinden het helemaal niet fijn... Dat er zo'n kind in de kerk zit. En dat vind ik juist hier: laat ze maar zien! En we zien dat deze mensen net zo goed mensen zijn als wij allemaal ook al zijn ze gehandicapt, oké, wie heeft geen handicap? We zijn allemaal... Zitten allemaal vol met, ja.... Onze goede en minder goede kwaliteiten. Dus ik vind het heel fijn dat deze mensen dus nu in de kerk en in de hele samenleving een volwaardige plek krijgen. [...] Wij hebben een

This visibility realized through the presence of a "substantial" number of people with disabilities in worship services in the Ontmoetingskerk therefore represents a first form of interaction that can have a large impact. One respondent noted that even though she herself did not interact personally with HVV residents a lot, their presence in worship services still had a very positive impact for her.[3]

Visibility and presence can only be realized on the condition of accessibility. We have already treated the measures for physical accessibility to the church building and sanctuary (cf. 4.5.1), as well as the discussions regarding possible adaptations in the liturgy (cf. 5.2.2). The current section underlines the importance of these measures and discussions by identifying them as not just technical issues, but as means facilitating meaningful interactions. We have also already noted that not all residents of HVV experience this accessibility to the same degree. The data reveals that the level of interaction differs depending on the resident. Some interviewees, like Ada, also noted this fact and reflected on it:

> On that women's night two years ago there was this one woman and she was ... well, I forgot here name, so let's just call her Truus. One person after another greeted her. And I thought: Truus has been doing something right, everybody knows Truus. And it wasn't like five people, it was at least 10. She was really being pampered, wallowing in bliss... And there are probably many others who think: why don't I get a pat on the shoulder? I think that's something we really have to avoid.[4]

Creating Space for Interaction in Communal Gatherings

In section 5.2, we already saw how attention for the personal is one important characteristic of worship in the Ontmoetingskerk. We also noted how this personal character expanded significantly as a result of the congregation's increased diversity. The attention for personal

---

paar van die gehandicapte meisjes met name die de tekst lezen van waar de preek over gaat. Nou, dat vind ik prachtig. Ze kunnen niet zo goed lezen soms, een beetje haperig, maar dat denk ik: doe dat alsjeblieft. Dat is, ja... Het wordt vrij normaal en ik denk dat het goed is."

[3]*Interview with B15, 2018-04-23, D100.*

6.2. Interaction

narratives in church services can be seen as a form of interaction as well. Sometimes, direct interaction takes place in the form of an interview between the pastor and a church member during the service. At other times, personal stories are shared as a part of the sermon. The latter case does not involve direct interaction between residents and non-residents, yet it can be seen as a enhancing the type of interaction we described above as visibility and presence. These personal stories contribute to fuller visibility in the sense that they surpass the superficial level of being together in the same room and noting certain differences in terms of appearance or behavior. The stories offer some insight into the person behind their outward appearance. As such, church members come to realize that they are not interacting with disabilities (or even people with disabilities), but with human beings who have complex and rich biographies. An example of this can be seen in the following excerpt from my fieldnotes. The fieldnotes were written based on observations of a worship service in which the theme of 'protecting life' was discussed, in relation to the ethical issues of abortion and euthanasia. Pastor Smit closed his sermon with the following, which I copied down word for word:

> Evan can sometimes be heard during the service, in the form of a kind of cough when he is short of breath. He does not speak, does not seem to make contact in other ways. He does watch what is going on. And you might say he doesn't have much else to contribute. He cannot sing along. And we cannot know what he does in his thoughts. I always find Evan's story moving. As a young man, [...] he was standing on a scaffold while working in construction. He fell down, on his head, and never recovered. And now we meet him here [...] as a congregation. Next week we will be celebrating the Lord's Supper, and

---

[4] *Interview with B7, 2018-03-07, D84.* Dutch original: "Op die vrouwenavond van twee jaar geleden was er 1 vrouw en het was he (ik weet niet meer hoe ze heet) Truus door de een, en he Truus door de andere. En ik denk: Truus heeft het goed voor elkaar, iedereen kende Truus. En dat waren er geen 5, maar dat waren er wel 10. Die werd lekker gepamperd, die wentelt zich helemaal om in de gelukzaligheid die ze krijgt. Er zullen er ook een heleboel zitten die denken: waarom krijg ik die klop niet op mijn schouders. Ik denk, daar moet je wel erg voor waken."

> he will receive the Lord's blessing. We are not going to start debates about what we find meaningful or meaningless [about his life], but we rather reach out to him and bless him. As a congregation, you open your heart to him in that way. You protect his life. And share that life with Jesus. I find that an incredibly moving event. In the most vulnerable sense, we share this life together, with Jesus, because we are loved by God, and because we, together, bear the image of the Creator. Also in all our vulnerability. And then, in faith, we stand on the side of the protector of life. We do not fall from His hand. Evan does not fall from His hand.[5]

The kind of interaction shown in this example can only exist if the one leading the communal gathering, like the pastor in this case, knows the personal narratives of the people present. Such interaction therefore has to be preceded by individual, pastoral interaction. This seems to be one of the reasons why the identity of the one leading worship services in the Ontmoetingskerk has such an impact. It also means that the leader must not be afraid to share personal stories and search for fitting language to describe experiences of people that are often very different from his own. This is a challenge, as numerous examples from my fieldnotes can prove. At certain times, the experience of people with disabilities was not mentioned where one might have expected it (cf. the example on page 144). In other cases, the experience of disability was automatically equated with suffering. For example, when resident Saakje celebrated her 65th birthday, the guest pastor in his prayer gave thanks for her birthday with the following words:

> We offer our heartfelt thanks together for Saakje Daams, who turned 65 today. That is very special. With her and her family members, we want to thank you for this, for your protecting hand over her life, with all its sadness and sorrow. Be near to her. Will you bless her, also in the evening of her life. Remember all those who surround her, as well as those who receive care together with her and those who give her care. Grant, Lord, that she might

---
[5] *Fieldnotes 2017-11-12, D69.*

6.2. Interaction

find rest and acceptance and peace and comfort with you, the Eternal One.[6]

The prayer's formulation makes it sound like Saakje is a deeply unhappy person and possibly seriously ill, given that she is apparently 'in the evening of her life' at age 65. None of this was actually the case. The example therefore shows how easy it is to frame people's experiences in inadequate ways. Such framing represents a hindrance to meaningful interaction, as it serves to sustain the imaginary boundary between those who are healthy, whole, and happy, and those who have a disability and are therefore broken and suffering. Such framing is not resolved by avoiding to talk about the experience of people with disabilities since, as we have seen, that too does not serve to enhance interaction. Rather, as we saw in the example of pastor Smit and his story about Evan, it seems important first to listen to the actual voice of the person involved, and where possible to actually let people speak for themselves. Moreover, pastor Smit, unlike the guest pastor from the example, employs a fundamentally reciprocal approach when he shares stories like this. Even when he says that Evan 'might not have much else to contribute', his use of the story in his message itself already indicates that the very fact of Evan's presence and participation in the sacrament in his eyes represents a huge contribution, since it opens up new ways for seeing God's protection of and provision for our lives in all their vulnerability.

This reciprocity in communal interaction is undergirded theologically by a specific understanding of *charismata*. Pastor Smit is attentive to the fact that these charismata may take different shapes than one would generally expect. In Reformed circles, for example, the charismata may be noticed most frequently if they are realized in verbal or cognitive gifts. Here the charismata of good speakers are generally recognized and valued highly, for example. However, as we saw on page 124, Pastor Smit also recognized the charisma of roaring with

---

[6]*Fieldnotes 2017-11-12, D69*. Dutch original: "We willen samen hartelijk danken dat Saakje Daams vandaag 65 jaar mocht worden. Dat is heel bijzonder. Met haar en met haar familie willen we samen u daarvoor danken, voor Uw bewarende hand over haar leven met alle verdriet en met alle zorg. Weest u haar nabij. Wilt u haar zegenen, ook in de avond van haar leven. Gedenk ook allen om haar heen, ook hen die met haar verpleegd worden en die haar verzorgen. En geef Here, dat ze rust en overgave en vrede en troost mag vinden bij U, de eeuwige."

laughter, just to mention one. At other times, Smit recognized other such 'unexpected' charismata, like the gift of weeping that another resident brings to the congregation.[7] This is not just a way of speaking, but represents something that both the pastor and other church members truly recognize as a way in which the congregation is growing. Such an eye and active attentiveness for the gifts that every member may have to offer creates a fundamentally reciprocal practice and therefore facilitates interaction.

6.2.2 Individual Interaction

Besides the forms of interaction that take place during communal gatherings, there are also many cases of interaction between residents and non-residents on the individual level. In general, the data show that these kinds of interaction can be much more transformative and powerful than the interaction in larger group settings. The other side to that is that interactions between individuals are much rarer.

"Having a Soft Spot for the Disabled"

One thing that interviewees noted numerous times is that in order to have meaningful communication with people with disabilities, one must have a kind of 'soft spot' for them. This is understood as either a natural inclination or aptitude towards communicating with 'these people', or something that is the result of one's biography, as for those who have a relative with a disability. Interacting with people with disabilities is seen as complex, requiring certain skills as well as a willingness to learn, which need to be present before one can embark on individual interaction. The following example from an interview with church member Jolien may serve to illustrate this point:

> It is quite difficult, because you really have to learn how to deal with people with disabilities. You should actually treat them in a very normal way, treat them as equals, but you also need to interact with them at their own level... And sometimes it is difficult to understand them, and that's something you have to learn. For some people that

---

[7]*Interview with C3, 2018-03-12, D88.*

6.2. Interaction

is very difficult to learn. So it makes me think, like, it's not like you can just offer a crash course or something like that.[8]

There are obviously all kinds of shallow interactions, like greetings or some small talk about the weather before and after worship services. But some interviewees have the impression that more profound interaction requires special skills and is therefore only within reach for a small group of people. In an interview, church member Marja reflected on this:

> I see that there is fortunately a large group of people who have some kind of interaction with [the residents]. But I cannot estimate the percentage of the congregation that really has meaningful contact with them. I think there are many like me, who exchange friendly greetings and say hello now and then, during coffee. But that it doesn't go much further than that. But I really couldn't tell you how many they are... I think there are many like me. And that there is a small group of people who have a lot of contact with them.[9]

Organized Forms of Individual Interaction

Marja's assessment of the situation seems to be in line with the picture emerging from the data. Many people who reported meaningful interaction had this interaction in a more or less organized setting,

---

[8] Interview with B16, 2018-05-03, D103. Dutch original: "...het is ook wel lastig, want je moet ook wel echt leren om met gehandicapten te kunnen omgaan. Je moet eigenlijk heel normaal tegen ze doen, je moet ze behandelen als gelijken, maar je moet wel met ze omgaan op het niveau dat ze hebben... En soms zijn ze ook heel moeilijk verstaanbaar en dat moet je ook leren begrijpen. En dat is voor sommige mensen heel lastig om te kunnen. Dus dan denk ik: ja... Je kan er niet zomaar een stoomcursus voor geven ofzo."

[9] Interview with B1, 2018-02-22, D76. Dutch original: "Ik zie, er is gelukkig een hele groep mensen die in ieder geval met een aantal wel lijntjes heeft. Maar ik kan niet inschatten hoe groot deel van de gemeente nou echt goed contact met ze heeft. Ik denk dat er veel zijn zoals ik die vriendelijk groeten en af en toe hallo zeggen bij de koffie. Maar dat het daar bij blijft. Maar ik kan echt niet inschatten hoeveel dat er zijn.

as a professional or as a volunteer in some capacity. While not all of them spoke of their predisposition as a 'soft spot' for people with disabilities, they did often either have personal biographical reasons for engaging in this interaction or else were given specific responsibilities. Examples include a mother of a child with a disability, who had an active role as an evening hostess in HVV's building, or Frederik, who taught a bible class for people with disabilities, or Henk, who is the elder for HVV, and of course pastor Smit himself.

As we have seen before (cf. 5.4.2), the organized nature of interaction does not make it meaningless, nor does it necessarily remain shallow or unreciprocal. Yet most respondents did not see organized forms of interaction as the ideal. As elder Henk put it, organized interaction runs the risk of feeling like an obligation: "When you really stimulate it - we do stimulate it - but if you go too far in that, people will start to feel uneasy, I think."[10] This perceived uneasiness on the part of church members is one thing, but Michiel, one of the initiators of HVV, had yet another reason for the importance of somehow surpassing the level of organized interaction. In his estimation, many people with disabilities already have a surplus of organized and 'professional' contacts. As such, their social circles often differ quite radically from that of the average person. Michiel drew these social circles on a piece of paper and explained:

> Here's your 'I' and around it are the people you are intimately connected with, your parents (or so I would hope), your girlfriend, your kids. And then around it is the circle of friends. And then there is a circle of acquaintances, and after that you get the circle of professionals. People you pay. [...] My dentist, [for example]. If you look at people who have care needs, they might have this [intimate circle], this circle [of friends] gets really small, and maybe they have a little bit of this [circle of acquaintainces]. But here [in the circle of professionals] there are many people. And they call those people in that circle 'friends'.

Ik denk veel. Zoals ik. En dat er een groepje mensen is die veel contact met ze heeft."

[10] *Interview with C1, 2018-02-21, D75.* Dutch original: "Als je dat heel erg stimuleert, we stimuleren het wel, maar als je dat heel erg doet, dan voelt men zich ongemakkelijk worden denk ik."

6.2. Interaction

> They figure they are here or even there [in the more intimate circles]. But the fact is that once you stop paying them, they are gone. Yet it [intimate social circles] is something you would wish everybody had. And I feel that the church as a community can be very valuable in creating these connections.[11]

As Michiel's example very clearly shows, the ideal is for true friendships and informal forms of interaction to begin in HVV and the Ontmoetingskerk, since exactly these kinds of interactions could be beneficial for the residents as well as rewarding for the others who are involved. At the same time, many respondents revealed they were not sure that such interactions can actually happen if people are not either somehow predisposed towards interaction with people with disabilities, or else have the appropriate professional skills. This seems to be a paradox.

Falsifying the 'Soft Spot Myth'

Notwithstanding the paradox described above, individual meaningful interactions between residents and non-residents *do* take place in HVV, even when the non-resident is not particularly disposed towards interaction with a person with a disability and does not have any professional skills. This can be illustrated by the story of church member Sam.[12]

Sam ten Hove is a 37-year old father, with a complicated history with the church. In the past he experienced church as a burden and

---

[11] *Interview with E2, 2018-04-18, D97*. Dutch original: "Je hebt je ik en daar omheen zitten de intimi, de intieme mensen, dat zijn je ouders, tenminste als het goed is, dat is je vriendin, je kinderen. Dan krijg je daar omheen een cirkel van vrienden. Dan krijg je daar omheen een cirkel van kennissen en dan krijg je hier een beetje de professionals. En deze huur je in. […] Mijn tandarts. Als je kijkt naar mensen met zorg, een zorgbehoefte, die hebben van dit nog wel, dit wordt heel klein, misschien hebben ze dit nog een beetje en hier zitten heel veel mensen. En die mensen hier, die noemen zij vriend. Zij noemen dat die hier zit, of misschien zelfs wel hier. Maar feitelijk: als je stopt met betalen dan zijn ze weg. Maar je gunt dit wel iedereen. En ik denk ook dat daarom de kerk als gemeenschap heel waardevol kan zijn door die verbindingen te leggen."

[12] The story is based on the interview with Sam and the quotations are taken from it: *Interview with B13, 2018-04-03, D93*.

was for a while "on the outskirts of the church". At the outset, Sam was not exactly enthusiastic about the plans for HVV, and certainly had no plans to get involved with the residents. However, at some point he came into contact with one of them, having been asked multiple times by one of the coordinators to make music with a resident. In a moment of weakness he said yes: "I felt like I got suckered into it. I was too self-involved. But well... So I did it." The interaction started off as a duty, but it did not end that way: "We became friends. And well, man... You come over for dinner sometime, that's how you start to bond and create a friendship." As a result, Sam developed a new outlook on people with disabilities:

> Maybe people with disabilities, as they are called on paper, lack one 'disability' that somebody without disabilities does have... They are so pure. When I look at the people here [residents], they are like children... So pure, so authentic, you won't find that in a world or society or environment without people with a 'disability', between brackets, for the record.

Sam said he learned a lot from people with disabilities, precisely at the point he found most important about being church: that the church should be a safe space of connection and authenticity. He therefore became an advocate for the participation of people with disabilities in church. He often visits the residential groups and tries to facilitate resident participation, for example in making music during worship services. Sam stated that people should almost be "required" to be "volunteers", although he realizes that there is a contradiction in these terms.

Sam's story illustrates a meaningful kind of interaction that did not start from some intrinsic motivation or 'soft spot'. Rather, the starting point was a strong aversion. A remarkable element in this story is that it started with *doing* something, and something that Sam was very good at, namely making music. He did not need to 'leave his comfort zone' to do this, even though the interaction with his new friend was challenging at first. Making music together created a safe space where this encounter could take place.

6.2.3 Experienced Benefits of Interaction

Respondents mentioned a number of ways in which they found interaction between residents and non-residents to be beneficial. These benefits were sometimes experienced by the respondents themselves. In other cases, they were formulated more like a desire than an actual experience. The benefits related to personal growth in spirituality and other areas of life, but were not limited to the individual level. Respondents saw how these interactions also had a positive effect on the congregation as a whole. An illustration of this can be found in the example of Sam discussed above.

Interaction Starts a Process

The data suggest that interaction between people 'with and without disabilities' starts a process that produces various kinds of perceived benefits at various stages of the process. The process starts with the actual interaction that is often framed as an *encounter*. This first step of the process is already experienced as beneficial, contributing to a feeling of being known and seen.

The interaction also produces a second step in the process, which is that of awareness. We saw examples of this stage in section 6.2.1. Abstract societal problems like policies concerning 'the disabled' become much more prominent in the minds of people as issues about a person they know. A very interesting example is found in an interview I had with Niels, a young church member.[13] When asked to reflect on the place of people with disabilities in society, he responded that an inclusive society with people with disabilities is "just not very practical... It's just that they are mentally handicapped. They are just like babies. It might sound harsh, but that is how it is."[14] But at the same time, Niels noted that "there are people who can't do anything at all, and then there are the people of HVV [...] For example those guys in our church, they understand me very well, and I can chat with them. [...] They can take care of themselves.""[15] This example is interest-

---

[13] *Interview with B5, 2018-02-28, D82.*

[14] Dutch original "Het is gewoon niet heel erg praktisch... Het is gewoon zo, ze zijn verstandelijk gehandicapt. Het zijn eigenlijk gewoon baby's. Het is gewoon hard gezegd, het is gewoon zo."

[15] Dutch original: "je hebt mensen die echt niks kunnen. En je hebt mensen van

ing, because the residents of HVV represent a rather wide spectrum of disabilities. Niels apparently had an image of people with disabilities that does not really match reality. It is people like 'those guys in our church' that we talk about when we discuss disability and disability policy. Niels's interaction with the residents of HVV, albeit limited, therefore changed his perspective on at least a part of 'the disabled'. It turned this abstract group into a concrete and personal reality.

Awareness may in turn lead to understanding. Some residents, for example, indicated that they would appreciate understanding of the often very practical difficulties they face in their participation in congregational life. This might be the time of day when activities are held, or the way worship services are conducted. We have seen examples of both in some of the things mentioned by residents like Simone and Tjalling. In their cases, solutions are often not very difficult to come by, although they do require a sense of understanding fed by an awareness of the issues at hand, which can only grow if there is interaction with the persons involved. Reflecting on this dynamic, church member Marja spoke of the importance of knowing people's stories:

> Yes, you need to invest a lot in campaigns and really show that they are just normal people who face normal challenges and who, notwithstanding their impairments, do their utmost to participate. This is what our society demands from them, so it really makes sense that it doesn't work out... So just to create more awareness with everybody. [...] Just share their stories. Make them visible. Because people on the streets only see a person acting

---

Hart van Vathorst... [...] Bijvoorbeeld zoals die jongens bij ons in de kerk, die verstaan mij heel goed, kan ik zeker een gesprekje mee hebben."

[16] *Interview with B1, 2018-02-22, D76*. Dutch original: "Ja, dan moet je heel veel gaan investeren in, ehm, denk ik wel campagnes en heel veel in beeld brengen van: dit zijn ook gewone mensen die tegen hele gewone dingen aanlopen en die met hun beperkingen hun uiterste best doen om mee te draaien en dit vraag je als maatschappij van ze en het is heel logisch dat dat niet kan ofzo. Dus dat je veel meer bewustwording gaat creëren bij iedereen. [...] Laat maar verhalen horen. Laat ze maar zien. Wat mensen op straat alleen maar zien is iemand die gek doet. En daar worden zo snel conclusies uit getrokken zonder dat ze daar het verhaal achter weten of weten waar iemand mee zit... [...] Dus dan zou je echt veel meer moeten investeren in laten zien wat voor mensen dat zijn en hoe dat dan gaat en ik denk dat er dan veel meer begrip zou ontstaan."

6.2. Interaction

> madly. And they draw their conclusions based on that, without knowing the story behind it or the problem they face … [...] So you would really have to invest in showing what kind of people they are and how this works. I think that would lead to a lot more understanding.[16]

As understanding grows, it can also produce an environment where there is acceptance of differences, where people feel safe to 'be themselves'. Church member Floris understood acceptance as an important basis for interaction:

> The question is: How do you look at these people? And how do they accept you? I think they just accept you, or me. Just as I am. And I want to accept them as they are. And that there are differences… Well, everyone differs from me. To me that doesn't make a difference.[17]

Interestingly, Floris did not start with the imperative of accepting others, but with the experience of being accepted by others, in this case the residents he meets in HVV. This experienced acceptance gives him room to be himself, realizing that everybody is fundamentally *different* from everyone else. Hvv is experienced by many respondents as a place where such acceptance of otherness is present. Resident Simone, for example, feels this acceptance of otherness. In places where she had lived before, she had not been accepted, because some of the things she did were considered childish by others there. These others even became abusive to her, as Simone recalled with some anxiety. But in HVV, she feels the freedom to be herself, which makes her very happy. She also recognized this in her fellow residents who, in her words, are "just themselves".[18] Taken out of their original context, these examples can make it seem as if acceptance is the end of the matter. But is not, as a number of other examples show. Acceptance is not always easy, especially if it is about accepting one's own limitations. At the end of a long and generally cheerful interview with one

---

[17] *Interview with B14, 2018-04-11, D94.* Dutch original: "Het is: hoe sta je zelf tegenover die mensen? En hoe accepteren die mensen jou? Ik denk dat die mensen jou, mij gewoon accepteren. Als degene die ik ben. En ik wil ze accepteren zoals ze zijn. En dat dat anders is… goed, ieder is anders dan ik zelf. Voor mij is dat geen verschil."

[18] *Interview with A5, 2018-06-28, D106.*

of the elderly residents of HVV, this resident reflected on how hard it is to accept the limitations that come with old age. He had recently sold his bicycle, for example, which meant diminished mobility.[19] Another example in which we can see that acceptance of certain limitations remains a struggle, notwithstanding HVV's character as a place of acceptance, can be found in the interview with resident Martin. Martin is a young man who is very creative and a skilled woodworker. Yet he has limited energy and now and then has to deal with very frightening experiences:

> Yes, I have already had moments where I just kind of spun out of control today... And then you see the space where you are and you see your own room as a kind of prison, that's how you see it. And you see things that aren't there at all, it's very scary. [...] And you just spin out of control, you can't control yourself. No, they are very frightening moments, I wouldn't wish them on anyone. [...] Even during dinner. We were sitting at the table with four or five people, well, I just had two or three moments where I spun out of control and really looked at my fellow diners, how do you say that, my housemates, as if they were scary people. So that is very tough. It's not easy to accept.[20]

Healing and Learning

Above we described the experienced benefits of interaction in HVV as a process. Given what people say about this process, it would seem that there are two important keywords to characterize the direction in

---

[19] *Interview with A1, 2018-05-01, D101.*

[20] *Interview with A2, 2018-05-31, D103.* Dutch original: "Ja, ik heb al veel momenten gehad dat ik gewoon helemaal wegdraaide vandaag... En dan zie je de ruimte waar je in zit en je ziet je eigen kamer dat is gewoon een soort van gevangenis, zo zie je het aan. En je ziet dingen die er helemaal niet zijn en dat is heel eng. [...] En je draait helemaal weg, je hebt jezelf niet onder controle. Nee, dat zijn hele angstige en rare momenten, dat wens ik niemand toe. [...] Zelfs met het eten. Toen zaten we met zijn vieren of vijfen, ja en daar heb ik gewoon twee of drie momentjes gehad dat ik echt helemaal wegdraaide en dan zie je je mede-eters, hoe heet dat, je huisgenoten ook als enge mensen. Dus dat is heel moeilijk. Dat kan ik niet makkelijk accepteren."

6.2. Interaction

which this process leads: first, it is understood as a process of *healing*; and, second, as a process of *learning*.

The concept of *healing* hardly ever surfaced in the sense of people expecting miraculous healing of disabilities (cf. 4.4.3). Yet healing in the sense of 'becoming whole', living well within the confinements of one's situation and health, was often mentioned in some way as a benefit of HVV. This is not only true for residents, like Simone who described her move to HVV as a move from hell to heaven (see 4.4.2). It is also true for church members, like Sam who felt that the congregation has become more 'complete' with the addition of new HVV-members (see page 191). Aspects that were considered to be healing include a sense of belonging, security, feeling at home, being known, being there for one another, and mutual support or care. The difficulties healed by these aspects included things like insecurity, loneliness, and a lack of social connectedness. Notably, these things have just as much, if not more, to do with HVV's micro context and its lack of connectedness, for example, than it does with the specific issues that HVV residents face. Down syndrome, autism, or dementia are not on the list of hardships that need healing, while loneliness is. This is not to downplay the often challenging reality of living with a disability, but just to highlight the light in which healing is understood in the data.

A second word that people used to describe the direction of HVV is *learning*. This learning process is reciprocal. Respondents mentioned that they learned a lot from interaction between people 'with and without disabilities', for example regarding trust, rest, genuineness, openness and space for otherness, and equality. Areas of learning also included aspects that relate directly to faith, such as unity, peace, discovering Christ and following him (discipleship), receptivity, cutting to the core of things and getting below the surface of outward appearance, and acknowledging one's own limitations. As with healing, this learning process is not limited to 'learning about disability'. It is learning about life, about faith, in a togetherness that includes people with disabilities. Through the involvement of people with disabilities, certain aspects of life and faith are highlighted that might otherwise remain underexposed.

We can conclude, then, that although some respondents would frame HVV above all as a project that is good for people with disabilities, the benefits really apply to the entire congregation and the wider surrounding community. As we noted above, the process is still ongoing, and the benefits described here are often a mix of reality and ideal. Yet the data clearly reveal that there are developments and that many people have already been impacted by these developments in significant ways, so that the Ontmoetingskerk is indeed different from the way it was before it embarked on participation in HVV.

6.2.4 Summary of Interaction

In this section, we explored the interactions that started to take place between people 'with and without disabilities' in HVV. Exploring these interactions is an important way of seeing how HVV's inclusive vision is being realized. We have seen that interaction for a sizeable group of the Ontmoetingskerk's members is experienced primarily in and around communal gatherings, such as church services. Nonetheless, this limited interaction has proved to have an impact in terms of visibility and presence, making it impossible to think of 'disability' as an abstract and distant reality. This communal interaction is supported by the leadership as an indispensable element. An important theological impetus for supporting interaction is the idea that each member of the body has gifts, or *charismata*, to contribute. We also looked at more individual kinds of interaction. We saw that it is not necessary to 'have a soft spot' for people with disabilities in order to experience meaningful interactions, nor is professional know-how in many instances a prerequisite. Nonetheless, as with communal interaction, it is important that there be leaders who support the interaction and challenge people to go outside their comfort zone. We also explored the benefits of these different kinds of interaction, and saw that they can best be explained as a process with various steps: from interaction in which people feel known and seen; to awareness in which issues become concrete and urgent; to understanding in which people also start to learn about the reasons for issues that others face and to look for possible solutions; to an atmosphere of acceptance in which there is room to be oneself and also to wrestle with one's own limitations that are hard to accept. From the data, it appears that this process can be framed as a process of healing, or as a process of learning *for all who are involved.*

6.3 Commitment

In the previous section, we explored interaction between people 'with and without disabilities' in HVV and the Ontmoetingskerk. This interaction is one of the main stated aims of HVV's vision as discussed above (see 4.4). In the current section we will look more closely at how and why people get involved in HVV (i.e. their commitment).

6.3.1 Different Levels of Commitment

This subsection will survey the kinds and levels of commitment people experience for HVV. The research here is not quantitative in nature, so that we cannot provide precise numbers and statistics for illustrating specific developments. Our focus is much more on the content of what people said with respect to their commitment. I distinguish between formal and informal commitment given the clear difference between these two kinds of community involvement. One can be a member and perform certain formal roles within the community. At the same time, one relates to this community in a specific way. One may feel emotionally or socially connected to what is going on in the community, or else remain a distant observer in spite of one's formal status as a 'member' or even a 'small group leader' or 'volunteer'. Both kinds of commitment are, to my mind, relevant to explore.

There are a number of ways in which commitment can be formalized. Such formal types of commitment can be measured quite easily, for instance by looking at the number of people involved in volunteer roles. We will briefly examine these formal kinds of commitment, before moving on to more informal kinds. The latter require conversations with people who are involved so as to understand how they relate to HVV apart from any formal role they might have in the project. After this overview of different kinds of commitment, we will detail a number of elements described by respondents as motivations for their involvement.

6.3.2 Formal Commitment

The most evident way in which people commit to HVV is by being or becoming a member of the Ontmoetingskerk. As we explained before (see 4.3.2), many people no longer simply join the local church of their denomination when they move to a new place. This applies to many respondents as well. When people described what stood out most about the Ontmoetingskerk, they often mentioned its involvement in HVV - to such an extent, in fact, that for some the Ontmoetingskerk has virtually become 'HVV's church'. This implies that when people choose to become members of the Ontmoetingskerk, they also choose to commit to HVV, albeit in different degrees. Given the fact that the Ontmoetingskerk is still a growing congregation in spite of the declining membership facing many churches in the Netherlands and the presence of another large and popular Protestant church in the direct vicinity (Kruispunt, cf. 4.3.1), one could say that people are indeed drawn to HVV and are willing to be a part of it. Church member Marja described her family's decision to join the Ontmoetingskerk on moving to Vathorst from a big city as follows:

> To be honest, we looked around [for other churches] for about a year here, because we really had to get used to 'middle-class Amersfoort', so we looked at other congregations and asked ourselves what a fitting place for us might be. And in the end we did pick the RCL. Well, also because of the plans for HVV. At that time, things were about to start. So that attracted us.[21]

Other formal indicators for HVV commitment leave a mixed picture. There seem to be high levels of commitment amongst the small group who have volunteering roles or hold leading positions in shaping the interaction between HVV and the congregation. Those in leading positions, like 'HVV-elder' Henk, sometimes regret that a large part of the congregation is not as heavily involved with HVV as one might wish.

> At some point, we tried to get the congregation, including the residents, together for an evening on the theme of inclusion. And as it turned out, after we had done a

---

[21] *Interview with B1, 2018-02-22, D76.* Dutch original: "En toen hebben we eerlijkheidshalve wel eerst een jaartje hier een beetje rondgekeken want we moesten een beetje wennen aan burgerlijk Amersfoort-Vathorst dus we hebben wel een beetje bij andere gemeentes ook gekeken van: wat past ons nou eigenlijk goed. En uiteindelijk toch voor de GKV dan gekozen. Ja, ook wel vanwege dat plan Hart van Vathorst. Dat ging toen eigenlijk bijna beginnen. Dus dat sprak ons wel aan."

6.3. Commitment

lot of advertising for this evening, there were 8 HVV residents and 8 other people from the congregation. And those were actually the people that didn't really need it anymore. We had a wonderful evening together, led by Thijs Tromp.[22] It really was what one might call 'inclusion'. But it was inclusion among 16 people, instead of 835, 900 church members and residents. To me, that was a disappointing sign indicating that we hadn't arrived yet.[23]

As we noted in section 4.6, Henk's assessment of the situation seems justifiable. It is indeed true that there is a relatively small group of church members who are actively and recognizably involved with HVV in some formal capacity. However, whether that should really be considered disappointing is another matter. First, Henk himself already noted that the picture does seem to be changing as the number of people actively involved is growing. The situation is also about sharing responsibilities, as Henk acknowledged. This was something he at first found quite difficult. The story we heard from Frederik, about how there was greater supply than demand when volunteers were needed to teach a bible class for residents, serves as an example of this. Secondly, as we saw in section 6.2.1, the fact that people are not involved with HVV in formal roles or do not have interactions with residents on an individual level does not mean that they are not impacted by HVV. Thirdly, it is also possible to view the differences in formal commitment with a level of understanding and realism, as pastor Joost Smit indeed does:

> I realize that my own position is a really privileged one:

---

[22]Thijs Tromp is a Dutch professor of diaconate and director of a Christian organization of care providers. He was also involved in the initial reading group in HVV that studied Hauerwas and Vanier, *Living Gently in a Violent World*.

[23]*Interview with C1, 2018-02-21, C1*. Dutch original: "Op een gegeven moment hebben wij geprobeerd om de gemeente met de bewoners samen een avond te laten samenkomen rondom het thema inclusie. En toen bleek dat er, na heel veel reclame gemaakt te hebben, 8 bewoners van Hart van Vathorst waren, en 8 mensen uit de gemeente. En dat waren ook de mensen die eigenlijk dat helemaal niet meer nodig hadden. En toen hebben we onder leiding van Thijs Tromp een hele mooie avond gehad. Dat was echt dat je zegt: dat is inclusie, maar dat was inclusie tussen 16 in plaats van 835, 900 kerkleden en bewoners. En dat was voor mij een teleurstellend teken dat ik denk van we zijn er nog lang niet."

I can just work here [in HVV] all day and just go and sit in the restaurant and talk to people. Some people do indeed take inspiration from that and have started to do the same. But if you spend your weeks working in Amsterdam and need your weekends just to rest... Well, I don't want to force people, like: everyone should be like Joost and spend their time in the restaurant.[24]

6.3.3 Informal Commitment

We turn from formal, measurable kinds of commitment to another, much more fluid kind of commitment which we have called informal commitment. People have the opportunity to be involved in HVV in very different ways, even if their 'formal' status of commitment is the same. This emerges from the following two reflections on HVV from two church members who are not formally involved with HVV in any other capacity than that of 'church members':

> Niels: Of course, my Christian perception of HVV is that what is happening there is really good. But anyhow...[25]

> Floris: And when you're in church, too, if you notice how Joost Smit, our pastor, how he deals with that, it's just fantastic. Because he addresses them by name. And sometimes they make noises and he responds. Those are beautiful things. I mean, that people with disabilities are given a fitting place in society, and particularly in church, I really find that wonderful.[26]

---

[24] *Interview with C3, 2018-03-12, D88.* Dutch original: "Ik besef ook wel dat mijn plek heel bevoorrecht is: ik kan hier de hele dag werken en ik zit gewoon een beetje in het restaurant te shinen en ik kan mensen aanspreken. Er zijn wel mensen die door dat voorbeeld geinspireerd zijn en die dat ook wel gaan doen. Maar als je de hele week zit te werken in Amsterdam en in het weekend gewoon ligt bij te komen op de bank... Ja, ik heb ook niet die heilige zweep van: we zullen en moeten nu allemaal net zoals Joost door dat restaurant lopen."

[25] *Interview with B5, 2018-02-28, D82.* Dutch original: "Mijn christelijke kijk is natuurlijk dat van Hart van Vathorst, dat is natuurlijk echt heel goed wat daar gebeurt. Maar ja."

[26] *Interview with B14, 2018-04-11, D94.* Dutch original: "En als je dus in de kerk zit ook, hoe Joost Smit, de dominee, hoe hij daarmee omgaat, dat is fantastisch. Want hij spreekt ze ook bij name aan. En ze maken geluiden en hij reageert daarop. Dat zijn

6.3. Commitment

Niels and Floris both 'agree' with what is going on in HVV, and are both appreciative in a way. But what also emerges from these short excerpts, and much more so from the entire interview transcripts, is that their appreciation of and commitment to HVV plays out on two very different levels. For Niels, HVV is a good idea according to his understanding of the Christian faith. His appreciation has a kind of normative quality; apart from his personal taste, this is how he believes things should be done. Floris, on the contrary, was deeply touched by some of the things he experienced in HVV. His appreciation takes its point of departure more in an emotional experience than a normative conviction. Niels and Floris are in very different phases of their lives, which might go some way in explaining some of the differences in their responses. But here they also represent two different ways of committing to HVV. Some people feel that they are more or less 'obliged' to say that HVV is a worthwhile addition to the life of their congregation. Others, however, experience the value of this addition personally and emotionally, and share their enthusiasm.

Experiences of emotions and enthusiasm surface remarkably frequently in our data. The unique selling point of Reformed churches is typically not the emotional quality of their church services. Yet during HVV's official opening worship service, for example, I noticed many people with tears in their eyes at different moments of the service.[27] The residents of HVV on average show more emotional responses during the services than other church members do. It seems as though they invite others in the congregation to do the same. This is what pastor Smit meant when he identified roaring with laughter and weeping as gifts (see 6.2.1). This increased space for emotions in congregational life also enables people to overcome thinking about HVV in purely cognitive or normative terms. For some respondents, this development has clearly changed their reflection on HVV. One example came from Floris, but also much earlier (p. 158) we already saw how Ada's recollection of an emotional moment during a worship service, for example, still caused tears during an interview much later. The space created for emotion thus enables people to commit themselves to HVV on an emotional level as well. The fact that the Ontmoetingskerk includes

---

hele mooie dingen. Ik bedoel, dat gehandicapte mensen in de samenleving en met name ook in de kerk op een gegeven moment een plek krijgen, dat vind ik heel fijn."

[27] *Fieldnotes 2016-04-17, D13.*

many professionals (cf. 4.5.2) explains why this is not the case for all respondents. For it is also a community with a large percentage of 'detached observers' who reflect on what is going on from a distance, and offer their feedback to those who are involved rather than becoming involved in the activities themselves. What remains an interesting question is whether this should be challenged, and if so, how this could be done.

As we have shown, levels of informal commitment vary, and are at one time guided more by emotional experiences and other times they are more rational and normative in nature. Some respondents really opened themselves up and immersed themselves, while others kept a greater distance. But for the vast majority, HVV has started a new way of reflection on important questions like unity and diversity, (dis)ability, the nature of the church, and the nature of faith. Elder Henk expressed it in the following way, although his words could also have been spoken by many other respondents: "We are all such unique human beings. It is truly unimaginable. But I only learned to speak of that since the launch of Hart van Vathorst. Before that, I didn't really think about it in that way."[28] Even if their commitment to HVV took no formal shape, most respondents were still influenced by HVV and started to reflect on important but previously neglected questions.

6.3.4 Motivations

Behind people's willingness to commit to HVV lies a certain motivation. Another research project, focusing more on the place that HVV takes up in the Vathorst neighborhood and applying more quantitative research methods, noted how an important question relating to HVV would be to investigate how people's involvement with HVV could be a *rewarding* experience for them. One outcome from the questionnaires was that people indicated they would primarily invest time in activities that they found rewarding. This is in line with broader societal developments, in which people act less upon what they feel *obligated*

---

[28] *Interview with C1, 2018-02-21, D75.* Dutch original: "We zijn allemaal zulke unieke mensen. Echt onvoorstelbaar. Maar ik heb wel geleerd om er zo over te praten sinds Hart van Vathorst hoor. Daarvoor dacht ik er eigenlijk niet op die manier over na."

6.3. Commitment

to do and more on what they consider rewarding.[29] This makes it important to explore what motivates people to become involved with HVV. Pastor Smit, for example, noted the importance of this when he jokingly wrote in a column that "the battle for the volunteer" will be the most important battle of our time.[30] People's commitment is not self-evident, especially on the long term. In the present section, we will describe some of the motivations unearthed by the data. In chapter 7, we will return to the question how these motivations can be employed and strengthened in projects like HVV.

A large part of people's motivation to commit to activities in HVV has already been discussed in section 6.2.3, where we looked at the benefits people experience when they participate in the interaction between residents and non-residents. These benefits were interpreted as a process of growth towards learning and healing. When people recognize growth, learning, and healing, it of course represents a major motivation for further involvement.

Another aspect of motivation is related to HVV's religious side. People sometimes experience what is going on as an act of God, in which they want to participate. There is little in the data suggesting that people experience participation in HVV as an obligation or commandment given them by God. But when they experience that God is somehow present and active in HVV, they too are inspired to commit. Quite frequently, the language respondents used gave proof of this. For example, respondents saw HVV as a reason of thanksgiving to God, or as a miracle or gift from him. Frederik, a church member and bible class instructor, thus described the realization of HVV in the face of many hardships as a true miracle:

> I would say: There have been people in the congregation who, well, have really given it their best. And sometimes, they were desperate. They lost sleep over it, I think. It was really complicated, extremely complex. New setbacks all the time, and so on. So it took loads of energy. But nonetheless, there were people who kept pushing forward. There were moments when they said it just wasn't going to work out... [...] And now it's a reality! That is

---

[29] Slenderbroek-Meints and Jager-Vreugdenhil, *Nulmeting Viaa*.
[30] *Column by Joost Smit, 2016-09-14, D25.*

truly a miracle, you know. A true miracle, yes.³¹

Frederik's description of the realization of HVV as a miracle is more than just a way of speaking. In other places in the data, one can similarly see certain respondents choosing faith language to describe the process that HVV went through.³² Such framing in language calling for attention to God's presence and activity acknowledges this presence and activity and turns it into a motivation for committing to the community.

A final aspect of motivation that is frequently mentioned in the data is the wide recognition of HVV as a meaningful project. This causes a sense of 'pride' about belonging to this project, as was true for resident Tjalling, who put up a very large picture of himself, some other residents, and pastor Smit in his apartment. This same picture has been used by Sprank as the cover on a magazine they publish. According to Tjalling, the picture was spread "all over Europe!"³³ Hvv is often visited by groups of interested people (e.g. politicians, government workers, people from other churches) who look to it as an example to emulate (see 4.3.3). These visits contribute to the recognition and pride of hvv, as do a number of awards which HVV has won, including a national 'social real estate award' and a social involvement award from a bank.³⁴ Another factor giving proof of HVV's recognition is the amount of media attention the project has received. There has been attention for HVV not only in Christian magazines and

---

³¹*Interview with B6, 2018-03-02, D83*. Dutch original: "Ik moet zeggen: er zijn mensen geweest in de gemeente die daar, nou, die zich daar helemaal voor ingezet hebben. En die waren soms ook ten einde raad, die sliepen er denk ik niet meer van. Het was echt heel ingewikkeld, uitermate ingewikkeld. Iedere keer weer tegenslagen enzo. Dus het heeft heel veel energie gekost. Maar er waren mensen die toch steeds doorgegaan. Er zijn echt momenten geweest dat ze zeiden: het wordt 'm niet. [...] En nu is het er toch! Dat is echt een wonder hoor. Dat is echt een wonder, ja."

³²E.g. how Floris speaks about the place of HVV residents in the congregation: "Those people have been put there by God as they are" (*Interview with B14, 2018-04-11, D94*), or how Henk speaks about about the origin of the contagious faith and discipleship of the some residents: "...it does not come from themselves. Regardless of the brokenness they live in, it comes from the Spirit of God."(*Interview with C1, 2018-02-21, D75*) .

³³*Interview with A6, 2018-07-23, D111*.

³⁴*Online post, 2018-04-11, D95* and *Blog about HVV Winning an Award*.

6.3. Commitment

newspapers, but also in a large secular newspaper[35] and on national televion.[36] All of this attention and recognition strengthens the feeling that something special is going on in HVV and that people want to be a part of it. The amount of attention HVV, with its values of community, sharing vulnerability, and appreciation for religion, is attracting is interesting. This in turn helps people involved with HVV to look upon the project with appreciation, as can be seen in the following excerpt from a radio interview with a young member of the Ontmoetingskerk broadcasted on national Christian radio:

> Interviewer: So discipleship is actually not all that hard in this, um, town?
>
> Joanna: It isn't, actually.
>
> Interviewer: It is just all around you.
>
> Joanna: Yes.
>
> Interviewer: And it seems as if almost everyone is participating, doesn't it?
>
> Joanna: Yes, there are a lot of people who make some sort of contribution here in this house.
>
> Interviewer: I think this is very special, but do you guys yourselves even still see how special it is?
>
> Joanna: Um, yes, I think you get used to it after a while. But the concept is very nice, of course, to be together with so many different people.
>
> Interviewer: Shouldn't it always be like that?
>
> Joanna: Yes, actually it should be.[37]

Something that people might have gotten used to is now revalued as something really special when they look at it from an 'outsider's per-

---

[35] The Algemeen Dagblad called HVV a "utopian mini-society": Maassen, "Hart van Vathorst".

[36] E.g. *1 Vandaag 2017-04-14, Nieuwsuur, 2018-12-19*.

[37] *Radio show Zin, zout en zegen, 2017-06-18, D54* Dutch original: "Interviewer: "Dus discipel-zijn is eigenlijk helemaal niet zo moeilijk in dit, eh, dorp." Joanna: "Nee, eigenlijk niet." Interviewer: "Het is allemaal om je heen." Joanna: "ja" Interviewer: "En iedereen doet het volgens mij, of niet?" Joanna: "Ja, er zijn heel veel mensen die

spective'. It must be noted that HVV has invested a lot in communicating its story, not only to those *within* the community, but also to people outside. These examples suggest that this outward communication also serves to reinforce the motivation of people 'inside'.

6.3.5 Summary of Commitment

In this section, we have explored how and why people commit to HVV. We saw two types of commitment: formalized commitment, as in defined roles, and informal commitments, as in the emotional commitment people experience towards the project and its mission. With respect to formal commitment, we have seen that both the modern context in which the choice of a church is a deliberate act and the Ontmoetingskerk's involvement with HVV is one of its main characteristics make church membership in itself already a form of formal commitment. More intensive formal commitment in the shape of volunteer work, for example, is restricted to a smaller group of people within the congregation. As our exploration of informal commitments shows, this does not mean that this small group is alone in being affected by HVV. In fact, all respondents in some way committed to HVV as something they considered or were supposed to consider important. People responded remarkably often in quite emotional ways when they were reflecting on HVV. Many respondents were therefore somehow committed to HVV on an emotional level. Important motivations for their commitment included the benefits they experienced in terms of spiritual and personal growth. People were also motivated by the religious dimension of HVV. In narrating HVV's story, they often used faith language, demanding attention for God's presence and activity in the reality of HVV. Lastly, the wide recognition garnered by HVV as a special and laudable initiative also proved to be a motivating factor.

---

hier in het huis wat doen." Interviewer: "Ik vind het wel heel bijzonder, zien jullie zelf nog wel hoe bijzonder dat is?" Joanna: "Ehm, ja, ik denk dat het op een gegeven moment ook wel went. Maar het concept hier is natuurlijk heel mooi, dat je met zoveel verschillende mensen bij elkaar bent." Interviewer: "Zo zou het eigenlijk altijd moeten zijn..." Joanna: "Ja eigenlijk wel.""

6.4 Resistance

6.4.1 Forms of Resistance

After this overview of how and why people commit to HVV, we will now focus on the opposite side, exploring why people do not get deeper involved or do not get involved at all. This resistance consists of many elements, such as frustration, disappointment, irritation, or skepticism. Elements like these prevent people from full participation in HVV. They voiced these elements in interviews in a number of different ways, whether as *concerns*, or *discontentment*, or outright *criticism*.

One *concern* that was sometimes expressed is that the attention garnered by HVV is getting in the way of other things people find important. The aspect most frequently mentioned in this respect was the attention for youth in the Ontmoetingskerk. Another area of concern was whether the limited resources were actually sufficient for the pastoral responsibilities.

Expressions of *discontent* sometimes related to very practical matters, such as the architecture or acoustics of the building. Dissatisfaction sometimes also related to more 'spiritual' matters, as when people alleged that the preaching was anthropocentric or claimed that the Encounter Group meetings were deficient in spirituality.

The data yielded much less outright *criticism* than concerns or discontentment. This might be because people typically do not use interviews to communicate their criticisms in outspoken fashion, but rather use words that take the form of discontentment or concern. One example of outright criticism can, however, be found in the responses of some people to the changes in the Lord's Supper celebrations in Vathorst (cf. 146 ff.). They voiced these criticisms in official letters to the church council (which, I should note, were not available to me to read).

Resistance to full participation in HVV seems to play out on at least three different levels. First, there are factors of resistance that have to do with general processes of change. Secondly, there are factors that are related to the specific cooperation of HVV's partners and related practical issues. Thirdly, there are also factors that have to do with people's theological or other conceptions of disability and their un-

6.4.2 Changes and Communication

A first level of resistance concerns the way people deal with changes in general. Respondents in leading positions and general respondents alike often mentioned that change takes time. They indicated that they or others need time to get accustomed to the new situation and to figure out the right way of doing things. However, this can cause resistance when people feel they are not being taken along in this process or experience a lack of clarity. Despite the efforts taken to inform people, many in church still felt they did not really know enough about the plans for HVV. This in itself already creates some resistance, because people are not really prepared to get involved. It also produced varying expectations. Many interviewees and other church members whom I encountered primarily considered HVV as a project separate from the church. I found this reflected during a number of meetings for small group leaders which I attended, for example.[38] Consequently, HVV was often understood as a burden drawing on the congregation's already limited resources. Originally, the congregation had just wanted to build a church building for itself, meaning that when HVV came into view, some still looked at it as a way to achieve that original goal. Of course, they were aware that the project would have impact on their life as a congregation, but according to church member Hannah, many people became quite hesitant once they learned that it entailed more than just 'sharing their roof':

> I was surprised when we had the first congregational meeting about this project and there was a lot of resistance. It really surprised me. Especially among young people. Resistance like: that means we'll have to do tons of volunteer work. And what about pastoral care...?[39]

---

[38] *Fieldnotes 2017-05-22, D52; 2017-09-18, D63.*

[39] *Interview with B3, 2018-02-27, D80.* Dutch original: "Ik was verbaasd toen de eerste gemeentevergadering was over dit project [...] dat er heel veel weerstand was. Dat verbaasde mij ontzettend. Bij de jonge mensen. Weerstand van: dan moeten we allemaal vrijwilligerswerk doen. En de pastorale zorg..."

6.4. Resistance

This conception of HVV as a *burden* emerges from later interviews as well. The origin of this conception seems to lie in the lack of clarity in the expectations at the outset, when HVV was imagined as a project apart from the Ontmoetingskerk. When the project proved to have considerable impact on congregational life, some respondents experienced and still experience this impact primarily as a burden, rather than an asset. This also implies that these respondents have not had any experiences over the course of the project to make them change their mind. Church member Jolanda put it as follows:

> For the pastor, it is quite a challenge. Many people with dementia, and all those handicapped people, not to mention all the autists... I mean: it is a very diverse home, right. It is very special, of course, but it is also... There is a big responsibility, for the congregation as well.[40]

Therefore, even though the vision (cf. 4.4) portrayed HVV as something profitable to the congregation, which was also communicated to the members during the process of preparation, not everybody seems to have understood it that way. While this perception was sometimes related to a degree of ignorance as to what HVV exactly was to be, it also means that their experience with HVV as a reality has still not yet changed their estimation.

The absence of change in people's perceptions seems to be related primarily to the way they experience their congregation's increased *diversity*. As noted by Jolanda, diversity can easily become burdensome; it makes things complex, and, in Jolanda's estimation, for example, demands specific approaches for the wide variety of 'categories of people' within the diverse congregation, such as those with dementia, with intellectual disabilities, or autism. On the other hand, diversity can also be understood as an asset, an opportunity to learn from otherness, or a fuller understanding of what it means that the body of Christ is comprised of different, but equally valuable members (cf. 6.2). The first understanding of diversity above sometimes surfaces as

---

[40] *Interview with B4, 2018-02-28, D81*. Dutch original: "Voor de dominee is het best wel pittig. En heel veel demente mensen nu en dan nog eens al die gehandicapten en dan nog al die autisten. Ik bedoel: het is een gevarieerd huis he. Het is wel heel bijzonder maar het is wel... er ligt wel een hele grote taak, voor de gemeente ook."

part of people's resistance against HVV, while the latter understanding is part of the vision of HVV and of how it is shared by pastor Joost Smit. It is precisely at this point that the vision of HVV has apparently not (or not yet) been communicated successfully to all involved.

Although this part of people's resistance has to do with the specifics of the HVV project, in essence it is something that is at play in any process of change. All change processes involve some groups of people more eager to join change than others. To describe this dynamic, the American communication theorist Everett M. Rogers designed a famous theory of the diffusion of innovations. He identifies five groups: innovators, early adopters, early majority, late majority, and laggards. On a graph, these groups are presented in a normal distribution.[41] The underlying questions in this respect concern the successful communication of the vision for the new before its implementation, and the realization of this vision as something that can be experienced by all involved. While we have also seen examples of people whose appreciation for HVV changed, two years into the church's new configuration this is still not the case for all members. These questions will therefore return in chapter 7.

6.4.3 Practical Concerns

Organizational aspects

In the previous paragraph, we explored the way dynamics surrounding change processes in general played their part in HVV and led to resistance on the part of some church members. Another set of elements that lead to forms of resistance has to do with HVV's specific nature as a cooperation project between very different organizations and with the complex context of healthcare legislation, finances, and other practical concerns. Church member Pieter described how such concerns in themselves already create tension and resistance, even apart from the implementation of HVV's vision:

> Look, of course it already creates a lot of tension and so on if you plan to build a church building... The financial responsibilities you take on, just to name one thing. And

---

[41] Rogers, *Diffusion of Innovations*.

6.4. Resistance

then also: how is the building supposed to look? Everybody has their own opinions on that...[42]

In section 4.6 we already saw that fruitful cooperation between the partners involved in HVV is not easy and remains a challenge. This relates to the fact that they all have their own ways of doing things as well as their own interests. At times, the problems in cooperation already presented themselves as an element of resistance, leaving the success of the project in limbo. Church member Frederik shared what he remembers from the process of developing HVV:

> It took terribly long because, of course, it was a really complex project. It's very complex. Especially legally. We have some lawyers in the congregation and it was really... There were lawyers [...] who really had no faith in it. So that creates some resistance to the plans. So you have to deal with all that. They found it way too risky. [...] It was complex in the sense that, well, as a church we ended up buying a part of the building. But initially the idea was for four partners to invest: the church, Sprank, Accolade, Bzzzonder. And they were all going to buy a part of the building. And that was very complicated, of course. Like, how do you separate that well? And how do you manage things if one of the partners quits? So one after the other just quit. In fact, we [as a church] were the only constant factor. We've always said: We want to buy own our own building. We want to buy. And so they had to find financing for the others. They managed, and so things were arranged the way they are now.[43]

Frederik's recollection exemplifies how practical and financial concerns can become important factors of resistance; things simply do

---

[42] *Interview with B8, 2018-03-08, D85* Dutch original: "Kijk, het geeft natuurlijk al een heleboel spanning sowieso, een kerkgebouw neerzetten... Een stukje financiën alleen al wat je aangaat. En dan nog eens een keer van: hoe moet het er uit komen te zien, daar heeft iedereen zijn mening over..."

[43] *Interview with B6, 2018-03-02, D83.* Dutch original: "Maar het heeft verschrikkelijk lang geduurd, omdat het natuurlijk een heel ingewikkeld project was. Het is heel ingewikkeld. Vooral juridisch. We hebben ook wel juristen in de gemeente en dat

not work out the way they were intended, people refuse to take certain risks, and processes are slowed down considerably or even stalled. Even though this is an issue primarily during the developmental stages of the process, practical issues remain influential for the way people look at HVV. This is true for the cooperation between the HVV partners, as well as for the residents, who sometimes complain about seemingly trifle matters like the direction in which the windows of their apartment open, or the failure of one of the partners to install blinds. While these matters might seem small, what stands out in interviews is that they can nonetheless have great influence on people's experience of HVV, their evaluation, and the extent of their commitment or resistance.

The Size of the Ontmoetingskerk

Another practical aspect of HVV often mentioned as an element of resistance is the size of the congregation. This makes it hard to get to know everyone, leaving people feeling very anonymous or not missed because it is so difficult to tell whether somebody is present or absent. The result is that some do 'not feel at home', which is of course problematic given the emphasis on mutual encounters and koinonia (cf. 5.5). For some of HVV's residents, the fact that the Ontmoetingskerk is a large congregation presents additional difficulties as they struggle with being in large groups due to sensory overload, for example. A resident named Martin, for example, was one of those who had such issues:

was echt... Er waren juristen [...] die zag[en] het helemaal niet zitten... Dus dan heb je ook weerstand tegen de plannen enzo, dus daar heb je allemaal mee te maken. Die vond[en] het veel te gevaarlijk. [...] Omdat het in die zin heel ingewikkeld was, kijk, nu is het zo dat wij als kerk een bepaald gedeelte gekocht hebben. Dus wij zijn eigenaar van een bepaald deel, van de kerkzaal he. Maar aanvankelijk was het de bedoeling dat er vier partijen mee zouden doen: de kerk, Sprank, Accolade, Bzzzonder. En die zouden allemaal een gedeelte kopen. En dat was natuurlijk heel ingewikkeld. Hoe onderscheidt je dat van elkaar, hoe regel je dat en wat gebeurt er als er eentje afhaakt. En wat je zag, op een gegeven moment: de een na de ander haakte af. Wij waren eigenlijk min of meer de constante factor. We hebben altijd gezegd: wij willen een eigen kerkgebouw hebben. Wij willen sowieso kopen. En toen moesten dus financiers gezocht worden voor die anderen. Dus dat hebben ze gedaan en dat is zo geregeld als het nu is."

6.4. Resistance

> Interviewer: And did you become a member of the Ontmoetingskerk at that time as well?
>
> Martin: I think so, but I never go there because it's too busy.
>
> Interviewer: Ok, so you never go there...
>
> Martin: Every gesture you make with your hands as you talk, and nodding yes or shaking no, really makes me go mad, my eyes get very tired from that, I get a headache and nausea. You can't help it, because I too use my hands to speak, but even that bothers me. I notice every fly that flies by. That's why I sometimes don't look at you, because it makes me too tired.[44]

Martin's response gives rich insight into the potential challenges that some face when they find themselves in large groups. If one-on-one conversations already cause so much stress, one can only imagine what it would be like for Martin to go to church on Sunday mornings, first making his way through a crowded hallway and restaurant, finding a place among hundreds of other churchgoers, experiencing music, singing, different actors during the liturgy, and so on. As Martin himself notes, it would not be right to 'blame' anyone for this, because it is simply impossible to design a communal gathering that would not be 'too much' for him. But still it is necessary to acknowledge that the massiveness of a (sometimes large) congregation can become a major element of resistance preventing people from participating in HVV. In Martin's case, for example, his participation would require other forms of (preferably individual) interaction which he does not really experience at this time. It should also be noted that many non-residents likewise find the size of the congregation to be something that, in their eyes, prevents certain aspects of HVV's vision from re-

---

[44] *Interview with A2, 2018-05-31, D103*. Dutch original: "En ben je toen ook lid geworden van de Ontmoetingskerk hier? R: Volgens mij wel, maar ik kom daar nooit omdat het me te druk is. I: Ok, dus je gaat daar nooit naar toe. R: Elke beweging die jij maakt met je handen bij het praten en je ja en nee schudden daar word ik al helemaal gek van, mijn ogen worden daar moe van, daar krijg ik hoofdpijn van en misselijk. En daar kan je niks aan doen want ik praat ook met mijn handen en zelfs dat zie ik. Ik zie elke vlieg die langsvliegt. Daarom kijk ik je soms niet aan, omdat ik daar gewoon te moe van wordt."

ally 'working'. They thus find it important to really get to know other people, and feel that the congregation is simply too big to make that possible. The fact that the congregation holds two separate worship services on Sunday mornings makes this an even more pressing issue.

The Scarcity of Time

A final practical issue sometimes mentioned as a factor of resistance is time. People feel that time is one of the most important ingredients to make HVV a success. Not only do they think that they, or others, should invest time in volunteer activities, but they also stress that it takes a lot of time to build relationships, especially with people who are very 'different' from them. Church member Jolien, for example, explained what she would have to do to really get to know a certain HVV resident with whom she now only experiences occasional, superficial encounters:

> In that case you'd really have to start and care for him, then you can find out more about him. Then you would see him day and night. Now I only see him during a church service, and sometimes he just falls asleep – currently that's the only time I see him. But if you were to start to care for him, work with him, then at some point you would start to understand him [...] So yes, you have to make time for it.[45]

Jolien thus underlines the importance of time. As we have seen, time is very scarce in Vathorst, as many people have demanding careers (cf. 4.3.1). This creates resistance. We will return to the question of time investment and its influence on HVV in chapter 7.

6.4.4 Conceptions of Disability

We have explored how elements present in any change process play a role in HVV and may create resistance. We have also looked at more

---

[45] *Interview with B16, 2018-05-03, D103.* Dutch original: "Dan moet je echt gewoon hem echt gaan verzorgen, dan kom je daar achter. Dan zie je hem dag en nacht. Nu zie ik hem in een dienst, soms valt 'ie dan gewoon in slaap, nu zie ik hem alleen dan.

6.4. Resistance

specific elements of resistance relating to the constitution of HVV and its context. Finally, we will be looking here at yet another kind of resistance, which is of a much more 'internal' nature. The way people think about what 'disability' means can also become a considerable factor of resistance, preventing them from participating in HVV's vision. The following elements emerging from our data will be discussed in greater detail below: inexperience, shame and embarrassment, fear, superficiality, and lack of respect for others.

These conceptions of disability or attitudes vis-a-vis people with disabilities were often mentioned in third-person accounts. That is to say, few would say, for example, that they are themselves afraid of people with disabilities, but they did name fear as an important element when speaking of what might be holding others back from participating in interaction. This applies in particular to the more unfavorable elements like 'lack of respect' and 'superficiality'.

Inexperience

One way in which conceptions of disability create resistance to the vision of HVV is when people feel that they lack the experience, knowhow, or skills to communicate with people with disabilities. Sometimes this is simply perceived as an unchangeable fact about disabilities. As such, people with disabilities are understood to be difficult to communicate with and to require specific skills for communication. Church member Hannah put it this way:

> Well, in the end you are handicapped, you just can't get around that fact. [...] I was in touch with one of the people who lives here now, not a church member. [...] But I cannot understand him... And that makes contact really difficult. So, well, it will never be 'ideal' for the disabled.[46]

For some respondents, the interview for this research project actually

---

Maar je echt hem zou gaan verzorgen, met hem bezig zou gaan, dan zou je hem op een gegeven moment wel begrijpen.[...] Ja, je moet er tijd voor vrijmaken."

[46] *Interview with B3, 2018-02-27, D80.* Dutch original: "Maar uiteindelijk ben je gehandicapt en kun je niet anders. [...] Ik heb contact gehad met een van de mensen die hier nu woont, geen lid van de kerk. [...] ik kan hem niet verstaan... En dat maakt het contact zo moeilijk. Dus, ja. Ideaal zal het nooit worden voor de gehandicapten."

made them reflect on why they did or did not get involved in interaction with HVV's residents. From church member Willem's reflection, it is very clear that inexperience or insecurities about communicating formed the main reason for not interacting with certain people. Up until the interview, he had not given any thought to this, but he now came to realize how this inexperience or lack of knowledge was driving his decisions:

> Of course, sometimes there are people who are more severely disabled. I actually don't speak with them all that much. They also sit in specific pews. I think it would be a bit harder to interact with them. It's not something I do consciously, it's not that I avoid it, but [...] I also don't choose to sit next to them or anything like that [...] Not because I wouldn't want to, or anything, but I don't actually know how I could deal with that in a proper way. [...] It's more that I don't have any experience with that [...], I don't know if it is a deliberate... Well maybe, I think you do it more unconsciously. Now that I think about it, I realize that I don't really sit next to them that often, [...] but I also don't enter the church like: oh, I don't want to sit next to them, I don't think like that. But I think you do it unconsciously. I don't know why. I think it's maybe a kind of restraint, like: what am I supposed to do?[47]

One result of inexperience is an insecurity about finding proper language to express oneself. An example of this can be found in the following excerpt from my fieldnotes of a church service. Pastor Smit

---

[47] *Interview with B11, 2018-03-16, D90.* Dutch original: "En soms heb je natuurlijk mensen die echt wat zwaarder beperkt zijn. Maar die spreek ik eigenlijk wel minder. Die zitten ook op een specifieke plek. Dat lijkt me wel lastiger om daar contact mee te leggen dan. Maar ik doe dat ook niet echt bewust, het is niet dat ik het mijd, maar [...] ik ga er dan ook niet zo bewust naast zitten ofzo [...]. Niet omdat je dat niet zou willen ofzo, maar ik zou eigenlijk niet weten hoe ik daar dan goed mee om zou moeten gaan. [...] Meer dat, omdat ik daar ook geen ervaring mee heb [...], ik weet niet of dat echt bewust... Ja misschien, ik denk dat je dat meer onbewust doet. Als ik er nu over nadenk denk ik: ja, ik zit daar eigenlijk niet vaak naast, [...] maar ik loop niet naar binnen van: o, daar wil ik niet naast zitten, niet zo'n gedachte. Maar ik denk dat je dat onbewust doet. Waarom weet ik eigenlijk niet. Ja, ik denk een soort terughoudendheid van: hoe moet je daar dan mee omgaan?"

6.4. Resistance

had shared with me ahead of time that they wanted to be more flexible about, for example, who would join the children's program during the church service. If there are HVV residents who would enjoy making crafts or listening to a Bible story and reporting about this back in the sanctuary, would there be any reason to have one program for the children and another one for HVV residents? Why not invite all who want to participate in these activities to what had up to then been called the 'children's program'? In the excerpt from my fieldnotes quoted below, we see one elder struggling to communicate this idea during a worship service because he apparently cannot find the proper language to name those for whom this invitation is meant:

> When the actual service starts, an elder welcomes us all. He also mentions that the children, who are sitting in the front of the room near the podium (I think there are around 70 of them), will have their own program. He mentions what Joost had told me earlier: if you prefer to do crafts, sports, or listen to a bible story instead of staying in the service - feel free to join! The thing is that the intended audience of this comment is not entirely clear. I expected that Joost would clarify this later on, but he didn't. Maybe he just forgot. In the end, none of the residents joined the 'children's program'.[48]

Shame and Embarrassment

Besides feelings of inexperience, feelings of shame or embarrassment can also inhibit people from full participation in HVV. A very clear example can be found in what two church members had to say about the collection of prayer requests during the services:

> Marja: They have no diffidence or shame! And we are just sober Dutchmen who don't dare to say anything, while they just share whatever's on their hearts. I think that's so cool, that they do that. We have a lot to learn from them. [...] Sure, especially when prayer requests are being collected, it makes me think that this is exactly what we

---

[48] *Fieldnotes 2017-10-01, D65.*

want. To share things together. They just do that, even if it's like: my sister had a baby. Well, fantastic, great! But the rest of us, we don't do that. We think: I don't want to stand up, I don't want to say anything. But they just do it. Super fun. [And then, in response to the follow-up question whether she has thought of doing the same thing herself:] No (laughing)! Not like that...[49]

Pieter: That they have the courage to mention those prayer requests... I myself am not really like that, like: I've got a request too...! You can learn a lot from them in that sense, the openness they dare to offer [...] Well, in fact I should actually have a bit more of that. But still, when the moment comes, I still think: I'm out... I'll share things like that in a smaller circle, not the full congregation.[50]

Both Marja and Pieter feel they can learn from some HVV residents in this respect, and would like to be more open during worship services. For them, this represents a valuable lesson for the entire congregation to learn. But when they reflect on whether they would follow the example of HVV residents, they respond that a certain level of shame prevents them from doing this. This sentiment is shared by church member Sam, who agreed that it is a big issue in the Ontmoetingskerk:

I miss that in myself, too, and when I look around... We

---

[49] *Interview with B1, 2018-02-22, D76.* Dutch original: "Ze zijn zo zonder schroom! Wij zijn vernuchterde Nederlanders die dan allemaal niks durven te zeggen enzo en zij zeggen gewoon alles wat in hun hart opkomt. Dat vind ik echt heel tof als ze dat doen. Daar kunnen wij echt heel veel van leren. [...] Ja, zeker. Zeker bij zo'n gebedsronde, dan denk ik: ja, je wilt toch met elkaar delen en zij doen dat gewoon ook al is het: ja, mijn zus heeft een kindje gekregen. Fantastisch, supermooi. Maar dat doen wij allemaal niet. Dan denken we: ik ga toch niet staan, ik ga toch niks zeggen, maar zij doen het gewoon, superleuk. I: Ja, en heb jij nog niet de neiging gehad om het zelf ook te gaan doen? R: [Lachend] Nee! Toch niet...."

[50] *Interview with B8, 2018-03-08, D85.* Dutch original: "Dat hun die gebedspunten zo durven noemen... Ik ben daar zelf ook niet zo van, van: he, ik heb nog wel wat... Daar kan je heel veel van leren eigenlijk, die openheid die hun daar in durven geven. [...] Ja, eigenlijk zou je dat wel meer moeten hebben. Maar toch, als het moment daar is denk ik: het is wel goed. Ik deel het inderdaad een wat kleinere kring, als inderdaad

6.4. Resistance

don't dare to be sincere at all anymore. And if something happens in church and it makes one of the residents happy, he'll start to clap and say: yeah! Not like we should all be doing that. I mean: do what feels right for you. But we are all so stiff and think, o boy, should we really be doing this? Maybe it's not allowed or something like that...[51]

Fear

Fear can also become a factor of resistance. Elder Gerrit stated that there is a certain fear in the congregation about really sharing life together, not just between people with and without disabilities, but in general. Becoming very close with one another, and sharing one's deepest convictions and questions is perceived to be a scary thing: "What we also see is that many people find it very difficult if you ask something like: how is your faith life? And when you come very close, people find it scary."[52]

Gerrit also sees how people are sometimes afraid of people who are different from themselves, like people with disabilities. This fear, so Gerrit and church member Pieter noted in their interviews, has a lot to do with inexperience in and lack of knowledge about communication.

> Gerrit: Well, that's hard. And think of someone in a wheelchair, what are you supposed to ask, and what if that person asks you something!? Some people find that quite scary. [...] Not me, but it is something I do notice about people in the congregation, that they find it scary.[53]

---

volop in de gemeente."

[51] *Interview with B13, 2018-04-03, D93.* Dutch original: "Dat mis ik in mezelf ook, en als ik om me heen kijk... Wij durven helemaal niet meer puur te zijn. En als er iets in de kerk gebeurt en een van de bewoners die zit en die wordt ergens blij van dan gaat 'ie klappen en zegt ie: yeah! En niet dat je dat met z'n allen moet gaan doen hoor. Ik bedoel: je moet doen waar je je goed bij voelt. Maar wij zijn allemaal stijf en dan denken we, o, kunnen we dat wel maken... Want straks mag het misschien ofzo niet."

[52] *Interview with C2, 2018-02-26, D78.* Dutch original: "Ook wel dat veel mensen dat ook wel heel erg moeilijk vinden als je zegt van: hoe is het nou met jouw geloof en als je heel dichtbij komt, dat mensen dat ook wel een beetje eng vinden."

[53] *Interview with C2, 2018-02-26, D78.* Dutch original: "Ja, da's moeilijk he. En dan

Pieter: No, well, it's like: What are you being confronted with? What kinds of people are there? People with disabilities, that's a bit scary... And we never came into contact with them... How do you interact with such people? So really, it involved some tension.[54]

In the estimation of Gerrit and Pieter, this fear can really prevent people from interacting, evidently making it a considerable factor of resistance. Interestingly enough, 'HVV-elder' Henk shared how fear of people with disabilities had been a real issue for him as well, until he started interacting with HVV residents:

If I just stick to myself: When I first encountered those residents, my brothers and sisters, I had no idea how to do it. I was afraid of them, I preferred to avoid them rather than meeting them and trying to create a connection. I was not the only one like that.[55]

Fear does not only play a role for people 'without disabilities', of course. Some residents I interviewed also reported how fear prevented them from participating in active roles in church services, for example. Ms. Wiertz reflected on whether the scripture reading during the worship services might be something she would want to do: "I have never done that. I don't think so. I don't know I would be any good... [...] I actually find it a bit scary."[56] Resident Simone said she

---

iemand met een rolstoel, wat ga je dan vragen en wat vraagt 'ie dan aan mij? Sommige mensen vinden dat best wel eng. [...] Ik vind het zelf niet eng. Maar ik merk wel aan mensen uit de gemeente dat ze dat wel eng vinden. De een is wat extravert en de andere is wat minder makkelijk in praten."

[54] *Interview with B8, 2018-03-08, D85*. Dutch original: "Nee, nou ja, wat komt er op je af he, wat voor mensen zitten daar, gehandicapte mensen, da's eng... en daar hebben we nooit mee in aanraking... hoe ga je met zulke mensen om, dus best wel een stukje spanning daar omheen."

[55] *Interview with C1, 2018-02-21, D75*. Dutch original: "En als ik even het dicht bij mijzelf houd, toen ik voor het eerst met die bewoners, en die broers en zussen in contact kwam wist ik eigenlijk niet hoe dat moest. Ik vond ze eng, ik ging het liefste met een grote boog om ze heen dan dat ik naar ze toe kwam en verbinding met ze probeerde te maken. Dat was ik niet de enige."

[56] *Interview with A4, 2018-06-28, D105*. Dutch original: "Dat heb ik nog nooit gedaan. Ik denk het niet. Ik weet niet of ik daar zo goed in ben... [...] Dat vind ik een

6.4. Resistance

would not dare to: "Well, sometimes we sing. But reading and stuff like that, I wouldn't dare that either. I am too afraid that I would start to stutter."[57]

Superficiality

Another potential factor of resistance is superficiality, meaning that people primarily 'judge the book by its cover'. This can be a real issue in preventing meaningful interaction, according to church member Mrs. De Vries, because you often need time to know a person's background as well as a willingness to explore it. She reflected on the example of a woman she knew who had very difficult behavior:

> But it's not something you immediately realize, it really is a process. But it is a beautiful thing, if you receive and take the time to discover that together, like: there's something behind this behavior that explains why she acts this way, it's not like she's a nasty woman. There is something behind it, so you go on to explore: what could that be?[58]

If people only interact superficially, those with more complex behaviors will keep struggling for acceptance. In pastor Joost Smit's estimation, the danger of superficiality is present in the Ontmoetingskerk on two accounts: On the one hand, the context of Vathorst as a neighborhood may influence people in valuing just the superficial ideal of perfection present in that context. On the other hand, simplistic theological ideas about faith as the end of all troubles and suffering can lead to another kind of superficiality, in which the hardships and complexity of everyday life are seen as a lack of faith and therefore not really meaningful.

---

beetje eng."
    [57] *Interview with A5, 2018-06-28, D106.* Dutch original: "Nou, ik heb wel eens dat we gaan zingen. Maar voorlezen ofzo dat durf ik ook niet. Dan ben ik bang dat ik ga stotteren."
    [58] *Interview with B15, 2018-04-23, D100.* Dutch original: "Maar dat heb je ook niet gelijk door hoor, dat is echt een proces. Alleen het mooie is als je daar ook de tijd voor krijgt en neemt om dat met elkaar ook te ontdekken zeg maar, van: er zit iets achter waardoor ze zo doet, het is geen nare vrouw. Er zit iets achter en dat je zoekt: wat zit er achter?"

Well, we discussed the word *vulnerability*. But I think the element of *suffering* also became a reality for the congregation, in a good way. Not suffering as in having no strength left at all, but suffering in the sense of the externality of living in a neighborhood like Vathorst, being between 30 and 50, your next career step, two incomes, an Audi, you have a house and are planning to buy a bigger house - well, all of that comes to be questioned the moment you see, either in your own existence or in that of another, that this is a very superficial ideal. Just wanting more in a material sense... What is left when you don't have possibilities like that in your life? What is left when everything is knocked from your hands? But in that dry desert God can still give connections, or new joy, or: how good is it to be together? Or: we share Christ in bread and wine. Well, I think that in suffering, God often speaks much more powerfully than he does in, well, a kind of triumphant faith, like: from now on everything will only get better. [...] So like: just a while and then the great healing of HVV will start. I don't believe in that. To receive God's strength within one's limitations, or in brokenness, is a much more powerful thing than it is to say

---

[59] *Interview with C3, 2018-03-12, D88.* Dutch original: "Nou, we hebben het woord kwetsbaarheid benoemd. Maar ik denk wel dat het element van lijden op een goede manier ook naar de gemeente toegekomen is. Lijden niet altijd in de zin van aan het eind van je krachten zijn ofzo, maar lijden in de zin van: de Vinex-buitenkant van tussen 30 en de 50, je carrièrestap, je hebt twee inkomens, je hebt een audi, je hebt een huis en straks nog een groter huis, ja, dat wordt natuurlijk wel doorbroken op het moment dat je, of in je eigen bestaan of in het bestaan van een ander ziet van: ja, dat is eigenlijk een soort heel oppervlakkig plaatje. Gewoon materieel meer willen of wat dan ook. Wat houd je over op het moment dat je in je hele leven die mogelijkheid niet hebt, of wat hou je over op het moment dat het je uit handen geslagen wordt. Maar in de woestijn kan God dan toch verbinding geven, of nieuwe vreugde, of: wat fijn om bij elkaar te zijn, of: we delen Christus in brood en wijn. Nou, ik denk dat in het lijden God vaak veel krachtiger kan spreken dan in het, nouja, een beetje een overwinningsgeloof van: nu wordt alles alleen maar beter [...] Dus dat is van: nog even en de grote genezing van Hart van Vathorst gaat beginnen. Dat geloof ik dus niet. Het is veel sterker om in de beperking, of in de gebrokenheid kracht van God te ontvangen in zwakheid, dan dat je zegt: eerst moet al die zwakheid weg zijn en dan pas zijn we zeg maar de goeie christen. Ik vind het voor [mensen die zo'n overwinningsgeloof hebben] ook wel confronterend om te zien dat dat niet overgaat hier, he."

6.4. Resistance

that all your weakness first has to go, and then you can be a proper Christian. For them [people who have such a triumphant faith], I find it to be quite a challenge when they see that those things [limitations, suffering] aren't going away here.[59]

Lack of Respect

Superficiality as we explored it above is an unconscious way of overlooking the complexity of reality and of others' lives. A lack of respect, or intolerance, is a more conscious way of *not being willing to* place oneself in the other person's shoes. Church member Marja has had some experience with the integration of people with mental health issues into a 'regular neighborhood' in another city. She noted that the intolerance of people in the neighborhood is a big problem she encounters, leading to a lot of tension:

> ...they went quite far with that project: a lot of people [with mental health issues] in the neighborhood and in society. But society isn't as tolerant as we all pretend it is, so to say. So what happens is that a lot of tension arises. And those people end up being the victims.[60]

However, this element of resistance is not only present outside of the church, in the neighborhood. According to Sam, a lack of respect sometimes surfaces in the church as well. The recollection of this lack of respect made him very agitated:

> Um, well, we sometimes have a few of those girls who like to read Scripture. And well, unfortunately, that leads to complaints. It makes me very sad [...] It means you're sitting there because you apparently want to hear the text read quickly and because you simply don't have the common decency to understand that it's very important for

---

[60] *Interview with B1, 2018-02-22, D76.* Dutch original: "...daar hebben ze dat project best wel ver doorgevoerd: heel veel mensen in de wijk en in de maatschappij. Maar de maatschappij is niet zo verdraagzaam als we met z'n allen doen alsof, zeg maar. Dus wat er gebeurt is dat er toch heel veel frictie ontstaat waar uiteindelijk die mensen weer de dupe van zijn."

the person doing the reading to have a place in the congregation. And they say: well, can't they do something else? No, let them read, let them sing, let them have a place of their own. And don't start complaining that it's monotone, or that it takes too long, or that someone has some struggles with the text. Yes, that makes me... It could make me very angry, let me put it that way, yes. And these things happen, right, it's happening here, this is a reality.[61]

6.4.5 Summary of Resistance

In this section, we explored elements that prevented people from committing to HVV and its mission. Such resistance surfaced in the data as outings of concern, discontentment, or, less frequently, outright criticism. Some elements of resistance can be explained as resistance elicited by process of change. Respondents indicated, for example, that they were not very well aware of the precise impact that HVV would have on congregational life. In part, and for some respondents, this led to evaluations of HVV as primarily a burden, instead of an asset. Another set of elements of resistance was grouped under the heading 'practical concerns': aspects such as finances, or the plans for a large building project like HVV, create their own dynamic of resistance. Another practical element producing some resistance was the size of the Ontmoetingskerk, which many considered too big to truly realize HVV's mission of encounters and sharing life. A last practical matter that functioned as an element of resistance was the scarcity of time. Many respondents noted that fulfilling HVV's mission demanded a lot of time for personal interaction, and that many people in the neighborhood of Vathorst lack the necessary time in their busy schedules.

---

[61] *Interview with B13, 2018-04-03, D93*. Dutch original: "Eh, ja we hebben wel eens wat meiden die gewoon de Bijbeltekst willen voorlezen. En ja, helaas komen daar klachten op. En dan wordt ik heel verdrietig. [...] Dan zit je daar dus omdat je kennelijk een snelle tekst wil horen en omdat je gewoon niet het fatsoen hebt om te snappen dat dat voor die persoon die dat wil voorlezen gewoon heel erg belangrijk is, om een plekje te hebben in de gemeente. En ze zeggen; ja, kunnen ze toch wat anders doen? Nee, laat ze lezen, laat ze zingen, laat ze een plek krijgen. En dan moet je niet gaan lopen mekkeren dat het op een toon is, of dat het te lang duurt, of dat iemand even er niet uit komt. Ja, daar word ik... Daar zou ik heel boos van kunnen

Lastly, there were conceptions, theological or otherwise, of disability that surfaced as resistance.

6.5 Summary

In this chapter, we explored the extent to which, and the way in which, the inclusive ideals of *hvv* have been realized in its life. First, we looked at interactions between people 'with and without disabilities' on the communal and individual levels. Although for the majority of respondents, as well as church members in general, interactions are mainly concentrated on the communal level, this does not mean that those interactions are without effect. Communal interactions have given 'disability' a concrete face and story. These communal interactions are dependent on a leadership that supports interactions, based on its theological vision. Interaction on the individual level also derives benefits from organized forms of interaction. We have seen that the 'spontaneous' forms of interaction by people who already 'have a soft spot' for others are not the only ones that prove fruitful. Communal and individual interactions are experienced to be beneficial. These interactions start a process that is understood to be *healing* and *instructive* for all who are involved. This process includes stages of familiarity, awareness, understanding, and acceptance.

Following this examination of interactions in hvv, we looked at how and why people were willing to get involved in hvv's mission. We looked at formal as well as more informal ways of commitment. We noted how every member of the Ontmoetingskerk was in fact already formally committed to hvv in the sense that they were members of this particular congregation, while choosing a church is as such hardly self-evident in the ecclesial context of the day. The group that committed itself more intensively in formal ways remains a minority, even though there were some developments and examples where an abundant supply of 'volunteers' proved to be available. In informal ways, every respondent we encountered was at least committed to hvv in a 'normative' way; they thought, or thought they were supposed to think, that hvv is an important and good initiative. Many respondents, however, also felt a warmer connection with hvv. Emo-

---

worden, laat ik dat zeggen, ja. En het gebeurt he, dat gebeurt, dat is hier."

tional responses surfaced remarkably often in the interviews. People were motivated in their commitment by the experienced benefits of interactions, by the fact that they connected what was happening in HVV to the work of God, and by the widespread attention for and recognition of HVV by outsiders.

Aside from commitment, there were also elements of resistance. These very diverse elements work to impede the realization of HVV's mission in more or less powerful ways. Although resistance is hard to grasp and different elements often co-exist, we saw how, in broad lines, three kinds of elements of resistance played an important part in the data. Resistance can thus be explained in part by dynamics that appear in all change processes. To deal with these elements of resistance, one can therefore be inspired by studying theories of change (or change management) and focusing, for example, on clear communication and on making people experience the benefits of the new situation. Other elements of resistance related more to practical concerns. These elements seem to point in the direction of organization and leadership for solutions. A final set of elements of resistance had to do with the way people think about disability and make sense of it theologically. These conceptions may be challenged by interactions, as we saw in section 6.2.3, but that does not mean that such conceptions obstructing HVV's mission no longer exist in the Ontmoetingskerk.

Chapter 7

Conclusions & Discussion

7.1 Introduction

In the first three chapters of this dissertation, I outlined the goal and method of this study and placed it in a broader theoretical framework. The next three chapters were to devoted to a thick description of life in Hart van Vathorst. What remains now is to take this thick description back to the questions we posed in the introduction; this will be done in section 7.2. Subsequently, in section 7.3 we will reflect further on a number of important themes arising from this research project. There we will zoom in on the themes identified, point out directions for dealing with them, and make a number of proposals for further study.

7.2 Conclusions

In section 1.4, I introduced this research project's main question together with its subquestions. Here I will answer them based on the results described in the previous chapters. We will first look at the descriptive subquestions, before moving on to the more interpretative subquestions and, finally, the main research question.

7.2.1 Descriptive Subquestions

The descriptive subquestions I formulated were the following:

1. What does the praxis of the Ontmoetingskerk in the context of Hart van Vathorst look like?

2. Which operant ecclesiological voices relating to inclusion can be heard?

3. Which espoused ecclesiological voices relating to inclusion can be heard?

4. Which formal ecclesiological voices relating to inclusion can be heard?

5. Which normative ecclesiological voices relating to inclusion can be heard?

Given the nature of this research project as a single case study in which we have focused on the specifics of lived reality in the Ontmoetingskerk and Hart van Vathorst (cf. section 3.5.2, the first question is a very difficult one to answer in a concise and satisfactory manner. A long answer can be found in chapter 4, which offers a general overview of life in Hart van Vathorst in four perspectives. The summary of that chapter (page 138) may serve as a concise, albeit not altogether satisfactory answer to the first subquestion. It shows how the praxis of the Ontmoetingskerk in the context of Hart van Vathorst must be understood in relation to its context in the neighborhood of Vathorst, in the RCL, and in its macro context which does appreciate social engagement, but remains uneasy when it comes to explicit religious motivations for this engagement. The summary also shed light on the way in which Hart van Vathorst's practice is rooted in explicitly Christian values as laid down in the vision statement, although some important theological questions remain unanswered for now. It subsequently explored the organization of life in Hart van Vathorst and the role that leadership plays in all of this.

Subquestions 2-5 are based on the model of theology in four voices developed by Helen Cameron and others that we introduced on page 15. Throughout the thick description in the previous chapters, I have sometimes referred to these voices to hint at tensions between them. With regard to the **operant voice**, we may note how the Ontmoetingskerk's practices have been impacted by its involvement with Hart van Vathorst. This emerged particularly in chapter 5. One example is

7.2. Conclusions

formed by the changes in the Lord's Supper celebrations in Vathorst. Just by observing the differences in the sacramental celebrations and how they changed over time, we can track ecclesiological convictions. The participation of HVV residents thus proves to be theologically significant enough to alter a standing practice. This example can be contrasted with another example highlighting another side of the operant voice, namely the fact that during social interactions following worship services, some people can be found standing on the sidelines by themselves without being talked to or even greeted. Apparently, for whatever good or bad reasons (which are not a part of the operant voice), people do not cross boundaries in order to include these people in their social interactions.

The **espoused** voice yields important insights in relation to this operant voice, as many people in the Ontmoetingskerk feel that the inclusion of people with disabilities is an important part of their church's calling, but not all respondents combine that conviction with an appreciation for the benefits of this inclusion. The espoused voice includes theological ideals like valuing every member of the body, welcoming those who are different, or serving each other and specifically those in need of extra support. Some church members combine such ideals with other ideals like learning from each other by not just giving, but also receiving. These church members often undergird these ideals by their own concrete experiences. For a sizable group, however, inclusion is primarily understood theologically (in terms of the espoused voice) as a task, and much less as a gift. Another important thing to note about the espoused voice is the persistent obscurity involved in some theological questions. This can be seen, for example, in the way church members think about ethical issues like euthanasia or frame (dis)ability in relation to faith.

The **formal voice**, in turn, shows much greater uniformity and is driven by a number of key convictions, such as the idea of the importance of receiving gifts or *charismata* in the church. A vision of the church that focuses on the reception of gifts leaves room for members to be surprised by what these gifts are and to whom they are given. The theme of reception is particularly prominent in the way pastor Joost Smit speaks about ecclesial life, but also surfaces in how other people in the congregation reflect on the church. Another key conviction in the formal voice is that the church best serves the world by being the church. In other words, the way in which the Ontmoetingskerk strives to be present in the neighborhood and interact with it, is not by continually reflecting on how it might be 'relevant'. Rather, according to pastor Smit, the Ontmoetingskerk does 'church things': preaching the Word, celebrating the sacraments. A final important part of the formal voice in the Ontmoetingskerk is the conviction that disability is not simply something that ought to be 'fixed' or 'cured'. Pastor Joost Smit showed himself critical of such thinking on multiple occasions, even though there is no clearly articulated theological rationale in the formal voice of what disability means theologically.

The role of the **normative voice** in the Ontmoetingskerk is difficult to describe. Elements from the normative voice surface in sermons, but also in interviews with individual church members. Furthermore, they come up as arguments in discussions. Our data show that Scripture is seen as normative. Scripture is read in a traditional Reformed way, with extensive attention to the 'history of salvation' as its overarching narrative. As such, elements like creation, sin, fallenness, and grace and forgiveness through Jesus's death on the cross are often mentioned as key elements of the normative voice. These Scriptural elements are sometimes used to put all humans on the same level from a normative point of view; in the end we are all part of God's good creation, while also limited in our abilities as creatures, and we are all sinners in need of grace, regardless of whether or not we are 'disabled'. This normative framework makes it possible for us to see each other as 'equal' in our created, fallen, and restored state, while also acknowledging the differences between us. Every creature of God is as such valuable, but also has her own specificity. Besides elements from Scripture, normativity was also attributed to elements from the Reformed and broader ecumenical theological tradition, such as the conviction that life is a gift and that every human being is created in the image of God.

7.2.2 Interpretative Subquestions

In addition to these descriptive subquestions, we posited a number of more interpretative questions:

6. How can the Ontmoetingskerk's approach for applying inclu-

7.2. Conclusions

sion to church life in the Hart van Vathorst context best be understood in relation to existing theory?

7. How can the Ontmoetingskerk's praxis in the Hart van Vathorst context be understood in relation to this approach?

8. What lessons can be learned from the Ontmoetingkserk in the Hart van Vathorst context?

Subquestion 6 can be answered by comparing the intentions of the Ontmoetingskerk and HVV with the overview of theological interaction on inclusion as we presented it in chapter 2. In that chapter, we showed how there are roughly three streams of theological interaction with inclusion. There is how-engagement, why-engagement (in minimal and maximal forms), and non-correlative engagement (cf. page 33). When we look at the Ontmoetingskerk and its interaction with inclusion, we can first of all conclude that it does not situate itself in the non-correlative camp, as it often uses the terminology of inclusion to describe its intentions and practice. Nor can its story be understood as a form of how-engagement, as there is clear and ongoing reflection on what inclusion actually means and how it relates to theological concerns. This places it in the middle, in the why-engagement category. Considering the fact that the Ontmoetingskerk has not become a 'target group'-church and remains clearly recognizable as a Reformed church, its why-engagement cannot be considered 'maximal'; ecclesiological reflection is not dominated by inclusion, but inclusion is rather just one aspect for reflection along with many other aspects that are relevant for what it means to be church. The story of the Ontmoetingskerk as it relates to inclusion must therefore be understood as a form of minimal why-engagement: there is an ongoing reflection on what inclusion means in relation to church. In this reflection, multiple interests are kept in balance, rather than one interest (such as inclusion) being prioritized over all others.

Chapter 6 reflected on how this story is put into practice in Vathorst and thereby offered an answer to subquestion 7. Life in the Ontmoetingskerk has undoubtedly undergone significant changes through its involvement with HVV. Even those who have little interaction with HVV residents were often changed in their perception of people with disabilities as well as their understanding of what it means to believe and to be church. The pursuit of a more inclusive congregation has therefore resulted in growing awareness and reflection. This growth must be understood as a process which is far from finished. As our explorations of factors resisting this growth show, in order for this process to be advanced, how-engagement questions must be addressed: How can we get everybody on board? How can we organize certain activities in more accessible ways? It is clear, however, that continued why-engagement remains necessary for addressing resistance also in challenging (and sometimes implicit) theological conceptions.

Consequently, the answer to subquestion 8 is that there are a number of lessons to be learned from the Ontmoetingskerk. Many aspects of the Ontmoetingskerk's life can be seen as examples for a church's engagement with the inclusion of people with disabilities. There are also lessons to be learned from things that are not (or not yet) working in satisfactory ways in Vathorst. These (positive and negative) lessons will be discussed under a number of themes in section 7.3. First, we will investigate what this study has taught us about what inclusion exactly is; what are the ways in which the vision and practice of the Ontmoetingskerk are 'new'? Next, we will examine ways in which this vision of inclusion is realized, as well as the organizational and leadership-related elements that play a part in this realization. Third, we will look at the way in which this inclusive vision can be embodied, made visible, and celebrated in ecclesial life. Fourth, there are also lessons to be learned regarding the way in which being an inclusive church relates to the surrounding world. Finally, we will look at what we can learn regarding the role of theological reflection in projects like HVV.

7.2.3 Main Question

The central question for this study was:

What contribution does the example of Hart van Vathorst make to theological reflection on the inclusion of people with disabilities in the church?

The answers to the descriptive subquestions have shown us much about the example of Hart van Vathorst and what it entails theologically. The answers to the interpretative subquestions yield a num-

7.2. Conclusions

ber of lessons, which will be discussed in further detail in the following section (7.3). In a more general sense, we can describe Hart van Vathorst's contribution to theological reflection on the inclusion of people with disabilities in the church in a threefold manner.

First, the study of Hart van Vathorst and the Ontmoetingskerk serves to reinforce the challenge that churches face. While not every church will find itself in a situation like that of the Ontmoetingskerk, statistics tell us that about 1% of people in the Netherlands have an intellectual disability, not to mention physical disabilities. This means that every church community should expect that people with disabilities, in the broadest sense of the term, will come to worship with them. However, there has been little reflection on what this means for the way we worship, the design of our church buildings (in relation to both physical and intellectual disabilities), and reflection on our missional calling.[1] The interviews with residents of Hart van Vathorst in this research project show that being intentional about the inclusion of people with disabilities in ecclesial life is of tantamount importance to these residents and their families. It answers a deep need and longing for fruitful participation in faith communities, which often becomes more ardent by past experiences of exclusion in other churches or society at large. This study has shown that becoming more inclusive is a difficult process that requires intentionality, leadership, and vision. The first contribution that the HVV example makes is thus a challenging call to action; much work remains to be done for churches to become accessible, and while this work is not easy, it is highly anticipated.

A second contribution is that HVV shows how many resources churches actually have available to them for responding to this challenge. Of course, the Ontmoetingskerk's situation was unique in the sense that it found itself in a position of having to build a new building and at that particular moment came into contact with HVV's other partners. We have seen how important it is that HVV's entire life happens under one roof. But this is not to say that other churches could not make similar efforts in their own situations. Notwithstanding everything that is specific about the situation of the Ontmoetingskerk,

---

[1] We have named some examples from the Dutch context in section 2.3. Internationally, the recent volume by Benjamin Conner must be noted here: Conner, *Disabling Mission, Enabling Witness*.

there is also much that is quite 'typical'. The Ontmoetingskerk was not a group of hyper-motivated people. Hvv is not a l'Arche community or a similar group of people who actively choose to be part of a community of people 'with and without disabilities'. Rather, the Ontmoetingskerk was very much a 'typical' congregation, and does not have a theology that is naturally inclusive; its traditional Reformed beliefs can easily result in various exclusions.[2] These beliefs were not given up. Yet the encounter with others and their desires and needs, combined with an awareness of its own resources, led the Ontmoetingskerk to invest these resources as it did. Besides the resources that churches themselves have in terms of people and finances, the current social context provides resources as well, as the government welcomes initiatives like HVV. The second contribution made by the example of HVV is thus the invitation it extends to churches to reflect creatively and critically on the way they invest their resources.

The third contribution of this study of HVV is an awareness of the impact that a project like this has on all of church life. As we saw in chapter 5, all aspects of ecclesial practice are challenged by the pursuit of greater inclusion. The church's liturgical life, its diaconal service, its witnessing aspects, and its ways of living life in communion with God and one another - all these things change as the congregation becomes more inclusive. The changes do not just impact 'target groups', but the entire congregation. This means that broad and conceptual ecclesiological reflection is needed to guide churches as they strive to become more inclusive.

7.3 Discussion

As we explained on page 234, there are a number of lessons to be learned from the case study presented in this dissertation. In the remainder of this chapter, we will discuss five themes that emerged from our analysis of the data and bring them into a broader conversation with the literature reviewed in chapter 2 as well as other relevant literature. By doing so, we seek to make the results of this study fruitful for broader discourse on inclusion and ecclesiology. As noted, the themes

---

[2] Cf. the criticisms launched against the terminology of inclusion in Reformed circles as they will be discussed in section 7.3.1.

7.3. Discussion

are:

1. Reflection on the meaning of inclusion for church life.

2. Organizational and leadership aspects.

3. How inclusion may be embodied in church life and how churches can celebrate inclusively.

4. Public-theological aspects of being an inclusive church.

5. The role of theological reflection in projects like Hart van Vathorst.

In the following subsections, these themes will be discussed in order.

7.3.1 Inclusion - What's New?

As we noted in chapter 2, inclusion has become a buzzword in today's society. Yet its meaning is often unclear. We did gain some clarity in the course of that chapter by offering a systematic overview of the way inclusion is understood both in society and in relation to the life of the church. Our exploration of life in Hart van Vathorst may shed new light on the meaning of the terminology of inclusion as it is embodied in its practices. What is different about the way people with disabilities participate in social and ecclesial life in Hart van Vathorst and the Ontmoetingskerk compared to other situations? What is 'new' about their approach? Why is this approach labeled as 'inclusion'? And how could this help churches in the Netherlands or in other contexts where there has been little reflection on the meaning of inclusion for church life?

Inclusion and a Receptive Ecclesiology

In broader societal discourse, *inclusion* is a term that conceptually belongs conceptually within the QOL framework (cf. section 2.2). Within this framework, it is a *domain* of the *factor* of *social participation*. In other words, the term inclusion is perceived as a kind of 'quality' of the way people with disabilities participate in social settings.[3] We speak of inclusive participation if people not only (a) receive ad-

---
[3] Schalock et al., "Cross-Cultural Study of Quality of Life Indicators".

equate support to participate in social settings and (b) are therefore present within these setting, but also (c) have valuable roles there. In broad lines, this third point is where inclusion can be contrasted with the somewhat outdated terminology of 'integration'. However, as we have shown in section 2.2, one can use the word inclusion and still work within an 'integration paradigm' and vice versa. We must therefore conclude that, as many authors have indeed argued, inclusion is a complex term that must be studied and subjected to further critique, specifically with a view to the social setting in which it is applied.[4]

With regard to the specific social setting studied in this research project (i.e. a church), this entails that we need to study and critique inclusion from a *theological* perspective, as theology is uniquely suited to interaction with the church's life. In Brian Brock's terms, we need to *theologize inclusion*.[5] This theologizing can be done from the perspective of many different theological disciplines, like ethics, systematic theology, and biblical studies. However, as we have argued in chapter 3, the life of the church as studied by practical theologians can also contribute meaningfully to this theologizing of inclusion. This is the contribution that the present study makes.

If we look at the life of the Ontmoetingskerk and how inclusion is embodied there, several things stand out. We see how inclusion is indeed a step forward from integration. If the goal were integration, one would expect ecclesial life to remain largely unchanged, with adaptations merely on the level of those with disabilities so that they could take part in this life 'as much as possible'. However, as our explorations have shown, ecclesial life has in fact changed in significant ways. These changes have therefore not only impacted individuals with disabilities (in older terminology: 'those who needed to be integrated'), but rather the entire congregation (which has therefore become more 'inclusive'). Even though we may be right to label the developments in the Ontmoetingskerk as developments towards inclusion, this does not per se make the congregation unique, as similar efforts are undoubtedly being undertaken elsewhere in the Netherlands. Nor does the application of the term 'inclusion' to the Ont-

---

[4]Cf. Martin and Cobigo, "Definitions Matter in Understanding Social Inclusion", Clapton, *Transformatory Ethic of Inclusion*, and Hall, "The Social Inclusion of People with Disabilities".

[5]Brock, "Theologizing Inclusion".

7.3. Discussion

moetingskerk mean that this congregation has reached some standard of perfection. The goal of this study never was to 'erect a monument' for Vathorst.[6] Nonetheless, the example of the Ontmoetingskerk does indeed clarify how inclusion differs from integration. As such, this study has led to greater clarity on the concept of inclusion within the context of the church. Using the terminology of inclusion has helped us to explore the specifics of the way people with disabilities participate in the life of the Ontmoetingskerk, even though this terminology needs to be further particularized in practice with more theological or Biblical concepts like 'love' in mind, as John Swinton (p. 32) and respondent Floris (p. 169) remind us.

An important aspect of what this inclusive social participation entails for the life of the church concerns the creation of room allowing valuable roles to be attributed to people with disabilities (point c of the above definition of inclusion). In the Ontmoetingskerk, a number of such roles can be identified. Some of them are formal roles (like specific tasks during the worship services), but there are also meaningful informal roles (like helping others realize and embodying the emotional impact of certain events in the life of the congregation). Whether the roles are formal or informal, they are theologically undergirded by a 'receptive ecclesiology'; receiving the gifts by which God builds up the church through the Spirit is a major focus in the way people in Vathorst think about the church. This seems to represent a central theological insight enabling churches to become inclusive in the sense of valuing each person's gifts, regardless of their (dis)abilities.

One could say that this idea of a 'receptive ecclesiology' as the theological core of inclusive practice is not a new insight, as it has been formulated in like manner by theologian Brian Brock.[7] However, it is interesting that Brock's article was not read by people in Vathorst, nor was its theological insight directly or explicitly formulated as a key belief in any mission or vision statement.[8] Rather, it flowed from

---

[6]The danger of idealization or romanticization is real, but it would be completely counter to the intention of this study to 'chasten the church's doctrinal selfunderstanding'. Cf. Healy, *Church, World, and the Christian Life*; Healy, "Ecclesiology, Ethnography, and God".

[7]We introduced Brock's article in section 2.3. See Brock, "Theologizing Inclusion".

[8]Cf. the discussion of these statements in section 4.4.

ecclesial practice as explored and analyzed in this study. This is in line with the way Stanley Hauerwas writes about the L'Arche communities. He argues that these communities must not be understood as embodiments of complex ideas, but rather as *sets of practices* flowing from a simple desire to follow Christ. Reflection on these practices, in turn, leads to the formulation of new concepts and ideas that are very relevant in relation to disability.[9] Yet in line with Hauerwas's argument, our exploration of HVV has suggested that it is more promising to start by doing, than it is to start by reflecting theologically, ethically, or otherwise. This practical ecclesiological study reinforces the importance of discerning the gifts of the Spirit to the congregation for being an inclusive church and in fact for being a church in general. This calls for a receptive ecclesiology. Ecclesiological reflection does not start with a doctrinal or inclusive ideal, but with the life of the church in which God is already present and active.[10]

Criticism and Discussion of Inclusive Ecclesiology

A receptive ecclesiology is by definition flexible and open as it understands the importance of being surprised by the gifts that God gives. Without these gifts, the church cannot be church. Yet the degree of flexibility is no easy matter. In fact, such flexibility and openness has led some to sound warnings against inclusive ecclesiologies. P.J. Vergunst, a leading figure within the conservative wing of the Protestant Church in the Netherlands (the mainline Protestant denomination), expressed some caution in a periodical regarding the use of the term inclusion in relation to the church. His concerns pertained not so much to the inclusion of people with disabilities, but rather to the church's stance on same-sex marriage. According to Vergunst, who cited the American evangelical theologian Tim Keller to make his point, communities can never be fully inclusive because they require certain convictions. Therefore, they always have an exclusive element to them.[11] There are also theologians who would strongly

---

[9]Hauerwas, "Seeing Peace".

[10]Or, as Jean Vanier puts it in relation to the L'Arche communities: "Communion is rooted in reality, not in dreams or illusions" (cited in Reinders, "Being with the Disabled", p. 467).

[11]Vergunst, "Een Inclusieve Kerk?"

7.3. Discussion

disagree with Vergunst, arguing that the church is ultimately not a community of people with the same convictions, but rather resembles something like a 'community of the question'.[12] However, it seems fair to acknowledge both sides of the debate and to admit that Vergunst is to some degree right in saying that 'full inclusion' is not a viable option for ecclesiology, since there are always basic convictions at stake. In this context, we might also recall Miroslav Volf's argument, which we quoted earlier, that "a consistent pursuit of inclusion places one before the impossible choice between a chaos without boundaries and oppression with them."[13] Nonetheless, there are some things to be said in response to this theological hesitancy to embrace inclusion.

In the first place, although inclusion is indeed a term that is used in relation to various social (minority) groups that are at risk of exclusion, it is not helpful to act as if they are all one and the same group. The theological issues at stake differ from group to group, and indeed from person to person. Inclusion has much more to do with the quality of the social participation of certain individuals than with some ideology that leaves no room for convictions or order. This realization may take away some of the worries of those who oppose inclusion out of a fear for chaos or the loss of key convictions. At the same time, it challenges those who advocate for more inclusive churches and societies on various terrains to explain what they mean by inclusion, what issues are currently preventing this inclusion, and how these issues ought to be resolved. Inclusion is not a one-word argument that can serve to settle every debate, but rather the starting point for a long and complex conversation in which at times conflicting interests must be openly addressed. These debates will have a different look depending on the social settings and the specific issues at stake in those settings.

Secondly, those who caution against an inclusive ecclesiology out of fear for chaos or the loss of key convictions must not overlook the opposing danger, either. Inclusion can be situated on a continuum between, on the one hand, 'total chaos' and the endangerment of what some perceive to be the church's key convictions, and, on the other hand, a church in which there is very little room for God-given diversity and only a very select group of people can in the end truly

---

[12]Shakespeare, "A Community of the Question"; Shakespeare and Rayment-Pickard, *The Inclusive God: Reclaiming Theology for an Inclusive Church*.

[13]Volf, *Exclusion & Embrace*, pp. 63–64.

belong. Both sides of the continuum are in fact caricatures, that is, in real life one seldom finds a church like it if one actually engages in the way these churches live. However, the caricatures do serve to explain why one could have worries about leaning too far to either one of these two sides. Inclusion is therefore always a concept entailing a certain *tension*. This tension can be understood as a tension between two elements that are at the heart of the church. As we saw in section 2.4.3, the church polity scholar Leo Koffeman describes these elements as relating to the church's *catholicity* and *holiness*. These two Nicene attributes of the church are translated by Koffeman into the so-called quality markers of inclusivity (catholicity) and integrity (holiness). Although Koffeman asserts that the quality markers are not to be equated with the Nicence attributes, his proposal does shed light on the tension that we have observed between 'radical' or 'full' inclusion and the fact that the church has certain key convictions that seem by nature exclusive. If Koffeman is right, then this tension is part of the church's core as it is formulated in the Nicene creed.[14] It therefore seems to be too easy simply to warn against inclusion and to leave it at that, because the pendulum may swing too far to the 'integrity side'. Rather, we must recognize that there is indeed a fundamental tension here which is woven into the very fabric of the church. The tension is consequently not something to 'get rid of'. Rather, it is a *dynamic tension*; it is precisely in this tension that we receive new things, gifts from the Spirit. The question is how we can find a balance while holding to this dynamic tension. In order to find this balance, do we need to lean more towards 'integrity' than we currently do, or should we lean more towards 'inclusivity'? If we turn to the statements from Koffeman on these two quality markers, as cited above, we may gain an idea of his own stance on the matter. Regarding 'inclusivity' he writes:

> As a community [the church] is called to, and it longs to embrace all people. If a church tries to live up to its destination, it cannot accept any limitation beforehand. So-called 'self-evident' boundaries, like social, cultural and economic dividing lines cannot be decisive. A church

---

[14] Koffeman, *In Order to Serve*. Koffeman also addresses the other two attributes, but they are less relevant to our discussion here.

7.3. Discussion

even knows of the relativity of its own historical limitations: it reaches out, beyond borders, and it is missionary and diaconal in nature.[15]

Regarding 'integrity', Koffeman states that "although [...] no limitation can be accepted at the outset, it is [...] true also that not 'everything goes' within the church. The Gospel implies limitations. Sometimes a clear 'no' has to be there, most of all in its internal life."[16]

Thirdly, then, reflecting on how the inclusivity and integrity of the church relate in Koffeman's thought, we suggest that the tension between them is not relieved by steering what one might perceive to be 'the middle course'. The two poles are not symmetric. About inclusivity, Koffeman writes that it is part of the church's calling and longing, and breaks "so-called self-evident boundaries". Inclusivity is, according to Koffeman, therefore at the church's core, yet it is also something that may often feel unnatural, going against the self-evident. Fundamentally, what we perceive as being self-evident must be challenged on the basis of the conviction that the church is catholic. On the other hand, Koffeman speaks about integrity as something that is just as much a part of the core of the church, but only becomes visible "sometimes", when the "clear no has to be there". Koffeman believes that this is mostly so when it comes to the church's "internal life". Thus, while he challenges the church to remind itself that it is indeed inclusive by nature, he also seems to be cautioning the church not to allow its conception of its own holiness to cause it to overstep its authority by drawing boundaries and being too quick in speaking the 'no'. This seems to suggest that if we, in our experience, were forced to lean in the direction of either one of these two poles (holiness-integrity and catholicity-inclusivity), Koffeman would encourage us to lean more in the direction of the latter.

This interpretation of Koffeman's work is in line with what the Old Testament scholar Frank Anthony Spina shows in his work *The Faith of the Outsider*. In it, he presents a close reading of six narratives in the Old Testament and one in the New Testament in which exclusion plays a role. Spina's focus on these stories, like that of Rahab, Ruth, or the Samaritan woman, shows a common thread to be woven

---

[15]Ibid., p. 132.
[16]Ibid., p. 133.

through them. Spina does not argue that the Bible has no exclusivist or excluding traces. It is very clear that one can belong to the people of God, but one can also find oneself outside of the boundaries of this people. But whenever people feel they can put their finger on the precise criteria for inclusion in or exclusion from God's people (like ethnicity, religious upbringing, ritual purity, health), the Biblical narratives overturn this construct. In chapter 2, we already saw how Spina reflects on the story of Naaman and Gehazi (2 Kings 5). Another example is taken from the story of Rahab and contrasted with the story of Achan (Joshua 2 and 7). On a surface reading, Rahab is the ultimate outsider, being a pagan, a woman with questionable ethical standards, and living in Jericho, the city of the enemy. Achan is a typical insider as a son of Israel, who commits what one could call a minor violation - taking things from the conquered city of Jericho that are not his, but technically also do not belong to anybody else, as Jericho's inhabitants are dead. However, in the end Achan and his family are stoned to death, while Rahab is included among the people of God and even appears in the genealogy of Jesus. According to Spina,

> the import of this text is that the community of faith must be constantly aware that outsiders are only a confession away from being included, while insiders are only a violation away (when it is a violation of Achan's magnitude) from being excluded. [...] It is a story in which the interplay of insiders and outsiders requires a reevaluation of the very nature of what it means to be God's people.[17]

Thus, in response to the hesitancy expressed by some theologians in regard to the use of inclusion-language in relation to the church, we can say that there is indeed a tension. Yet this tension must not be made bigger than it is; the theological issues at stake are not a massive construct that inevitably rob the church of her key convictions. Rather, the inclusion of certain groups will start to question some of these convictions, which might seem self-evident. As the Ontmoetingskerk shows, such questioning does not mean that one must immediately abandon one's convictions. The critical dialogue evolving from inclusive practices can also be seen as a positive product of catholicity,

---

[17]Spina, *The Faith of the Outsider*, p. 71.

7.3. Discussion

instead of an outside threat. As Spina's survey of biblical narratives shows, there *are* boundaries to the people of God. However, following his exegesis of these narratives as well as our own experience, we must acknowledge that it is often very hard, if not impossible, to draw these lines exactly. In those cases where self-evidences are questioned, the preceding argument suggested that we choose to give the benefit of the doubt to the person questioning us, rather than perceiving them as outsiders who have nothing to offer. In other words, it means that when in doubt, we ought to choose inclusion, rather than exclusion. This does not mean that "anything goes", to use Koffeman's terms. But it does mean that churches ought to exert maximal efforts for being places where all people are welcome, in order to receive the gifts that God may bring through them. As Spina shows, in the Biblical narrative it is often through the faith of 'outsiders' that God brings salvation to His people. As suggested by Koffeman's survey of some of the ecclesiological foundations in the Nicene Creed's formulations, together with his survey of elements from Scripture as divine revelation, the tension presented by inclusion must not be understood as an ecclesial peripheral issue that is to be eliminated. Rather, the tension shows itself to be at the very heart of what it means to be church in this world. This case study has given ample examples of how this tension can be fruitful, rather than burdensome. In fact, referring back to what Brock wrote about 1 Corinthians 12, it would seem to be in line with the New Testament witness about the church to argue that it is precisely in this tension that the Holy Spirit may bring unexpected yet vital gifts.

Summary

This subsection addressed the question of what this case study could teach us about inclusion in relation to church life and how this could help other churches to reflect on inclusion. We have seen that the example of the Ontmoetingskerk shows clearly how inclusion is indeed distinct from integration, mainly in terms of the reciprocity of people with disabilities who are not just present but also have valuable roles. Theologically, this asks for what we have called a receptive ecclesiology, open to the gifts that God gives to the church in every member of the body, through the Holy Spirit. Criticism of or hesitancy towards such a receptive ecclesiology is understandable, but can be addressed by noting that 'inclusion' is not a concept of universal application; it looks different depending on the social setting and the people 'to be included'. Additionally, one must understand that the tension that becomes apparent in reflecting on inclusion is indeed a fundamental tension in ecclesiology, and that it is neither possible nor desirable to relieve this tension by simply 'steering a middle course'. Eliminating the dynamic tension runs the risk of ignoring the work of the Spirit. Therefore, churches must make sure they make efforts to receive all God's people, and through them His gifts. This does not mean that they have to give up their core beliefs, but it does mean that they must have the courage, or faith, to bring these convictions into critical dialogue when this is called for by 'outsiders'. The church is a community of disciples that is fundamentally open, as Koffeman says. Everyone is welcome, but there will also always be transformation in the life of each and every disciple. Every church member is an 'insider' by virtue of her baptism, but even those who are 'outsiders' might be 'insiders' in God's eyes, as Spina's reading of Old Testament narratives suggests. The church as a community of disciples moves in a certain direction - 'not everything goes'. But as soon as the church starts to draw precise boundaries, she runs the risk of excluding the wrong people.

7.3.2 Organization and Leadership Towards Inclusion

In the previous subsection, we have explored how this case study has helped us understand inclusion in relation to church life. Here we will focus on what we can learn with respect to the realization of an inclusive vision. We will look at organizational aspects as well as the role of leadership.

The Church and Social Enterprise

Looking at Hart van Vathorst, one of the most unusual things about it is the partnership between (commercial) health care service providers, a (commercial) daycare center, a (commercial) restaurant operator, and a (non-commercial!) church. In today's context of declining church membership and therefore declining resources for churches to realize their mission, some reflection has arisen regarding the way church

7.3. Discussion

and commerce relate. One example of such reflection can be found in the work of HeartEdge, an organization originating in the church of St. Martin-in-the-Fields in London. Samuel Wells, a theologian and vicar at St. Martin, is one of the leaders of this organization, where four C's take center stage:[18]

- Congregation: Inclusive approaches to liturgy, worship, and day-to-day communal life.

- Commerce: Commercial activity and social enterprise generating finance, creatively extending and enhancing mission and ministry.

- Culture: Art, music, and ideas to re-imagine the Christian narrative for the present time.

- Compassion: Models of outreach serving local need and addressing social justice.

According to HeartEdge's philosophy, the classical models for funding ecclesial life are no longer working, leaving many church buildings in poor shape and church dreams unfulfilled. For this reason, the organization is encouraging churches to engage in commercial activity generating the financial resources needed to realize their mission. For HeartEdge, all these C's can be equally valued as 'church'. On face value, there seems to be a lot of overlap between what HeartEdge envisions and what is happening in Vathorst. Hart van Vathorst has commercial aspects to it, while it also strives to embody what it understands to be a Christian mission. On closer inspection, however, there is also an important difference, in that the church and the other partners are in many ways separate organizations. The Ontmoetingskerk focuses primarily on congregation and compassion, while the other partners focus more on commerce. The C of 'culture' is less present, although one might recognize it in some of the activities that take place in HVV's building, like concerts.

The HVV case study may offer some challenges to approaches like that of HeartEdge. Leading a church is something quite different from

---

[18]Taken from HeartEdge's 'membership pack', which can be downloaded from their website: *HeartEdge*.

running a business, as people in Vathorst have come to experience. We have already described some of the tensions that this can produce (see for example 6.4), although we also saw how partnering with the other patrons in Hart van Vathorst has provided the Ontmoetingskerk with unique opportunities to interact with people who would normally not find their way to church. There are thus obvious ways in which some of the commercial aspects of being part of a project like HVV may enhance the church's mission. On the other hand, the fact that the Ontmoetingskerk is not itself involved in 'running businesses' serves to safeguard its freedom to focus on what it perceives to be the core of being church, namely the preaching of the Word of God and the celebration of the sacraments. When we look at the practices of the Ontmoetingskerk, we see that this basic idea about the core of what it means to be church does not translate into a narrower church life; in fact, the Ontmoetingskerk is quite active in many areas. Its life is not confined to a weekly sermon and sacramental celebration. However, it does feel the freedom to invest in what it perceives to be important for the life of the church, like growing in inclusive practice and reflecting on that practice from the perspective of its own values, without worrying too much about finances or business interests. It has to be noted here, of course, that this is apparently due in part to the fact that the 'traditional' way of funding the church (through member contributions) allows the Ontmoetingskerk to realize its mission. Therefore, it may not experience the same urgency that has driven HeartEdge to include the C of commerce in its model. However, what is also at stake here is the more fundamental question of what the church's calling is. Is *commerce* really to be equally valued as church as *congregation*, for example? In the debates surrounding the place of churches in the current Dutch social landscape, a number of authors have cautioned churches to stick to their core responsibilities.[19] This is also how the rcl tradition in which the Ontmoetingskerk participates has often spoken about the relation between church and world; the church's main responsibility is to share the Gospel and as such to shape Christians to live out their calling in the world. In a recent dissertation, Marinus de Jong has shown this line to be present in the

---

[19]Examples include some of the contributors to the collected volume Bernts, *Boodschap aan de kerken?*

7.3. Discussion

thought of the theologian Klaas Schilder, one of the RCL's founding fathers, and connected it to the current day 'ecclesial turn' most famously represented by the American ethicist Stanley Hauerwas. De Jong shows that notwithstanding the many points of divergence between Schilder and Hauerwas, they do share a common interest in the formative nature of basic ecclesial life for the life of Christians in the world.[20]

The question whether and how the church should be partnering with other organizations in projects like HVV, or whether it should include commerce among its own responsibilities, is deserving of further attention. This question becomes relevant in the life of HVV in at least two ways. In the first place, as the description of the cooperation between the partners and their leadership (cf. 4.5 and 4.6) shows, the commercial partners sometimes have competing interests, but the position of the church is less complex because of the absence of immediate commercial interests in HVV. Similarly, in some of the forms of resistance against HVV's mission explored in section 6.4, we recognize the complexity of legal and financial constructions that arise in projects like HVV, not to mention all the practical issues related to building accessibility. Briefly stated, the Ontmoetingskerk seems to have a kind of freedom that may end up becoming endangered if it were itself actually in charge of running HVV as a business. As a second and related point, the question also becomes relevant for leadership (cf. 4.6). As we have seen, leadership for the partners is quite different from ecclesial leadership. Whereas the leaders of the different partners primarily need to 'run their business', in the current situation the church's leadership has the freedom to focus on leading the congregation itself. This includes making efforts towards more inclusive practices by the attention it gives to inclusion in sermons, etc., as well as the embodiment of inclusive values in their ways of leading. In relation to HVV, the church's leadership take their responsibilities in continued reflection on HVV's mission as established in its initial mission statement. They can do so without formal authority over any of the other partners. This means that the church's leadership does not have formal power over HVV, but a more testifying kind of voice. If the church were itself actively involved in the commercial side of HVV,

---

[20] De Jong, *The Church is the Means.*

this would complexify the power dynamics. The church would then not only have a 'ministerial authority' (as it now does with respect to its own church members), but also a more 'commercial authority'. This raises questions of a theological nature and also represents a possible source of power abuse.

The question of if and how the church should partner with other organizations in projects like HVV, or whether she should include commerce in her own responsibilities deserves further attention. This question becomes relevant in the life of HVV in at least two ways. In the first place, as the description of the cooperation between the partners and their leadership (cf. 4.5 and 4.6) shows, interests sometimes compete amongst the commercial partners, but the church has a less complex position in this because they don't have immediate commercial interests in HVV. Similarly, in some of the forms of resistance against HVV's mission that we explored in section 6.4, we recognize the complexity of legal and financial constructions that come up in projects like HVV, not to mention all the practical issues related with building an accesible building and keeping it accesible. Concludingly, it seems that the Ontmoetingskerk has a kind of freedom that might be endangered if they were actually in charge of running HVV as a business themselves. Secondly, related to the first point, the question also becomes relevant in relation to leadership (cf. 4.6). As we have seen, the leadership for the partners is quite different from the ecclesial leadership. Whereas the leaders of the different partners need to primarily 'run their business', in the current situation the church's leadership has the freedom to focus on leading the congregation itself. This includes making efforts towards more inclusive practices by giving attention to inclusion in sermons et cetera, as well as by embodying inclusive values in their ways of leading. In relation to HVV, they take their responsibilities in continued reflection on the mission of HVV as it was laid down in the initial mission statement. They can do this without having formal authority over any of the other partners. This means that the church's leadership does not have formal power over HVV, but rather has a more testifying voice. If the church would itself be actively involved in the commercial side of HVV, this would complexify the power dynamics. The church would then not only have a 'ministerial authority' (as they have now regarding their own church members), but also a more 'commercial authority'. This raises theo-

7.3. Discussion

logical questions and is also a possible source of power abuse.

A big contribution of HeartEdge's four C's is its acknowledgement of the necessity of reflection on the financial resources necessary for realizing the church's mission. However, provided that traditional ways of funding remain adequate, our case study suggests that these traditional ways have their benefits in terms of the church's freedom to focus on what it perceives to be its core responsibilities, and a separation between 'ministerial authority' and 'commercial authority'. These questions are deserving of further study as other local congregations wishing to embark on a similar journey might choose other organizational forms.

Inclusion in All Programs

Aside from the organizational form chosen in HVV, we can reflect also on the question whether its approach has resulted in 'enough' inclusion. As we have seen in chapter 6, it is very difficult to set a standard for what is 'enough'. We saw that inclusion is an ongoing process, in which new lessons are continuously being learned. Our purpose is therefore not to judge whether the Ontmoetingskerk has reached 'satisfactory' levels of inclusion. Even if this were possible, it never was the present study's intention. What we can do, however, is to reflect on the breadth of the inclusive ideal's application.

On a number of occasions over the course of our explorations, we noted how inclusion did *not* seem to shape certain aspects of church life. We can think, for example, of the way in which involvement with HVV seems at times to be competing for attention with youth work. In section 4.6, we thus saw how the church decided to invest separately in youth work by hiring a youth worker. In section 5.4.2, we similarly saw in relation to teaching practices that there is little overlap between the inclusive vision and the educational programs for young people and adults alike. In section 6.4, we saw how the perceived competing interest of attention for youth and attention for the residents of HVV also became a factor of resistance. The choices that the Ontmoetingskerk has made with respect to this tension are all very understandable. However, in light of the ideas on inclusion developed above (7.3.1), there are also a number of critical questions we can ask. First, if it is indeed true that inclusion teaches us new and unexpected things about fundamental aspects of what it means to be part of the Body of Christ, is it not remarkable that it is precisely those aspects of church life with the greatest focus on learning and formation that witness the greatest difficulties in making room for this inclusion? Secondly, if the major challenge for becoming more inclusive is indeed to 'question self-evidences', then what does that mean for the way we think about education in the church? On the basis of the stories we have heard in this study, it is clear that the Ontmoetingskerk has received an unusually rich potential in HVV for learning from others. This is also recognized at times, as when people responded emotionally during church services when personal testimonies were being shared (cf. 5.2). However, in order to derive full benefit from this potential, it is necessary to think creatively about how, for example, youth work could be structured differently to that end. In an article on Christian discipleship and ministry, Eeva John, Naomi Nixon, and Nick Shepherd sum up four pedagogical tools which can make learning a transformative experience, based on a qualitative research project carried out among theological educators. Transformative learning, in their words, "opens learners to the transformative work of the Holy Spirit by enabling them to bring their whole selves - intellect, affections, spirit and bodies - as well as their relationships to the learning experience."[21] According to their study, one of the pedagogical tools is the encouragement of real encounters. The authors point out that encounters take place on different levels. In education, we are used to the idea of relations between teachers and students, and students amongst each other, as when they work together on a project. But deeper and more meaningful encounters can take place "when opportunities are created for learners to wrestle with different (often contrary) perspectives. Teaching and learning that confronts learners with the view and interpretations of others is hard and even painful - but is transformative when learners are willing to see the Holy Spirit at work within the reality of those encounters."[22] Reflecting on the findings of these articles and relating them to HVV, it is not hard to identify 'different perspectives' that are challenging. If students learn in relation to people whose perspective on life is clearly different from their own, they are

---

[21] John, Nixon, and Shepherd, "Life-Changing Learning", p. 3.
[22] Ibid., p. 12.

7.3. Discussion

expected to learn much more and in much more transformative ways than if they were to be placed in their own separate groups. This challenges existing practices in the Ontmoetingskerk, but it also invites others who are thinking of how their faith community could become more inclusive to reflect from the very beginning on the breadth of their inclusive vision: inclusion relates to all aspects of church life.

Similar observations could be made for some other aspects of ecclesial life, like that of mission and diaconate.[23] Does the way in which these aspects are structured really allow for reciprocity? Does it enable the church to receive all the gifts that the Spirit gives?[24] The underlying question seems to be a simple one: are the self-evidences really questioned? That is, although it seems practical and self-evident to structure teaching programs according to intellectual levels, what does such structuring say about what we value most in learning and about what we perceive discipleship to be? And although it seems practical and self-evident for the 'strong' to contribute and the 'weak' to receive, what does such a vision say about the gifts we value most and about what it means to contribute to the church?

Dealing with Resistance

Apart from the organizational approach chosen and the breadth of the inclusive vision, another aspect that has a bearing on the extent to which the inclusive vision is realized is the handling of resistance (cf. 6.4).

Looking at HVV, first of all, it seems important to be realistic. Considering the context, one should expect to encounter resistance. In the micro context of the Vathorst neighborhood, for example, time is scarce. This means that even if people were to be positive about HVV's

---

[23]Cf. Conner, *Disabling Mission, Enabling Witness*.

[24]James R. Nieman writes about his experiences trying to change some of the liturgical customs surrounding the offertory in his first congregation. These seemingly innocuous changes opened up a world of hurt feelings for two of his congregants and their daughter, who has Down syndrome. Based in part on the rejection of their daughter's participation in a church Christmas play decades ago, these congregants wondered whether their money was not "good enough to be brought forward during worship". Nieman concludes: "It was all about whether gifts are received with dignity, and what that says in turn about basic human value." See Nieman, "Dancing: Moves and Rhytms That Engage Local Wisdom", p. 106.

intentions, they still might not have the opportunity to be as involved as they would want to be due to simple time restrictions. In *Becoming Friends of Time*, John Swinton has argued that our present day conceptions of time put people with disabilities at risk of exclusion. Informed by their experiences and in conversation with the Christian tradition, he provides a theological critique of how people in today's Western world look at time. But paradoxically, a 'redeemed' perception of time as a gift to be shared can only be discovered if we first take the time for this discovery, for example by becoming friends with someone who lives at a much 'slower pace'.[25] In some of our interviews, we saw that people in the Ontmoetingskerk have made this discovery and decided to invest their time differently as a result. However, this is not the case for everyone, nor is it realistic to expect this to be so. Another example of a form of resistance that will likely remain a part of the life of the Ontmoetingskerk has to do with koinonia. Reflecting on what community is and inspired by his experiences at L'Arche, Jean Vanier writes that personal sympathies or antipathies can not be decisive factors in true community. Rather, the *spiritual level* of community binds together, regardless of these sympathies and antipathies.[26] However, as we observed above, it is also in this regard that the Ontmoetingskerk as an 'average' congregation differs from a more 'high-commitment setting' like L'Arche.[27] In the Ontmoetingskerk, we have seen a lasting tension as to whether koinonia is indeed experienced by all, or whether there are smaller subgroups in which the communal aspect of church life is experienced. The latter seems to be the case, at least in part. In a way, this could be seen as a form of resistance against inclusion; are these subgroups sufficiently open to allow the inclusion of others? At the same time, it seems inevitable for subgroups like this to exist in churches as large as the Ontmoetingskerk, and they

---

[25]Swinton, *Friends of Time*. Cf. Reinders, "Watch the Lilies of the Field". Swinton writes in like manner about the relationship between time and our conception of dementia; see Swinton, *Dementia*.

[26]Vanier, *Community and Growth*, pp. 31–35.

[27]Vanier would probably agree with this, as he stresses the differences between 'communities' (like L'Arche) and the church. L'Arche is, in his estimation, not a church (cf. for example how he writes about the necessary connection between *communities* like L'Arche and the institutional stability of the Roman Catholic Church in ibid., pp. 8–10). But the church *can* indeed learn from communities like L'Arche; cf. Hauerwas and Vanier, *Living Gently in a Violent World*.

7.3. Discussion

can also do much good in providing settings where people trust each other enough to share life and faith. The tension we see here is thus not simply a 'negative' tension, but has fruitful sides as well (cf. 7.3.1).

Without becoming unrealistic in one's expectations, one must continue to address resistance in order to realize the inclusive vision. In this, as Kathleen S. Smith argues, effective Christian leadership is indispensable:

> Effective leaders believe certain things deeply and commit themselves selflessly to realizing certain ends. [...] For Christian leaders, such conviction has the greatest potential for long-term good when it arises out of a strong vision of the church's mission and a thorough grasp of the biblical, pastoral, and theological contours of the Christian faith and church. This must be combined with an ability to communicate these contours in meaningful and relevant ways through sound preaching and teaching and imaginative pastoral leadership. [...] Effective leaders are capable of informing and guiding an ongoing "argument" between competing convictions. At such points conviction requires a deep grounding in and understanding of the faith tradition, as well as a lively imagination and capacity for thinking creatively. Effective Christian leaders think deeply, theologically, integratively, and creatively.[28]

Connecting Smith's ideas back to the Ontmoetingskerk and its inclusive ideal, or to other faith communities wishing to become more inclusive, it is of tantamount importance for leaders to think about the way inclusion relates to "the church's mission, and the biblical, pastoral, and theological contours of the Christian faith." This will enable leaders to navigate the "competing convictions" that drive factors of resistance. Leaders will have to think "creatively" as well in how they communicate this vision so as to facilitate its realization. As we observed in section 6.4, this includes naming the ways in which the desired new situation is benefitting to all, and maximally facilitating opportunities for all to experience these benefits. What stood out is that intrinsic motivation on the part of church members was not

---

[28] Smith, *Stilling the Storm*, pp. 202–203.

a necessary condition for them to experience these benefits. On the other hand, when we consider some of the stories in which church members came to experience these benefits, what stood out is that they were often 'helped' in one way or another; someone may have asked them to volunteer for a certain task, or else they participated in a church service that left a big impression on them. One interviewee thought it might be necessary to 'force' people into interactions with people with disabilities, although he himself also problematized this coercion. However, this case study suggests that facilitating people as much as possible, albeit without coercion, is an important aspect of realizing the inclusive vision.

The American theologian Andrew Root writes in this respect that one of the pastor's primary tasks is to "curate [...] in-between spaces, through facilitation of locales that allow people to share in each other's needs, to see each other as persons."[29] By these 'in-between spaces', Root means relationships between people: "The space between us is the relationship that makes us *us*. This between is a spiritual reality where tangible faces encounter each other."[30] It is in this space that Jesus can be encountered, for Jesus promises "to be present in the place where the face of two or three are gathered."[31] Therefore, 'curating' these places or relationships is not a side business for Christian communities. Facilitating relationships should be at the very core of their ministry.[32]

Our case study serves to underline and confirm Smith's thoughts on the importance of effective leadership. For a congregation to become more inclusive, leadership is indispensable and must be grounded theologically, creative, and integrative; the realization of the vision requires not only the formation of abstract ideas, but also very concrete facilitations which are put in place. Much of the resistance we encountered had to do with very practical concerns. For this reason, we can also point back to the organizational structure chosen by HVV as we studied it in the beginning of this subsection; in order to think through the practicalities of becoming accessible and inclusive, it is important to involve professionals and to listen to the experiences of

---

[29]Root, *The Relational Pastor*, p. 163.
[30]Ibid., p. 155.
[31]Ibid., p. 157.
[32]Cf. also Moltmann, "Liberate Yourselves", pp. 112–114.

7.3. Discussion

experts. Inclusive ideals, no matter how lofty, simply cannot be realized in a building that does not provide access to people with mobility impairments.

Summary

In this subsection, we have explored the lessons that can be learned and the questions that still remain for HVV and the Ontmoetingskerk's pursuit of the realization of their inclusive vision. We have seen that partnering with other organizations with expertise and experience makes it easier for the church itself to focus on its core responsibilities, while learning from others in the many practical difficulties that surface over the course of a project like HVV. We have seen that it is easy to overlook certain areas of ecclesial life in realizing an inclusive vision. If you want to receive the gifts of all the members of the body, it is important to question self-evidences creatively in all aspects of church life. On the way to the realization of such an inclusive vision, many forms of resistance arise. Even as you acknowledge that this tension between ideal and resistance to the ideal as a lasting aspect of ecclesial life and thus remain realistic in your expectations, it is important for leadership to continue to engage this resistance and to take the lead in establishing a solid grounding for their vision and to communicate it clearly, while facilitating opportunities for church members to experience the benefits of a more inclusive congregation. An important theological motivation for this facilitation of encounters is found in Andrew Root's reflections on the presence of Jesus in the spaces in-between people.

7.3.3 Inclusive Celebration

In the previous subsections, we have looked at the lessons this case study has to offer for the concept of inclusion in relation to the life of the church and for the realization of an inclusive vision. In the current section, we will explore how inclusion is embodied and becomes visible in the life of the Ontmoetingskerk. Our primary focus in this will be on liturgical life.

Lessons From Vathorst for Inclusive Liturgy

There are a number of resources available about how worship can be made more inclusive. In the Dutch context, we can think of several resources from Johan Smit.[33] An example for the American context is Barbara J. Newman's work on inclusive worship.[34] When we interrogate our data on the point of what it says about liturgy, there are four characteristics that stand out:

1. **Participatory liturgy:** One element that people frequently named was the involvement of a broad group of church members in the liturgy. In Vathorst the liturgy is not led by the pastor alone, but many others have responsibilities in reading, leading worship, sharing testimonies, etc. If the contributions from a wide group of people are valued in liturgy, it is also much easier to value the contributions of people with disabilities, who are, of course, in the first place also just 'church members'. As one of the interviewees put it, with such a vision in place their participation is not considered something special (cf. p. 151). Liturgy is both the expression and formation of the congregation's faith, and the data suggest that making the expression of a broad group of believers visible in liturgy really does contribute to this formative aspect. After all, respondents often remarked that it was not just about *what* happens during a service (e.g. the reading of a text), but also about *who* is doing it.[35] Liturgy is thus more than the performance of a set of (ritual) functions; when a text from Scripture is read, there is more going on than just the communication of some written words in audible words (or visible gestures). It is good to be mindful of this and to be intentional in thinking about how the roles in the liturgy are

---

[33] Smit, *Zo gewoon mogelijk*; Smit, *Sociale integratie in de geloofsgemeenschap*; Smit, *Vademecum voor een inclusieve kerk*; Smit, "Competenties voor de pastorale communicatie met mensen met een verstandelijke beperking".

[34] Newman and Grit, *Accessible Gospel, Inclusive Worship*.

[35] We saw in section 6.2.3 how the mere presence, visibility, and participation of people with disabilities in communal worship gatherings changed people's perspectives on disability in significant ways. It is as Bill Gaventa writes: "Unless they have the opportunity to participate, people with disabilities will remain a class of people rather than becoming James, John, Susan, and Diane, individuals with unique interests, gifts, and needs." (Gaventa, "Learning from People with Disabilities", p. 111).

7.3. Discussion

distributed. Below, we will point to pastoral liturgy as a useful field for guiding reflection on this.

2. **Valuing the entire liturgy**: For many respondents, as indeed one might expect in a Reformed church, the sermon forms the center of the liturgy. The rest of the church service is then understood as a framework around that main event. Such a sermon-centric liturgy does, however, make it difficult to include everyone, especially if the sermon is understood as a verbal form of communication that is largely aimed at cognition. Behind this centrality of the sermon is an appreciation for the Scriptures as the Word of God that the congregation must give a central place. However, it remains possible for this theological conviction to be honored in other ways. In Vathorst, the sermon remains an important part of the worship service. In his sermons, pastor Smit often shares stories and makes personal connections. This makes it easier for his listeners to feel part of what is going on, even if they cannot follow the line of reasoning (which is sometimes abstract) throughout the entire sermon.[36] Even if the sermon may not be as accessible to everyone as one might wish, this does not have to mean that the entire worship service is inaccessible. Some respondents did not identify the sermon as the center, but pointed rather to the worship of God in song and prayer, or the celebration of the sacraments. These other 'centers' are much better suited to the inclusion of people of all abilities: singing, giving praise, receiving bread and wine, giving thanks, lamenting, or offering petitions to God in prayer - all these things can be done in a variety of ways, leaving room for the personal expressions and experiences of each and every person. What this entails is that inclusive liturgy must value the whole of liturgy, for if it focuses on a single center like preaching, it will inevitably be on just one track and therefore exclude

---

[36]In our discussion here, we are focusing primarily on the accessibility of sermons in terms of their comprehensibility. Another important element for the accessibility of sermons is for people with disabilities to feel that their experiences are understood by the preacher, rather than being neglected (cf. 5.2) or reduced to, for example, suffering or brokenness alone (cf. 6.2.1). An interesting discussion of the accessibility of sermons in this way and in relation to scriptural images of human impairments can be found in Black, *Healing Homiletic*.

certain groups. For this reason, it is necessary to reflect on what the constitutive elements of the liturgy are. Barbara Newman gives an example of this in her work when she refers to what she calls 'vertical habits', which can be seen as basic elements of any worship service that can easily be translated into forms suited to the entire breadth of any congregation. She lists eight such habits: Love You (Praise); I'm Sorry (Confession); Why? (Lament); I'm Listening (Illumination); Help (Petition); Thank You (Gratitude); What Can I Do? (Service); Bless You (Blessing).[37]

3. **As normal as possible**: Even though a number of things in the liturgy have clearly changed, most respondents reported that there is little that is special about their church services. The services feel quite 'normal' to them. In the tradition of the RCL and many other churches, special services have historically been organized from time to time to accommodate people with 'special needs'. These services were clearly recognizable as being 'different'. As we noted in section 5.2.2, the Ontmoetingskerk does sometimes still host such services in compliance with existing agreements with its classis. But as its other services show and as its vision entails, the intention is for everyone to feel welcome also in 'normal' services. It must be noted that the Ontmoetingskerk seems to have succeeded in this. Most people I spoke to, residents and non-residents alike, value the services, even if there are parts that they themselves find less inspiring or rewarding. Rather than designing special programs or liturgies, what seems to matter most is that a person is welcomed and experiences opportunities to express their faith and to be shaped in it. The adaptations necessary to achieve this are often quite minor, and must be discovered in conversation with the people requiring them.

4. **From special needs to universal needs**: Many respondents, including both residents and non-residents, indicated that ever since the Ontmoetingskerk's involvement with HVV, its worship services have become more interactive, and more embodied or

---

[37]Newman and Grit, *Accessible Gospel, Inclusive Worship*, pp. 33–75.

holistic, involving one's entire being instead of just the mind. They said that there is much more attention for the body and for emotion. Some respondents noted that they have been impacted significantly in the way they worship by what they have learned from the example of certain residents. So, as we saw in the first characteristic described above, the services *have* changed in some ways, but these changes have not just impacted a small 'target group'. Rather, they have impacted the entire congregation. The desire for a liturgy in which one's entire humanity is involved has nothing to do with special needs, but is better described as a universal need.

These four characteristics of the Ontmoetingskerk's inclusive liturgy could help others who are considering ways in which their worship might be made more accessible. Potential lessons for them are to keep things as normal as possible; to make sure that the liturgy offers opportunities for the formation and expression of the faith of the breadth of the congregation; to think about how the entirety of the liturgy can be valued without certain parts being overemphasized; and, finally, to realize and communicate that the development of an inclusive liturgical practice is not for the benefit of a small 'target group', but fosters the worship of the entire congregation.

Pastoral Liturgy

The approach to liturgy chosen in Vathorst can best be understood from the perspective of pastoral liturgy. Pastoral liturgy can be defined as

> the study and application of liturgy in the actual life of the church. It explores the nature of worship as constitutive and expressive of the Christian faith and applies these insights and commitments in concrete worshiping communities. Pastoral liturgy grounds practice in the history of liturgy and the theology of worship while being sensitive to the needs and resources of the local community of faith.[38]

---
[38] Senn, *Introduction to Christian Liturgy*, p. 1.

Pastoral liturgy is a term that has its origins in Roman Catholic circles after the Second Vatican Council as a way to put into practice the lines drawn in the Council's *Constitution on the Sacred Liturgy (Sacrosanctum Concilium)*.[39] An important message of this document is that all believers should be able to participate fully in the liturgy and that the liturgy should be reformed accordingly.41 In broad lines, in the pastoral liturgical approach, the main focus of liturgical training has shifted from knowledge of the liturgical tradition to the formation of liturgical leaders and their equipping with the skills necessary to lead meaningful worship in a local parish.[40] This emphasis on the local, practical dimension of worship in which all believers should be able to participate can still be seen as a characteristic of much pastoral liturgical scholarship that has emerged in Roman Catholic and Anglican circles following Vatican II.[41]

Anglican scholar Mark Eary uses the term pastoral liturgy in a more restricted sense, defining it as "worship that cares". He stands in the tradition of pastoral liturgy but introduces a focus on the pastor as caregiver. Eary states that worship is an important part of a believer's life, having the potential to change and shape it. Therefore, it is important for the task of leading worship to be taken seriously, and to ensure that believers are actually cared for or 'pastored'. It is not surprising then that Eary identifies inclusion as an important aspect of pastoral liturgy; one form of caring for all people is actively and consciously including all believers, with a sensitivity to the unwitting exclusion of certain groups.[42] By pointing to inclusion as an important factor in pastoral liturgy, Eary reinforces and underlines the Council's original call for the full participation of all believers.

The Reformed liturgist John Witvliet does not use the term pastoral liturgy as such, but in his book *Worship Seeking Understanding* he does devote the final four chapters to the connection between liturgy and pastoral studies.[43] The background to Witvliet's reflection is very different from that of Vatican II or the pastoral liturgical scholarship that followed the council in Roman Catholic and Anglican circles.

---

[39] Text can be accessed online: *Sacrosanctum Concilium - English Text*.
[40] Earey, *Worship That Cares*, pp. xiii–xiv.
[41] E.g. Perham, *New Handbook of Pastoral Liturgy*.
[42] Earey, *Worship That Cares*, pp. xiii–xx, 1, 8.
[43] Witvliet, *Worship Seeking Understanding*, pp. 269–308.

7.3. Discussion

While the latter two can be seen as a response to a liturgical praxis that had become uniform and was in need of reform, Witvliet's Reformed context never had a very strict and prescribed uniform liturgy. Rather, Witvliet's reflection on the relation between pastoral studies and liturgy flows out of a chaotic pluriformity in worship styles, leading to so-called worship wars. Notwithstanding the very different backgrounds, the result of Witvliet's reflections seems to be very similar to that of pastoral liturgy. Witvliet calls for discernment and wisdom in a time of extensive liturgical change. He issues a primary call to those who lead worship, both the theologians amongst them and other parties like the musicians, to conceive of themselves as pastors, rather than looking at their liturgical tasks as either a merely technical activity, or, on the contrary, an overly spiritual one. A pastor can be expected to have expertise in his field, but also a love for his flock. Witvliet argues for investment in pastoral training, so that the kind of values that enable worship leaders to act as pastors can be fostered:

> What the church needs most is not another hymnal, a new sound system, a revised prayer book, or another set of published scripts. What the church needs most are discerning, prayerful, joyous people who treat their work as worship planners and leaders as a holy, pastoral calling.[44]

This Reformed perspective shows that pastoral liturgy is not just a name for arbitrary liturgical changes in some specific ecclesial context. The pastoral liturgical perspective transcends its specific context and makes us aware of the complex dynamics between the available liturgical scripts (whether they be narrow, as in the pre-Vatican II Roman Catholic Church, or manifold, as in Evangelical and Reformed churches) and the worship as it is performed by a congregation on Sunday morning. Furthermore, the pastoral liturgical perspective points to the central role of the pastors (understood in the broad sense of the term, referring to all those who have some responsibility of leadership in worship) in working with these dynamics to care for the congregation. This pastoring or caring is not a soft form of caring, but also implies pointing in a certain direction, which may sometimes conflict with popular opinion. Thus, pastoral liturgy does not mean

---
[44]Ibid., p. 284.

the end of organized worship, handing this central task of the church over to the contingent desires of local believers. Witvliet's description of the Reformed context shows that it might even mean the opposite, reinforcing carefully planned and performed worship as a wise and discerning form of pastoral response to worship wars.

The perspective of pastoral liturgy sheds light on the liturgy in Vathorst. We can apply it, for example, to the changes in the praxis of the Lord's Supper which were made over time (cf. 5.2.1). The way in which the Ontmoetingskerk's leadership reflected on the changes in this practice can be seen as a textbook example of pastoral liturgy; its leaders took their role as shepherds of the flock seriously in their careful reflection on liturgical practice. They did so motivated by the conviction that all members of the flock should have access to the sacrament of the Lord's Supper. This conviction challenged existing practice and as such represented a critique on the normative backgrounds of this practice. However, this did not mean that all of these normative backgrounds were thrown overboard in a kind of ruthless worship war. Rather, following upon its criticism the leadership adjusted the form used in the invitation for identifying those who are welcome to join the celebration of the Lord's Supper, thereby acknowledging that it is something sacred that should not be thought of too lightly. However, by offering the possibility of receiving a blessing by the laying on of hands, and thus expanding the celebration of the sacrament with an added liturgical practice, the leadership also succeeded in still communicating the inclusive message that all are welcome. In this way, the celebration of the Lord's Supper is not just the performance of an old ritual, but a lived practice aimed at pastoring the flock in a certain direction, in this case (amongst other things) towards a more inclusive congregation. The changes in liturgical praxis therefore do not reduce to simply doing whatever the congregation or just a part of it wants, but keep in place the dynamic tension between human desires and the existing, normatively laden liturgical practices. In line with what we have said in the previous subsection about the importance of effective leadership in growing towards inclusive practices, finding a balance in this tension is a pastoral calling.

Summary

In this subsection, we saw what is characteristic about the Ontmoetingskerk's inclusive liturgical life and reflected on the possible lesson to be derived. We explored four elements: celebrating the liturgy in a manner that is as ordinary as possible, ensuring liturgical participation for all believers, valuing the entire liturgy, and realizing that inclusive liturgy does not aim at a small target group but seeks the benefit of the entire congregation. A helpful field of reflection on such liturgy was found in the pastoral liturgical approach. This approach has the potential to help the Ontmoetingskerk on its way forward, but it can also help other churches, regardless of how far they have already come on the road to a more inclusive worship.

7.3.4 Inclusive Church in the World

So far in this discussion section, we have explored the contributions that the present case study makes to our understanding of inclusion in relation to church life, the organizational forms that can be applied to bring this to realization, and the way inclusion looks when it is embodied in the church's liturgical life. We now turn to the meaning such inclusive communities can go on to have for the society around them of which they are themselves a part.

Churches as Uneasy Allies

As we saw in section 1.2.2, recent changes in social policy in the Netherlands underscore the need for strong local communities. The infrastructure of such communities is often described as civil society, although this term is debated. As Martin van der Meulen writes, we can understand civil society in a minimal sense to mean "a network of associations of citizens that try to achieve common goals set by themselves. This network can be distinguished, but not separated from the domains of state, market and the private sphere."[45] However, as was similarly noted in section 1.2.2, it is questionable whether this civil society is strong enough to compensate for the government's withdrawal in terms of social services. In section 2.2.2 we saw the possible

---

[45] Van der Meulen, *Vroom in de Vinex*, p. 174.

consequences for the inclusion of people with disabilities in society, for example. The Swedish sociologist of religion Per Pettersson observes that governments in Western Europe are increasingly calling upon churches to play a role in this, both as 'welfare agents' and as creators of social cohesion to strengthen communities.[46] As Marten van der Meulen shows for the Dutch context in his book *Vroom in de Vinex*, and Paul Lichterman does for the American context in his *Elusive Togetherness*, churches are indeed trying to play these roles in society.[47] Lichterman conducted an ethnographic study in nine liberal and conservative churches in a city and came to a number of conclusions about the way churches can contribute to the creation of social cohesion. One of them was the following:

> My findings lead me to propose that a community group's own togetherness shapes the kind of togetherness it can try to create with the world beyond the group. That does not mean that a society with more tightly knit groups is a society with more togetherness over all. Rather, the different kinds of togetherness within civic groups shape the possibilities for spiraling relationships outward.[48]

This case study has shown that Hart van Vathorst plays a similar role for its direct Vathorst neighborhood as well as for wider society, and is being recognized for this by the government (cf. 4.3.1, 4.3.3). Through its pursuit of greater inclusion for itself, it contributes to a more inclusive neighborhood with more social cohesion. At least, this is its goal and some are recognizing it. The methodological limitations of this study mean that it cannot confirm or deny such recognition. Regardless, it must be noted that Hart van Vathorst is not so much trying to *create* an inclusive neighborhood as pursuing an inclusive community within the neighborhood. It is also clear that this is being recognized by some, and that it is drawing people to Hart van Vathorst and the Ontmoetingskerk. In this sense, HVV and the Ontmoetingskerk are acting in line with what the German theologian Jürgen Moltmann wrote as early as 1989:

---

[46]Pettersson, "Church as Welfare Agent", p. 15.
[47]Van der Meulen, *Vroom in de Vinex*; Lichterman, *Elusive Togetherness*.
[48]Lichterman, *Elusive Togetherness*, p. 15.

7.3. Discussion

> Community can heal our divided society, and it can do so on both sides. It is only in fellowship with one another that both the person with disabilities and the one without can experience a new humanity. So may we, with all our strength, build such communities of persons with and without disabilities! This is a task for church communities.[49]

As our explorations of Hart van Vathorst's mission statement and the way that mission is lived out have shown, this vision of inclusive community is explicitly grounded in Christian faith (cf. 4.4). It 'goes against the grain' of society and can therefore create tensions with the wider context, as we have shown in section 4.3.3. However, it seems that this religious motivation is indispensable for Hart van Vathorst and is also part of its communal resources for becoming more inclusive. It is the grounding in Christian faith that makes people in the Ontmoetingskerk willing to get involved in this project. It is their religious practice of coming to church, at least on Sunday mornings, that provides HVV residents with a pattern of weekly opportunities for social interaction with the congregation. Even if the secularization context may result in societal unfamiliarity and unease with religion in general, or with Christianity (and a rather orthodox form of it at that) in particular, a project like Hart van Vathorst would look significantly different without that religious dimension, as indeed many respondents also formulated it (cf. 4.3.3). In his work on the role of a number of church-related projects in civil society in another newly built neighborhood in nearby Utrecht, Marten van der Meulen writes that

> ...the distinction made in civil society theory between religious and socio-cultural functions is questionable. Dividing the mission of these projects in a socio-cultural and a religious part, in which only the former can be seen as a contribution to society, does not do justice to the views of the two projects. They both take their religious activities to be important contributions, inseparable from the

---

[49]Published in English translation as Moltmann, "Liberate Yourselves", quotation from p. 122.

whole of their public mission.[50]

Learning from Vathorst, and specifically in relation to the work of Lichterman and Van der Meulen, we can thus suggest that if churches are to contribute to social cohesion and growth towards a more inclusive society for people with disabilities, they must first work critically on their own 'cohesion' and inclusivity, informed by their theological convictions on how their communities should be structured. This makes churches somewhat uneasy allies for governments; they have a high potential in terms of building social cohesion, but they may also have unpopular or misunderstood religious convictions. A question for further study within the field of public theology is thus what this tension entails for the cooperation of churches with other (religious or non-religious) partners, whether private or governmental, specifically in strengthening social cohesion.

A Particular Place

The above exploration of the role of the church in society might make it seem as if it is really the social aspect of church life that can have an impact on society. However, this case study has shown that other, more tangible aspects of ecclesial life in fact play a big part as well. It took considerable investments and courage to build the HVV building, and one could say that these resources could or perhaps even should have been invested otherwise, since a church is not a building. However, there is some sense in which the church *is* indeed the building. As one of HVV's residents put it, "I live in the same building as God does" (cf. 4.4.2). Oftentimes people mentioned how important it was to the residents that the different partners of HVV share the same roof, making church and other activities taking place in the building highly accessible (cf. 4.5). People from the neighborhood use Hart van Vathorst's building in several ways. The building is a place of meeting, of relaxation in the restaurant, of interaction with residents, or even of business. But it is also a building that holds religious value, as people know they may run into pastor Joost Smit there to talk about life, or can enter the prayer room to pray or light a candle. It was one of Vathorst's non-religious residents, who called himself a

---

[50] Van der Meulen, *Vroom in de Vinex*, p. 177.

typical Vathorster, who expressed the concern that his neighborhood lacked the soul which the church building in the village of his youth used to have (cf. 4.3.1).[51]

This raises questions for those who reflect on mission in current-day urban or suburban environments. Even though churches may have less available resources and people may be less willing to commit to 'heavy' communities, serving to make the concept of owning a church building increasingly outdated, the benefits of ownership for the way HVV and the Ontmoetingskerk live out their mission are clear. In an article on the early phases of HVV's development, Hans Schaeffer already pointed to the importance of the building itself in terms of the community's potential 'social capital'. As many authors have observed that the building itself, for example, opens up possibilities for cooperation between church and non-church partners. So too ownership of a building, whether full or partial, means that church communities can communicate their theology through the building.[52] As we have seen in section 4.5, this is also the case in HVV.

Summary

In this subsection, we have seen how the inclusive vision and practice of HVV and the Ontmoetingskerk may have an impact on broader society in strengthening social cohesion. We have seen that the social contribution of projects like HVV cannot be separated from their religious contributions, as religious convictions form important motivations for people to commit to these projects, as well as guidelines for the way churches like the Ontmoetingskerk think critically about their own 'togetherness', which in turn may 'spiral outward' as a contribution to togetherness in society at large. This makes churches important but slightly uneasy allies for governments looking to tap into the strength of local communities. We have also seen that projects like HVV benefit greatly from having their own building, and that this is a factor that must not be overlooked in reflection on the place of churches in newly built urban or suburban environments.

---

[51] Koelewijn and Remie, "Vinex-verdriet".
[52] Schaeffer, "Hospitable Church", pp. 187–190.

7.3.5 Theological Reflection

We have explored how this case study can help us understand inclusion in relation to church, its realization in practice, its embodiment in liturgy, and its impact on the world. Lastly, we will reflect on the role that theological reflection plays in this process.

Do We Need Theology?

As the model of theology in four voices shows, theology is woven throughout the life of the church, and is not something that happens only in an academic vacuum. An examination of the ways in which churches interact with inclusion, as we did in chapter 2, makes the question of the importance of theology all the more pressing. If we adopt a how-engagement, it would seem that we do not need any theology at all. We would then be able to make do with a pragmatic approach and look at 'what works' in order to promote inclusion. And is the how-engagement not the kind of engagement that *actually* makes a practical difference?

This case study suggests that it would be a mistake to underestimate the value of theological reflection. First, we saw how the Ontmoetingskerk adopted an 'on the go'-view on theology (cf. 4.4). Rather than starting with a fully worked out vision, it envisioned learning by doing and being in conversation *with* one another. It felt that this was much more in line with an inclusive vision - not designing a program *for* people, but working together with people. There are many benefits to this approach. However, we have also seen that it meant that some difficult theological questions remain unanswered relating, for example, to the way sense can be made from a Christian perspective of the existence of something like disability in this world. Such questions may lie behind problematic conceptions of people with disabilities that surfaced as part of what we have called 'resistance' against the project (cf. 6.4). To address such conceptions theologi-

---

[53]Reinders, *Disability, Providence, and Ethics*, pp. 1–29 argues that, even if people relate theological reflection (in his case on divine providence) to the experience of people with disabilities, they seldomly reflect critically on their own able-bodied position and perspective. This results in theological thought that, even if aimed at people with disabilities, does not actually reflect their experience and is therefore not helpful for "empowering them in living their daily lives" (p. 13).

7.3. Discussion

cally, for example, is not self-evident. For many people, disability is not a theme that they would relate to their thinking about God and the world.[53] Therefore, notwithstanding the importance of efforts to learn on the go, it is also necessary to take time to reflect theologically on questions that one sees coming up in reality.[54]

A second and related point is that HVV was in many senses a unique project when it started due to the combination it embodies of inclusive ideals and a rather 'typical' congregation. For this reason, it has had to learn many things on the go and wrestle with theological questions as they come up. However, part of the import of this case study is that other congregations may have something to learn from Vathorst. Therefore, by learning from HVV's story in this dissertation, they can anticipate a number of theological questions. It would be good, therefore, for reflection on these questions to become a part of such projects from their very start. Such reflection could take the form of a study group like the one they had in Vathorst, but the fruits of these studies would then also have to be presented to the entire congregation, for example through explicit attention to these matters in sermons.

Thirdly, in a number of places we have seen how theological reflection is indispensable for handling certain tensions. In section 4.3.3, for example, we noted how certain elements of the macro context are incompatible with the Christian convictions of the church. We also saw that in some cases, such as those relating to ethical issues like euthanasia, the espoused and operant theological voices of the Ontmoetingskerk show clear similarities with the macro context, even if these similarities are actually at odds with the normative and formal voices. Tensions like this show are indicative of the necessity of theological reflection. It is necessary not only to 'find the right answer' to questions like this one relating to ethics, but even more so to ask the right questions. This brings us to the issue of what we actually mean by theological reflection.

---

[54]Brock and Swinton, *Disability in the Christian Tradition* gives an overview of how theologians throughout the Christian tradition relate to what we now call 'disability'. This volume is a good aid in engaging theological conceptions of disability in one's own faith tradition. For example, there are contributions in the volume on Luther (Heuser, "The Human Condition as Seen from the Cross") and Calvin (Craemer, "John Calvin and Disability").

What Kind of Theological Reflection?

Up to this point, we have used the expression 'theological reflection' quite loosely. However, as the third point discussed above shows, what we understand theological reflection to mean is a very relevant question. This HVV case study has revealed that it does not have to mean that the congregation, or at least its majority, should have the right set of beliefs about disability before we can set out on the journey towards greater inclusivity. Some of the scholarship in the field of disability theology might make it feel like this is the case. That may be because it understands 'critical denunciation' to be part of its task; aspects of mainstream theology that represent 'ableist' biases must be critized.[55] Without denying the value of this approach for the development of theology as an academic discipline, an analysis of our data suggests that the kind of theological reflection needed at a local level is somewhat different.

A useful typology of different theological reflection methods has been designed by Elain Graham, Heather Walton, and Frances Ward:[56]

- **'Theology by Heart': The Living Human Document** - In this type of theological reflection, much emphasis is placed on the religious experience of individuals, as God is perceived primarily as an immanent force, knowable through the study of a person's inner world. This inner world is made accessible through things like journals or autobiographies.

- **'Speaking in Parables': Constructive Narrative Theology** - Theology of this type contrasts Scripture with human experience that might challenge or augment the Scriptural narrative. It thus studies Scripture, but do so always in relation to specific human experiences.

- **'Telling God's Story': Canonical Narrative Theology** - This type of theology places greater emphasis on the authoritative nature of canonical Scripture. Here human experience is not so much something that enriches our theological understanding as something that can only properly be understood from the

---

[55]E.g. Hull, *Disability*, pp. 61–76.
[56]Graham, Walton, and F. Ward, *Theological Reflection*.

7.3. Discussion

perspective of 'God's story' as found in Scripture.

- **'Writing the Body of Christ': Corporate Theological Reflection** - This type of reflection starts from the faith community as the Body of Christ. This community produces a theology through its life, which can be studied. This is not only a pragmatic step for understanding the community or changing it, but actually a way of doing theological reflection.

- **'Speaking of God in Public': Correlation** - This type of theological reflection understands theology's task to be to start a conversation between the surrounding culture and what Christians understand as revelation. That conversation is understood as a two-way process in which culture may also help theologians come to a better understanding of revelation.

- **'Theology-in-Action': Praxis** - The authors understand this type of theological reflection to be primarily about recognizing God's activity in reality. The call is then for Christians to grow in discipleship by following where this saving activity of God can be recognized. According to the authors, this discipleship often entails being with those who suffer and promoting justice.

- **'Theology in the Vernacular': Local Theologies** - Within this type, there is great emphasis on the contextuality of theology as an expression of the Gospel in a given culture, time, and place. An important question in this type of theological reflection is the extent to which the context determines theology.

This overview of types of theological reflection helps us to grasp the breadth of what we can call theological reflection, and also to understand how different these types may be from one another. There is not one 'right' way to answer the question what theological reflection is.

However, when we consider what has been done in this case study and reflect on what has the potential to help churches like the Ontmoetingskerk as well as other churches that have yet to start their journey towards greater inclusivity, it is clear that the 'writing the Body of Christ'-type of theological reflection can be a very helpful tool. Within such theological reflection, the congregation as a whole is invited to understand itself as the Body of Christ, and to realize the importance of the theological contributions made by all the members of the body as ways to grow in knowledge of the fullness of this Body. This type of theological reflection is therefore by nature inclusive (at least in Brock's 'theologized' conception of that word). It helps us realize that inclusion is not only a *goal*, but also *a way of reaching that goal*. It will inevitably lead to tensions and difficult theological questions, but treating these tensions and questions is then part of what it means to be the Body of Christ. Tensions and difficult questions are not 'attacks' from outside, but constitute hurting body parts that have truths to share with the rest of the Body. Theological reflection in this sense is helpful and even indispensable for congregations that want to become more inclusive. To be able to contribute fruitfully, it is important for this kind of theological reflection to study the Body of Christ in its complexity; that is, it should not only be after the 'opinions' of a limited group of people, but rather reveal a multifaceted construct of practices and reflection on these practices through time and space. Theology in this sense does not speak with one voice, but with at least four voices (cf. figure 1.1). The espoused and operant voices are not the only ones that are heard. They are always heard together with the formal and normative voices. As this case study has shown, even these four voices are not enough to fully grasp the Body's theology, as they all break down into many more individual voices and experiences. However, it is when these voices are carefully heeded and a dynamic conversation is constructed that the contours of the Body's theology start to reveal themselves in greater clarity. Both the *process* of bringing about this conversation and the preliminary *product* of these contours are immensely relevant for the life of the church. They help the church to live a "faithful" life, in recognition of and "participation in God's redemptive practices in, to and for the world."[57]

Summary

In this final subsection of the discussion section, we have looked at what we could learn from this case study about the necessity and role of theological reflection. We saw that theological reflection was indispensable in Vathorst, even if no fully worked out theological vision was in place at the outset of the project. Nonetheless, on-the-go the-

---

[57] Swinton and Mowat, *Practical Theology and Qualitative Research*, p. 7.

ological reflection was a necessary tool in handling tensions and difficult questions. Other faith communities may benefit from the Ontmoetingskerk's example so as to start reflecting on these questions and tensions before they arise in their own situations. We saw that it is important for this theological reflection not just to be about having the right 'theological positions' on certain themes, but to be more concerned with asking the right questions and providing church members with the tools to handle these tensions and questions. An awareness of what it means to be the Body of Christ may serve as a starting point for such theological reflection and assist the church in living faithfully in light of God's active salvific presence in the world.

Appendix A

Code Groups

This table provides an overview of the code groups that resulted from the analysis of the data through inductive open coding and consequent axial coding. The first eleven groups were visualized in networks in Atlas.ti. Due to the high number of codes, these networks cannot be printed in this book. The last group (i.e. rest) was not visualized in a network because the codes in it only provide background information for the other codes (see 3.5.5). The second column in the table shows the chapters in which the code groups and networks were primarily used.

Group	Name	Chapter
1	Context	4
2	Identity & Culture, Vision	4, 6
3	Leadership	4
4	Structure & Resources, community structures	4
5	Structure & Resources, organization	4
6	Atmosphere	4, 5
7	(Christian) practices	5
8	Commitment	6
9	Intended outcome, desire	6
10	Resistance	6
11	Interaction	6
12	Rest	4, 5, 6

Figure A.1: Distribution of code groups over chapters

References

Ammerman, N. et al., eds. *Studying Congregations: A New Handbook.* Nashville: Abingdon Press, 1998.
Angrosino, M. and J. Rosenberg. "Observations on Observation". In: *The SAGE Handbook of Qualitative Research.* Ed. by N.K. Denzin and Y.S. Lincoln. 4th edition. Los Angeles: SAGE, 2011, pp. 467–478.
Bach, U. *Ohne die Schwächsten ist die Kirche nicht ganz: Bausteine einer Theologie nach Hadamar.* Neukirchen-Vluyn: Neukirchener, 2006.
Bainbridge, W.S. *The Sociology of Religious Movements.* London: Psychology Press, 1997.
Barnes, C. "Understanding the Social Model of Disability: Past, Present and Future". In: *Routledge Handbook of Disability Studies.* Ed. by N. Watson, A. Roulstone, and C. Thomas. London/New York: Routledge, 2014, pp. 12–29.
Bass, D.C., K.A. Cahalan, et al. *Christian Practical Wisdom: What It Is, Why It Matters.* Grand Rapids: Eerdmans, 2016.
Bass, D.C. and C. Dykstra, eds. *Practicing Our Faith: A Way of Life for a Searching People.* 2nd edition. San Francisco: Jossey-Bass, 2010.
Bavinck, H. *Gereformeerde dogmatiek.* 7th ed. Kampen: Kok, 1998.
Bazzell, P. D. *Urban Ecclesiology: Gospel of Mark, Familia Dei and a Filipino Community Facing Homelessness.* London/New York: T&T Clark, 2015.
Bernts, T. *Boodschap aan de kerken? Religie als sociaal en moreel kapitaal.* Zoetermeer: Meinema, 2004.
Bernts, T. and J.T. Berghuijs. *God in Nederland: 1966-2015.* Utrecht: VBK Media, Mar. 15, 2016.
Black, K. *A Healing Homiletic: Preaching and Disability.* Nashville: Abingdon Press, 1996.

Bolwijn, R. *Armoede in Nederland 2019: Onderzoek Naar Hulpverlening Door Diaconieën, Parochiële Caritasinstellingen En Andere Kerkelijke Organisaties in Nederland*. Utrecht, 2019.

Bosman, J.A.G. *Celebrating the Lord's Supper in the Netherlands: A Study of Liturgical Ritual Practices in Dutch Reformed Churches*. Netherlands Studies in Ritual and Liturgy 22. Amsterdam/Groningen, 2020.

Bretherton, L. *Christianity and Contemporary Politics : The Conditions and Possibilities of Faithful Witness*. Chichester: Wiley-Blackwell, 2010.

Brock, B. "Theologizing Inclusion". In: *Journal of Religion, Disability & Health* 15.4 (2011), pp. 351–376. DOI: 10.1080/15228967.2011.620389.

Brock, B. and J. Swinton, eds. *Disability in the Christian Tradition: A Reader*. Grand Rapids: Eerdmans, 2011.

Brouwer, R. "Detecting God in Practices: Theology in an Empirical-Theological Research Project". In: *HTS Teologiese Studies/Theological Studies* 66.2 (2010), p. 5. DOI: 10.4102/hts.v66i2.805.

— *Geloven in gemeenschap: het verhaal van een protestantse geloofsgemeenschap*. Kampen: Kok, 2009.

Brouwer, R. et al. *Levend lichaam: dynamiek van christelijke geloofsgemeenschappen in Nederland*. Kampen: Kok, 2007.

Burger, H. "Theologische Hermeneutiek in Soteriologisch Perspectief". In: *Gereformeerde Hermeneutiek Vandaag: Theologische Perspectieven*. Ed. by A.L.Th. de Bruijne and H. Burger. Barneveld: Vuurbaak, 2017, pp. 35–66.

Cahalan, K.A. "Three Approaches to Practical Theology, Theological Education, and the Church's Ministry". In: *International Journal of Practical Theology* 9.1 (2005), pp. 63–94. DOI: 10.1515/IJPT.2005.005.

Calvin, J. *Institutes of the Christian Religion: In Two Volumes*. Ed. by J.Th. MacNeill. Trans. by F.L. Battles. Philadelphia/London: The Westminster Press, 1960.

Cameron, H. *Studying Local Churches: A Handbook*. London: SCM Press, 2005.

Cameron, H., D. Bhatti, and C. Duce. *Talking About God in Practice*. London: Hymns Ancient & Modern Ltd, 2010.

Campbell-Reed, E.R. "The Power and Danger of a Single Case Study in Practical Theological Research". In: *Conundrums in Practical Theol-*

ogy. Ed. by J.A. Mercer and B. Miller-McLemore. Brill, 2016, pp. 33–59.

Carter, E.W. *Including People with Disabilities in Faith Communities: A Guide for Service Providers, Families, and Congregations*. Baltimore: Brookes Publishing, 2007.

Cartledge, Mark J. *Testimony in the Spirit: Rescripting Ordinary Pentecostal Theology*. Farnham: Ashgate Publishing, 2010.

Clapton, J. *A Transformatory Ethic of Inclusion: Rupturing Concepts of Disability and Inclusion*. Rotterdam: Sense Publishers, 2008.

Conner, B.T. *Disabling Mission, Enabling Witness: Exploring Missiology Through the Lens of Disability Studies*. Downers Grove: IVP Academic, 2018.

Craemer, D.B. "John Calvin and Disability". In: *Disability in the Christian Tradition: A Reader*. Ed. by B. Brock and J. Swinton. Grand Rapids: Eerdmans, 2011, pp. 216–250.

Crijns, H., ed. *Diaconie in beweging*. Kampen: Kok, 2012.

Crutzen, O. and L. van der Linden. *Armoede in Nederland 2016: Onderzoek Naar Hulpverlening Door Diaconieën, Parochiële Caritasinstellingen En Andere Kerkelijke Organisaties in Nederland*. Utrecht, 2016.

De Bruijne, A.L.Th., ed. *Gereformeerde Theologie Vandaag : Oriëntatie En Verantwoording*. Barneveld: De Vuurbaak, 2004.

De Hart, J. and P. van Houwelingen. *Christenen in Nederland: Kerkelijke Deelname En Christelijke Gelovigheid*. Den Haag: Sociaal en Cultureel Planbureau, Dec. 2018.

De Jong, J.M. *The Church is the Means, the World is the End: The Development of Klaas Schilder's Thought on the Relationship between the Church and the World*. Kampen: Theological University, 2019.

De Jonge, A.M., H. Wijma, and J.H.F. Schaeffer. *Chocoladereep of - hagelslag? Literatuuronderzoek naar Ontwikkeling van "Gereformeerde Identiteit" in zeven decennia*. Zwolle: Praktijkcentrum, 2016.

De Roest, H.P. *Collaborative Practical Theology: Engaging Practitioners in Research on Christian Practices*. Leiden/Boston: Brill, 2019.

De Ruijter, C.J. *Meewerken met God: ontwerp van een gereformeerde praktische theologie*. Kampen: Kok, 2005.

Deddens, D and M. te Velde, eds. *Vrijmaking - Wederkeer: vijftig jaar vrijmaking in beeld gebracht, 1944-1994*. Barneveld: De Vuurbaak, 1994.

Douma, J. *Hoe gaan wij verder? Ontwikkelingen in de Gereformeerde Kerken (vrijgemaakt)*. Kampen: Kok, 2001.

— ed. *Om de ware oecumene: de Gereformeerde kerken (vrijgemaakt) in Nederland*. 1980.

Dulles, A. *Models of the Church*. 2nd ed. New York: Bantam Doubleday Dell, 2000.

Earey, M. *Worship That Cares: An Introduction to Pastoral Liturgy*. London: SCM Press, 2012.

Eiesland, N.L. *The Disabled God: Toward a Liberatory Theology of Disability*. Nashville: Abingdon Press, 1994.

Eiesland, N.L. and D.E. Saliers, eds. *Human Disability and the Service of God: Reassessing Religious Practice*. Nashville: Abingdon Press, May 1, 1998.

Emerson, R.M., R.I. Fretz, and L.L. Shaw. *Writing Ethnographic Fieldnotes*. Chicago: University of Chicago Press, 1995.

Fackre, G. *The Church: Signs of the Spirit and Signs of the Times*. Grand Rapids: Eerdmans, 2007.

Flyvbjerg, B. "Case Study". In: *The SAGE Handbook of Qualitative Research*. Ed. by N.K. Denzin and Y.S. Lincoln. 4th ed. Los Angeles, CA: SAGE, 2011, pp. 301–316.

— "Five Misunderstandings About Case-Study Research". In: *Qualitative Inquiry* 12.2 (2006), pp. 219–245. DOI: 10.117/1077800405284 363.

Gaventa, W.C. "Learning from People with Disabilities: How to Ask the Right Questions". In: *The Paradox of Disability: Responses to Jean Vanier and L'Arche Communities from Theology and the Sciences*. Ed. by J.S. Reinders. Grand Rapids: Eerdmans, 2010, pp. 154–168.

Geertsema, H. *Jaarplan 2016 Praktijkcentrum: Geloven... in werkelijkheid*. Zwolle: Praktijkcentrum, 2015.

Graham, E., H. Walton, and F. Ward. *Theological Reflection: Methods*. London: SCM Press, 2005.

Hall, S.A. "The Social Inclusion of People with Disabilities: A Qualitative Meta-Analysis". In: *Journal of Ethnographic & Qualitative Research* 3.3 (2009), pp. 162–173.

Hauerwas, S. "Seeing Peace: L'Arche as a Peace Movement". In: *The Paradox of Disability: Responses to Jean Vanier and L'Arche Com-

munities from Theology and the Sciences. Ed. by J.S. Reinders. Grand Rapids: Eerdmans, 2010, pp. 113–126.

Hauerwas, S. and J. Vanier. *Living Gently in a Violent World: The Prophetic Witness of Weakness*. Ed. by J. Swinton. Downers Grove: IVP Books, 2008.

Hay, P.L. *Negotiating Conviviality: The Use of Information and Communication Technologies by Migrant Members of the Bay Community Church*. Mankon: Langaa RPCIG, 2014.

Healy, N.M. *Church, World, and the Christian Life: Practical-Prophetic Ecclesiology*. Cambridge/New York: Cambridge University Press, 2000.

— "Ecclesiology, Ethnography, and God: An Interplay of Reality Descriptions". In: *Perspectives on Ecclesiology and Ethnography*. Ed. by P. Ward. Grand Rapids: Eerdmans, 2011, pp. 182–199.

Hegstad, H. "Ecclesiology and Empirical Research on the Church". In: *Explorations in Ecclesiology and Ethnography*. Ed. by C.B. Scharen. Grand Rapids: Eerdmans, 2012, pp. 34–47.

— *The Real Church: An Ecclesiology of the Visible*. Eugene: Wipf and Stock, 2013.

Heuser, S. "The Human Condition as Seen from the Cross: Luther on Disabilty". In: *Disability in the Christian Tradition: A Reader*. Ed. by B. Brock and J. Swinton. Grand Rapids: Eerdmans, 2011, pp. 184–215.

Hitzert, F. *Relatieontbinding in Vinex-Wijken, 2014 versus 2008*. CBS, Aug. 2016.

Hull, J.M. "'Sight to the Inly Blind'? Attitudes to Blindness in the Hymnbook." In: *Theology* 827 (2002), pp. 333–341.

— "A Spirituality of Disability: The Christian Heritage as Both Problem and Potential". In: *Studies in Christian Ethics* 16, 2 (2003), pp. 21–35. DOI: 10.1177/095394680301600202.

— "Blindness and the Face of God: Towards a Theology of Disability". In: *The Human Image of God*. Ed. by H.G. Ziebertz et al. Leiden: Brill, 2001, pp. 215–229.

— *Disability: The Inclusive Church Resource*. Ed. by B. Callaghan. London: Darton, Longman & Todd, 2014.

— "Open Letter from a Blind Disciple to a Sighted Saviour: Text and Discussion." In: *Borders, Boundaries and the Bible*. Ed. by M. O'Kane. Sheffield: Sheffield Academic Press, 2001, pp. 154–177.

Hütter, R. "The Church - The Knowledge of the Triune God: Practices, Doctrine, Theology". In: *Knowing the Triune God: The Work of the Spirit in the Practices of the Church*. Ed. by J.J. Buckley and D. Yeago. Grand Rapids: Eerdmans, 2001, pp. 23–47.

Ideström, J. "Implicit Ecclesiology and Local Church Identity: Dealing with Dilemmas of Empirical Ecclesiology". In: *Ecclesiology in the Trenches: Theory and Method under Construction*. Ed. by S. Fahlgren and J. Ideström. Eugene: Cascade Books, 2015, pp. 121–138.

Jager-Vreugdenhil, M. "Zo hoort het: Sociale regels in een samenleving in transitie." Lectoral speech VIAA (Zwolle). Jan. 13, 2015.

John, E., N. Nixon, and N. Shepherd. "Life-Changing Learning for Christian Discipleship and Ministry: A Practical Exploration". In: *Practical Theology* (Apr. 2018), pp. 1–15. DOI: 10.1080/1756073X.2018.1458178.

Jongeling, P, J. P. de Vries, and J. Douma. *Het vuur blijft branden: geschiedenis van de Gereformeerde Kerken (vrijgemaakt) in Nederland, 1944-1979*. Kampen: Kok, 1979.

Keller, T. *Center Church: Doing Balanced, Gospel-Centered Ministry in Your City*. Grand Rapids: Zondervan, 2012.

Kennedy, J.C. *Stad op een berg: de publieke rol van protestantse kerken*. Zoetermeer: Boekencentrum, 2012.

Koffeman, L.J. *In Order to Serve: An Ecumenical Introduction to Church Polity*. Zürich: LIT, 2014.

Kooiman, A. et al., eds. *Leren transformeren: hoe faciliteer je praktijkinnovatie in tijden van transitie?* Utrecht: Movisie, 2015.

Kuiper, J., ed. *Handboek 2018 van de Gereformeerde Kerken in Nederland*. Bedum: Print Media, 2018.

Kuiper, R. and W. Bouwman, eds. *Vuur en vlam: Aspecten van het vrijgemaakt-gereformeerde leven 1944-1969*. Amsterdam: Buijten & Schipperheijn, 1994.

Kunz, A.J. "Als een prachtig boek: Nederlandse Geloofsbelijdenis artikel 2 in de context van de vroegreformatorische theologie". Zoetermeer: Boekencentrum Academic, 2013.

Kunz, R. and U. Liedke, eds. *Handbuch Inklusion in der Kirchengemeinde*. Göttingen: Vandenhoek & Ruprecht, 2013.

Lakeland, P. *Postmodernity: Christian Identity in a Fragmented Age*. Minneapolis: Fortress Press, 1997.

Lichterman, P. *Elusive Togetherness : Church Groups Trying to Bridge America's Divisions.* Princeton: Princeton University Press, 2011.

Luiten, M. "Unieke maatschappelijke samenwerking". In: *Gereformeerd Kerkblad* (May 2016).

Lutheran World Federation. "Nairobi Statement on Worship and Culture: Contemporary Challenges and Opportunities". In: *The Ecumenical Review* 48.3 (July 1996), pp. 415–417.

MacIntyre, A.C. *After Virtue: A Study in Moral Theory.* Notre Dame: University of Notre Dame Press, 1984.

Martin, L. and V. Cobigo. "Definitions Matter in Understanding Social Inclusion". In: *Journal of Policy and Practice in Intellectual Disabilities* 8.4 (Dec. 1, 2011), pp. 276–282. DOI: 10.1111/j.1741-1130.2011.00316.x.

McGrath, A.E. *A Scientific Theology: Reality.* Vol. 2. London: T&T Clark, 2002.

— *The Science of God: An Introduction to Scientific Theology.* Grand Rapids: Eerdmans, 2004.

Meininger, H.P., ed. *Van en voor allen: wegwijzers naar een inclusieve geloofsgemeenschap met mensen die een verstandelijke handicap hebben.* Zoetermeer: Meinema, 2004.

Modderman, J. *Kerk (in) Delen : Van Leergemeenschap Naar Ontmoetingsgemeenschap.* Kampen: Kok, 2008.

Moltmann, J. "Liberate Yourselves by Accepting One Another". In: *Human Disability and the Service of God: Reassessing Religious Practice.* Ed. by N.L. Eiesland and D.E. Saliers. Nashville: Abingdon Press, 1998, pp. 105–122.

Newman, B.J. and B. Grit. *Accessible Gospel, Inclusive Worship.* Scotts Valley: CreateSpace Independent Publishing Platform, 2016.

Nieman, J.R. "Dancing: Moves and Rhytms That Engage Local Wisdom". In: *Christian Practical Wisdom: What It Is, Why It Matters.* Ed. by D.C. Bass et al. Grand Rapids: Eerdmans, 2016, pp. 88–118.

Noordegraaf, H. *Kerk en Wmo: de eerste vijf jaren (2007-2012): een onderzoek naar (kritische) participatie van kerken in de Wmo.* Groningen: Stichting Rotterdam, 2012.

Nouwen, H.J.M. *Adam: God's Beloved.* London: Darton, Longman & Todd, 1997.

O'Reilly, K. *Ethnographic Methods.* 2nd ed. London/New York: Routledge, 2011.

Osmer, R.R. *Practical Theology: An Introduction*. Grand Rapids: Eerdmans, 2008. 264 pp.

Paas, S. "Ecclesiology in Context: Urban Church Planting in the Netherlands". In: *Evangelical Theology in Transition: Essays under the Auspices of the Center of Evangelical and Reformation Theology (CERT)*. Ed. by C. van der Kooi, E. van Staalduine-Sulman, and A.W. Zwiep. Amsterdam: VU University Press, 2012, pp. 131–147.

Paas, S. and J.H.F. Schaeffer. "Reconstructing Reformed Identity: Experiences from Church Planting in the Netherlands". In: *Journal of Reformed Theology* 8.4 (2014), pp. 382–407. DOI: 10.1163/15697312-00804004.

Parmenter, T.R. "Inclusion and Quality of Life: Are We There Yet?" In: *Public Health Journal* 6.4 (2014), pp. 413–428.

Perham, M. *New Handbook of Pastoral Liturgy*. London: SPCK, 2000.

Pettersson, P. "Majority Churches as Agents of European Welfare: A Sociological Approach". In: Bäckström, A. *Welfare and Religion in 21st Century Europe*. Farnham: Routledge, 2011, pp. 15–59.

Pew Research Center. *America's Changing Religious Landscape*. 202.419.4372. Pew Research Center, May 12, 2015.

Pickel, G. and O. Müller, eds. *Church and Religion in Contemporary Europe: Results from Empirical and Comparative Research*. Wiesbaden: VS Verlag für Sozialwissenschaften, 2009.

Piper, J. *Let the Nations Be Glad!: The Supremacy of God in Missions*. 3rd ed. Grand Rapids: Baker Academic, 2010.

Reinders, J.S. "Being with the Disabled: Jean Vanier's Theological Realism". In: *Disability in the Christian Tradition: A Reader*. Ed. by B. Brock and J. Swinton. Grand Rapids: Eerdmans, 2011, pp. 467–511.

— *Disability, Providence, and Ethics: Bridging Gaps, Transforming Lives*. Waco: Baylor University Press, 2014.

— *Receiving the Gift of Friendship: Profound Disability, Theological Anthropology, and Ethics*. Grand Rapids: Eerdmans, 2008.

— "Watch the Lilies of the Field: Theological Reflection on Profound Disability and Time". In: *The Paradox of Disability: Responses to Jean Vanier and L'Arche Communities from Theology and the Sciences*. Ed. by J.S. Reinders. Grand Rapids: Eerdmans, 2010, pp. 154–168.

Reynolds, T.E. *Vulnerable Communion: A Theology of Disability and Hospitality*. Grand Rapids, Mich: Brazos Press, 2008.

Robben, A.C.G.M. and J.A. Sluka, eds. *Ethnographic Fieldwork: An Anthropological Reader*. 2nd ed. Malden: Wiley-Blackwell, 2012.

Robson, C. *Real World Research: A Resource for Users of Social Research Methods in Applied Settings*. 3rd ed. Chichester: Wiley, 2011.

Rogers, E.M. *Diffusion of Innovations*. New York: Free Press, 2003.

Root, A. *The Relational Pastor: Sharing in Christ by Sharing Ourselves*. Downers Grove: IVP Books, 2013.

Roulstone, A., C. Thomas, and N. Watson. "The Changing Terrain of Disability Studies". In: *Routledge Handbook of Disability Studies*. Ed. by N. Watson, A. Roulstone, and C. Thomas. London /New York: Routledge, 2014, pp. 3–11.

Sadiraj, K., S. Hoff, and M. Versantvoort. *Van Sociale Werkvoorziening Naar Participatiewet: Hoe Is Het de Mensen Op de Wsw-Wachtlijst Vergaan?* Den Haag: Sociaal en Cultureel Planbureau, Sept. 2018.

Saldaña, J. *The Coding Manual for Qualitative Researchers*. 3rd ed. Los Angeles: SAGE, 2016.

Schaeffer, J.H.F. "The Practice of Being a Hospitable Church". In: *Mercy: Theories, Concepts, Practices (Proceedings from the International Congress TU Apeldoorn/Kampen, NL June 2014)*. Ed. by J.H.F. Schaeffer, G. den Hertog, and S. Paas. LIT Verlag Münster, Apr. 2018, pp. 177–194.

— "Theologie en etnografie. Een eerste verkenning voor gereformeerde praktische theologie in Kampen". In: *Instemmend luisteren: studies voor Kees de Ruijter*. Ed. by M. Beute and P.W. van de Kamp. Utrecht: Uitgeverij Kok, 2014, pp. 239–257.

Schalock, R.L. et al. "Cross-Cultural Study of Quality of Life Indicators". In: *American journal of mental retardation* 110.4 (July 2005), pp. 298–311. DOI: 10.1352/0895-8017(2005)110[298:CSOQOL]2.0.CO;2.

Scharen, C. and A.M. Vigen, eds. *Ethnography as Christian Theology and Ethics*. London/New York: Bloomsbury Academic, 2011.

Schippers, A. and L. van Heumen. "The Inclusive City Through the Lens of Quality of Life". In: *Public Health Journal* 6.4 (2014), pp. 311–322.

Schuurman, M., M. Speet, and M. Kersten. *Onderzoek Met Mensen Met Een Verstandelijke Beperking: Handreikingen Voor de Praktijk*. Utrecht: Nederlands Instituut voor Zorg en Welzijn (NIZW) / Landelijk KennisNetwerk Gehandicaptenzorg (LKNG), 2004.

Scott-Jones, J. and S. Watt, eds. *Ethnography in Social Science Practice*. London/New York: Routledge, 2010.

Senn, F.C. *Introduction to Christian Liturgy*. Minneapolis: Fortress Press, 2012.

Shakespeare, S. "A Community of the Question: Inclusive Ecclesiology". In: *Church and Religious 'Other'*. Ed. by G. Mannion. London/New York: Bloomsbury T&T Clark, 2011, pp. 156–167.

Shakespeare, S. and H. Rayment-Pickard. *The Inclusive God: Reclaiming Theology for an Inclusive Church*. Norwich: Canterbury Press, 2012.

Siebe, P.H. "Tussen wereldkerk en ware kerk: kerk, kerkverband en de Open Brief van 1966". In: *Vuur en vlam: Aspecten van het vrijgemaakt-gereformeerde leven 1944-1969*. Ed. by R. Kuiper and W. Bouwman. Amsterdam: Buijten & Schipperheijn, 1994, pp. 203–253.

Slenderbroek-Meints, J. and M. Jager-Vreugdenhil. *Hart van Vathorst: van droom naar werkelijkheid. Nulmeting onder wijkbewoners van de Amersfoortse wijk Vathorst naar sociale samenhang en betrokkenheid bij Hart van Vathorst*. Zwolle: Centrum voor Samenlevingsvraagstukken, Oct. 2016.

Smit, J. "Competenties voor de pastorale communicatie met mensen met een verstandelijke beperking: een praktisch-theologisch onderzoek naar leerprocessen van pastores". Amsterdam: Vrije Universiteit, 2011.

— ed. *Sociale integratie in de geloofsgemeenschap: zestien praktijkverhalen*. Utrecht: Instituut voor Theologie en Sociale Integratie, 2008.

— ed. *Vademecum voor een inclusieve kerk*. Utrecht: Instituut voor Theologie en Sociale Integratie, 2011.

— *Zo gewoon mogelijk: tien theologische tips voor inclusie*. Utrecht: Intstituut voor Theologie en Sociale Integratie, 2006.

Smith, K.S. *Stilling the Storm: Worship and Congregational Leadership in Difficult Times*. Herndon: Rowman & Littlefield Publishers, 2006.

Sol, C.Chr. "De geschiedenis van de gereformeerde diakonie, 1945-1964". In: *Diakonie in verleden en heden*. Ed. by G. Harinck. Barneveld: De Vuurbaak, 1992, pp. 125–169.

Spina, F.A. *The Faith of the Outsider: Exclusion and Inclusion in the Biblical Story*. Grand Rapids: Eerdmans, 2005.

Stone, B.P. *A Reader in Ecclesiology*. Farnham/Burlington: Ashgate, 2011.

References

Swinton, J. ""Where Is Your Church?" Moving toward a Hospitable and Sanctified Ethnography". In: *Perspectives on Ecclesiology and Ethnography*. Ed. by P. Ward. Grand Rapids: Eerdmans, 2011, pp. 71–92.
— *Becoming Friends of Time: Disability, Timefullness, and Gentle Discipleship*. London: SCM Press, 2017.
— *Dementia: Living in the Memories of God*. Grand Rapids: Eerdmans, 2012.
— "Disability, Ableism, and Disablism". In: *The Wiley Blackwell Companion to Practical Theology*. Ed. by B.J. Miller-McLemore. Wiley-Blackwell, 2014.
Swinton, J. and H. Mowat. *Practical Theology and Qualitative Research*. 2nd ed. London: SCM Press, 2016.
Tamminga, K.S. "Countering Ableism Through Embodiments of the Gospel: The Roles of Practice and Reflection". In: *Dignitas* (Forthcoming).
— "De evangelische paradox van geven en ontvangen: Risico en kracht van diaconale barmhartigheid belicht vanuit een theologie van beperking". In: *Verhalen om te delen: bij het afscheid van Peter van de Kamp*. Ed. by J.H.F. Schaeffer and G.M. Tamminga-van Dijk. Vol. 21. TU-Bezinningsreeks. Amsterdam: Buijten & Schipperheijn, 2018, pp. 15–22.
— "Een beetje kerk is inclusief". In: *Onderweg* (June 2017).
— "Gids in een onbekende stad: waarde en valkuilen van een 'single case study'". In: *Handelingen* 46.2 (2019), pp. 51–59.
— "Receiving the Gift of Laughter: How Joy Transforms the Life of an Inclusive Congregation". In: *Journal of Disability & Religion* 24.3 (2020), pp. 300–316. DOI: 10.1080/23312521.2020.1750533.
Tamminga, K.S., J.H.F. Schaeffer, and J. Swinton. "Potential Roles of Churches and Ecclesiology for Disability Inclusion". In: *International Journal of Practical Theology* 24.1 (2020), pp. 89–110. DOI: 10.1515/ijpt-2019-0007. URL: https://www.degruyter.com/view/jo urnals/ijpt/24/1/article-p89.xml.
Timpe, K. *Disability and Inclusive Communities*. Calvin College Press, 2019.
"Troonrede 2013". Speech (Den Haag). Sept. 17, 2013. URL: https://ww w.rijksoverheid.nl/documenten/toespraken/2013/09/17/troonrede -2013 (visited on 11/13/2019).

United Nations. *Final Report of the Ad Hoc Committee on a Comprehensive and Integral International Convention on the Protection and Promotion of the Rights and Dignity of Persons with Disabilities.* A/61/611. New York: United Nations, Dec. 6, 2006.

Van den Brink, G. and C. van der Kooi. *Christelijke dogmatiek: een inleiding.* Zoetermeer: Boekencentrum, 2012.

— *Christian Dogmatics: An Introduction.* Trans. by R. Bruinsma and J.D. Bratt. Grand Rapids: Eerdmans, 2017.

Van der Meulen, M. *Vroom in de Vinex: Kerk En Civil Society in Leidsche Rijn.* Maastricht: Shaker, 2006.

Van der Woud, L., I. van Bokhoven, and V. van Grinsven. *Monitor Passend Onderwijs, Leerkrachten Basisonderwijs.* Utrecht: DUO Onderwijsonderzoek & Advies, Oct. 2018.

Van Bekkum, K. "Verlangen naar tastbare genade: achtergrond, geschiedenis en typologie van spiritualiteit in de Gereformeerde Kerken (vrijgemaakt)". In: *Proeven van spiritualiteit: bijdragen ter gelegenheid van 160 jaar Theologische Universiteit Kampen.* Ed. by P. Niemeijer and J. de Wolf. Barneveld: Vuurbaak, 2014, pp. 131–157.

Van Deusen Hunsinger, D. *Theology and Pastoral Counseling: A New Interdisciplinary Approach.* Grand Rapids: Eerdmans, 1995.

Van Echtelt, P. et al. *Eindevaluatie van de Participatiewet.* Den Haag: Sociaal en Cultureel Planbureau, Nov. 19, 2019.

Van Loon, J. and A. Steglich-Lentz, eds. *Geloven in inclusie: Over zingeving en participatie van mensen met een verstandelijke beperking.* Antwerpen/Apeldoorn: Garant, 2012.

Vanier, J. *Community and Growth.* 2nd ed. London: Darton, Longman & Todd, 2007.

Vergunst, P.J. "Een Inclusieve Kerk?" In: *De Waarheidsvriend* (Feb. 22, 2018), pp. 4–5.

Volf, M. *Exclusion & Embrace: A Theological Exploration of Identity, Otherness, and Reconciliation.* Nashville: Abingdon Press, 1996.

Volf, M. and D.C. Bass, eds. *Practicing Theology: Beliefs and Practices in Christian Life.* Grand Rapids: Eerdmans, 2001.

Wall, B.S. *Welcome as a Way of Life.* Eugene: Cascade Books, 2016.

Ward, P. *Introducing Practical Theology: Mission, Ministry, and the Life of the Church.* Grand Rapids, Michigan: Baker Academic, 2017.

— ed. *Perspectives on Ecclesiology and Ethnography.* Grand Rapids: Eerdmans, 2011.

Watkins, C. et al. "Practical Ecclesiology: What Counts as Theology in Studying the Church?" In: *Perspectives on Ecclesiology and Ethnography*. Ed. by P. Ward. Grand Rapids: Eerdmans, 2011, pp. 167–181.

Watson, N., A. Roulstone, and C. Thomas, eds. *Routledge Handbook of Disability Studies*. London /New York: Routledge, 2014.

Webb-Mitchell, B. *Beyond Accessibility: Toward Full Inclusion of People with Disabilities in Faith Communities*. New York: Church Publishing, 2010.

Webster, J. ""In the Society of God": Some Principles of Ecclesiology". In: *Perspectives on Ecclesiology and Ethnography*. Ed. by P. Ward. Grand Rapids: Eerdmans, 2011, pp. 200–222.

Weiss Block, J. *Copious Hosting: A Theology of Access for People with Disabilities*. New York: Continuum, 2002.

Williams, M.D. *Community in a Black Pentecostal Church: An Anthropological Study*. Prospect Heights: Waveland, 1984.

Witvliet, J.D. *Worship Seeking Understanding: Windows into Christian Practice*. Grand Rapids: Baker Academic, 2003.

Yong, A. *The Bible, Disability, and the Church: A New Vision of the People of God*. Grand Rapids: Eerdmans, 2011.

Zuijderland, M. *Gentest of Geen Test?* Amsterdam: Amsterdam University Press, 2017.

Newspaper article references

ANP. "Overheid zoekt banen voor gehandicapten". In: *Nederlands Dagblad* (Nov. 3, 2018).
— "Welk Recht Heeft Kind Met Down?" In: *Trouw* (Mar. 4, 2017).
Bezemer, M. "'Kubo leert het meest op een gewone school'". In: *Trouw* (Apr. 4, 2017).
— "Steunt mensenrechtencollege kind met beperking bij schoolkeus?" In: *Trouw* (Apr. 4, 2017).
"Complex met GKv kerk Vathorst in gebruik". In: *Reformatorisch Dagblad* (Sept. 28, 2016).
De Korte, G. "Gerard de Korte: Armoedebestrijding hoort bij het hart van het Christelijk geloof". In: *Nederlands Dagblad* (Nov. 7, 2019).
De Korte, G. and R. de Reuver. "Kerk als bondgenoot en luis in de pels". In: *Trouw* (Nov. 1, 2016).
De Reuver, R. and G. de Korte. "Zelfredzaamheid Is Een Mythe". In: *Trouw* (Nov. 9, 2019).
Dujardin, A. "Leraren zuchten onder passend onderwijs". In: *Trouw* (Nov. 1, 2018).
Julen, J. "Arbeidsbeperkte lijkt pion". In: *Trouw* (Oct. 11, 2018).
Koelewijn, J. and M. Remie. "Vinex-verdriet in Vathorst". In: *NRC* (June 25, 2016).
Maassen, W. "Hart van Vathorst is een utopische mini-samenleving". In: *Algemeen Dagblad* (Jan. 26, 2019).
Meijer, H. "'Trots is terug in verpleeghuizen'". In: *Nederlands Dagblad* (Jan. 30, 2018).

Remie, M. "'Amsterdam is de scheidingshoofdstad'". In: *NRC* (May 11, 2016). URL: http://www.nrc.nl/next/2016/05/11/amsterdam-is-de-scheidingshoofdstad-1617791.

Ter Horst, G. "Een beetje Vathorst in het Engelse zuiden". In: *Nederlands Dagblad* (Aug. 17, 2016).

Trouw. "'Kubo terecht verwezen naar speciaal onderwijs'". In: *Trouw* (Apr. 5, 2017).

Van der Graaf, T. and D. Dijkstra. "Heden en geschiedenis in Eemland". In: *Nederlands Dagblad* (Oct. 25, 2017).

Van Soest, A. "Mensverbetering is hét debat van de 21e eeuw". In: *Nederlands Dagblad* (Oct. 6, 2017).

Visser, M. "'Toegang tot gebouwen is voor mij het grootste probleem'". In: *Trouw* (Dec. 3, 2019).

— "Positie mensen met beperking is verslechterd". In: *Trouw* (Dec. 3, 2019).

Waterval, D. "Wat bedrijven kunnen, moet overheid ook: meer arbeidsgehandicapten in dienst nemen". In: *Trouw* (Sept. 13, 2019).

Weel, I. "Arbeidsbeperkte werkt wel, maar zonder rechten". In: *Trouw* (Feb. 9, 2018).

— "Arbeidsbeperkten hebben even werk, raken dan weer uit beeld". In: *Trouw* (Nov. 8, 2018).

— "Banenplan leidde tot creatieve constructies bij overheid". In: *Trouw* (Oct. 13, 2018).

— "Blinde en dove mensen tellen nu ook mee voor het banenplan". In: *Trouw* (Jan. 6, 2020).

Wolff, J. "Waarom mijn Down-zoon er is?" In: *Nederlands Dagblad* (Sept. 21, 2017).

Online References

Amersfoort in Numbers. URL: https://amersfoortincijfers.nl/ (visited on 01/16/2019).
Blog about HVV Winning an Award. URL: http://www.hartvanvathorst.nl/uncategorized/hart-van-vathorst-winnaar-abn-amro-social-award-2016/ (visited on 06/15/2016).
Blog about liturgy in HVV. URL: https://www.opkijken.nl/mensen-met-een-beperking/avondmaal/ (visited on 11/13/2019).
Blog about liturgy in HVV. URL: https://www.opkijken.nl/Nieuws/hart-en-hokje/ (visited on 11/13/2019).
Blog about plans for HVV. Apr. 8, 2016. URL: http://www.denieuwekoers.nl/we-hoeven-elkaar-niet-dood-te-knuffelen (visited on 04/20/2016).
Dutch senate ratifies UN treaty. URL: https://www.eerstekamer.nl/nieuws/20160412/eerste_kamer_steunt_ratificatie_vn (visited on 11/02/2016).
HeartEdge. URL: https://heartedge.org/ (visited on 11/13/2019).
HVV's website. URL: http://www.hartvanvathorst.nl/ (visited on 11/13/2019).
Noordegraaf, H. *Blog about churches and the participation society.* URL: http://www.socialevraagstukken.nl/betrek-de-kerken-meer-bij-de-wmo/ (visited on 11/13/2019).
RCL Website. URL: http://www.gkv.nl/ (visited on 07/13/2016).
Sacrosanctum Concilium - English Text. URL: http://www.vatican.va/archive/hist_councils/ii_vatican_council/documents/vat-ii_const_19631204_sacrosanctum-concilium_en.html (visited on 02/23/2017).

Index

Ammerman, N., 11, 74, 77, 78, 82
Angrosino, M., 75
ANP, 24, 25

Bach, U., 28
Bainbridge, W.S., 6
Barnes, C., 35
Bass, D.C., 56, 59, 91
Bavinck, H., 48
Bazzell, P. D., 140
Berghuijs, J.T., 4
Bernts, T., 4, 5, 248
Bezemer, M., 23, 24
Bhatti, D., 15, 60
Black, K., 259
Bolwijn, R., 9
Bosman, J.A.G., 61, 149
Bouwman, W., 94
Bretherton, L., 39, 105
Brock, B., 28, 39, 238, 239, 271
Brouwer, R., 11, 50, 74, 82, 84
Burger, H., 49

Cahalan, K.A., 5, 56, 91
Calvin, J., 48, 49, 52
Cameron, H., 11, 15, 60, 82
Campbell-Reed, E.R., 14
Carter, E.W., 28, 34
Cartledge, Mark J., 52, 74

Clapton, J., 26, 238
Cobigo, V., 23, 238
Conner, B.T., 235, 253
Craemer, D.B., 271
Crijns, H., 9
Crutzen, O., 9

De Bruijne, A.L.Th., 51
De Hart, J., 108
De Jong, J.M., 249
De Jonge, A.M., 93
De Korte, G., 9
De Reuver, R., 9
De Roest, H.P., 47, 50, 61, 65, 66, 80
De Ruijter, C.J., 46, 50, 53
De Vries, J. P., 93
Deddens, D, 93
Dijkstra, D., 101
Douma, J., 93, 94
Duce, C., 15, 60
Dujardin, A., 24
Dulles, A., 7
Dykstra, C., 56, 59

Earey, M., 262
Eiesland, N.L., 36, 57
Emerson, R.M., 75

Fackre, G., 140

Flyvbjerg, B., 14, 72
Fretz, R.I., 75

Gaventa, W.C., 258
Geertsema, H., 4
Graham, E., 272
Grit, B., 258, 260

Hall, S.A., 23, 238
Hauerwas, S., 3, 66, 120, 201, 240, 254
Hay, P.L., 74
Healy, N.M., 13, 31, 32, 66, 70, 239
Hegstad, H., 67, 68
Heuser, S., 271
Hitzert, F., 85
Hoff, S., 25
Hull, J.M., 28, 36, 57, 272
Hütter, R., 20, 49, 59

Ideström, J., 74

Jager-Vreugdenhil, M., 9, 205
John, E., 252
Jongeling, P, 93
Julen, J., 25

Keller, T., 7
Kennedy, J.C., 11
Kersten, M., 77
Koelewijn, J., 85, 269
Koffeman, L.J, 37, 242, 243
Kooiman, A., 8
Kuiper, J., 29
Kuiper, R., 94
Kunz, A.J., 52
Kunz, R., 28, 34

Lakeland, P., 56
Lichterman, P., 266

Liedke, U., 28, 34
Luiten, M., 99
Lutheran World Federation, 42

Maassen, W., 207
MacIntyre, A.C., 58
Martin, L., 23, 238
McGrath, A.E., 64
Meijer, H., 101, 103, 104
Meininger, H.P., 17, 28
Modderman, J., 130
Moltmann, J., 256, 267
Mowat, H., 55, 58–64, 79, 274
Müller, O., 7

Newman, B.J., 258, 260
Nieman, J.R., 253
Nixon, N., 252
Noordegraaf, H., 9, 10, 33
Nouwen, H.J.M., 1, 2

O'Reilly, K., 69
Osmer, R.R., 50

Paas, S., 10, 93
Parmenter, T.R., 26
Perham, M., 262
Pettersson, P., 5, 266
Pew Research Center, 5
Pickel, G., 7
Piper, J., 7

Rayment-Pickard, H., 35, 39, 241
Reinders, J.S., 2, 36, 240, 254, 270
Remie, M., 85, 269
Reynolds, T.E., 37
Robben, A.C.G.M., 69
Robson, C., 69, 72, 74–78
Rogers, E.M., 212

Index

Root, A., 256
Rosenberg, J., 75
Roulstone, A., 35

Sadiraj, K., 25
Saldaña, J., 78
Saliers, D.E., 36
Schaeffer, J.H.F., 19, 54, 69, 93, 99, 269
Schalock, R.L., 21, 237
Scharen, C., 69
Schippers, A., 23, 26
Schuurman, M., 77
Scott-Jones, J., 69
Senn, F.C., 261
Shakespeare, S., 35, 39, 241
Shaw, L.L., 75
Shepherd, N., 252
Siebe, P.H., 93
Slenderbroek-Meints, J., 205
Sluka, J.A., 69
Smit, J., 28, 33, 258
Smith, K.S., 255
Sol, C.Chr., 11
Speet, M., 77
Spina, F.A., 38, 244
Steglich-Lentz, A., 21, 111
Stone, B.P., 6
Swinton, J., 19, 32, 35, 55, 58–64, 67, 70, 79, 254, 271, 274

Tamminga, K.S., 19, 74, 99, 100, 122, 158
Te Velde, M., 93
Ter Horst, G., 99
Thomas, C., 35
Timpe, K., 36
Trouw, 24

United Nations, 8, 21

Van Bekkum, K., 92, 93
Van Bokhoven, I., 24
Van den Brink, G., 51
Van der Graaf, T., 101
Van der Kooi, C., 51
Van der Linden, L., 9
Van der Meulen, M., 8, 85, 265, 266, 268
Van der Woud, L., 24
Van Deusen Hunsinger, D., 64
Van Echtelt, P., 25
Van Grinsven, V., 24
Van Heumen, L., 23, 26
Van Houwelingen, P., 108
Van Loon, J., 21, 111
Van Soest, A., 106
Vanier, J., 3, 120, 201, 254
Vergunst, P.J., 240
Versantvoort, M., 25
Vigen, A.M., 69
Visser, M., 26
Volf, M., 40, 56, 241

Wall, B.S., 2
Walton, H., 272
Ward, F., 272
Ward, P., 13, 60, 67, 69
Waterval, D., 25
Watkins, C., 60, 68
Watson, N., 35
Watt, S., 69
Webb-Mitchell, B., 35
Webster, J., 67, 68
Weel, I., 25
Weiss Block, J., 36
Wijma, H., 93

Williams, M.D., 74
Witvliet, J.D., 262, 263
Wolff, J., 107

Yong, A., 38

Zuijderland, M., 106

CPSIA information can be obtained
at www.ICGtesting.com
Printed in the USA
JSHW031519041120
9271JS00001B/1